Marc Monnier

Brigand life in Italy : a history of Bourbonist reaction

Marc Monnier

Brigand life in Italy : a history of Bourbonist reaction

ISBN/EAN: 9783337229467

Printed in Europe, USA, Canada, Australia, Japan

Cover: Foto ©ninafisch / pixelio.de

More available books at **www.hansebooks.com**

BRIGAND LIFE IN ITALY:

A HISTORY OF BOURBONIST REACTION.

EDITED FROM ORIGINAL AND AUTHENTIC DOCUMENTS.

BY

COUNT MAFFEI.

IN TWO VOLUMES.

VOL. II.

LONDON:
HURST AND BLACKETT, PUBLISHERS,
SUCCESSORS TO HENRY COLBURN,
13, GREAT MARLBOROUGH STREET.
1865.

CONTENTS

OF

THE SECOND VOLUME.

CHAPTER I.

The Brigandage of the Present—Appointment of a Parliamentary Commission—Value of the Moral Support of England—The Chief Home of Brigandage—Reception of the Commission in Southern Italy—Deputations—The Causes of Brigandage—Influence of the Feudal System—Brigandage in the Reign of Ferdinand II.—The Assertions of Wienspeare—Re Marcone and Abate Cesare—Honours Conferred on Brigand Chiefs—Brigandage under the Spanish Rule at Naples—Regions Infested by the Brigands—Want of Means of Communication . 3

CHAPTER II.

Conduct of the Deposed Dynasty—The Band of Lagrange—Giorgi—Complicity between Bourbonism and Brigandism—Crocco—Renewal of Reactionary Efforts—Conduct of the Clergy—Pasquale Romano—Remarks on the Attempt of Borjès the Spaniard—Complication of Affairs—Brigandage Strengthened by Municipal Dissensions—The Communal Administrations—Defects in the Public Administration—The Old and New Magistracy—The System of Trial by Jury—The Police Administration—Facility in the Payment of Ransoms—The Attractions of Brigandage 33

CHAPTER III.

Brigandage and the Catholic Priesthood—The Brigands' Mass—Superstition of the Brigands—The Influence of Religious Fear—Services Rendered by the Priests to Brigandage—Complicity of the Bourbon Committees with Brigandage—Pilone—Giuseppe Tardio's Proclamation to the People of the Two Sicilies—Illustration of Administrative Corruption—Tristany—Encouragement of Brigandage by Francis II.—Arrangement of Expeditions from the Pontifical Territory—Predicted Return of Francis II. to Naples—Tenacity of Brigandage in the Neapolitan Provinces—Formation of Brigand Bands at Rome—Their Military Equipment and Organization 63

CHAPTER IV.

Important Documents—Reparation for an Insult to the Italian Flag—Cucitto—The Murder of Spina—Necessity of Rome to Italy—The French Protectorate an Encouragement to Brigandage—Sympathy between Italian and French Soldiers—Furtive Landings on the Coast—Patient Heroism of the Italian Army—Its Sufferings from the Climate, Sickness, and Privations—General Lamarmora—Inferior Morale of the Brigands—Origin of their Chiefs—Religious Experience of a Brigand—The Foreign Bandits—Haunts of the Brigands—Eradication of Brigandage . 89

CHAPTER V.

Connection of the Roman Government and of the Bourbon Committees with Brigandage—The Revelations of Ettore Noli—Traitors among the Employés of the Italian Government—Caracciolo's Interview with Francis II.—De Gottedon, De Lupé, and De Christen—Pecuniary Aid from the Ex-king Francis—De Luca—Instructions from Rome—The Depositions of Pasquale Scuotto—Testimony as to the Invasion of General Borjès—The Adventures of Mr. Bishop—The Process against the Baron Achille Cosenza—Revelations made by Eusebio Capitaneo—The Case of the Marquis Avitabile 125

CONTENTS. vii

CHAPTER VI.

Trials Continued—Arrest of the Princess Barberini Sciarra—Opposition of the Clergy to the New Italian Government—The Reactionary Press—Letters in Cipher to Father Clarenzio—Correspondence between the Conspirators of Naples and of Rome—Important Depositions—Religion and Policy—Examination of Pasquale Forgione—The Oath of Fealty taken by the Brigands 157

CHAPTER VII.

Measures for the Repression of Brigandage—Gradual Improvement of the Country—Beneficial Influence of Works of Public Utility—Organization of a Vigilant Police—Improved Administration of Justice—Necessity of the Removal of Francis II. from Rome—Vigorous Military Action—Losses of the Italian Army and of the Brigands—The National Guard in the Southern Provinces—Cavalry Volunteers—Respect for the Laws—Official Connivance with Brigandage—Local Exile—Capital Punishment—Honour among Brigands 183

CHAPTER VIII.

The Last Stage of Brigandage—Successful Results of the New System of Repression—Atrocities Committed by Caruso—Report of General Pallavicini—Sketch of the Life and Character of Caruso—The Slaughter of Mellanico—Ricciardelli—State of the Province of Beneventum—Disaster near Torre Palazzo—Giulio Videmari—Anecdotes of Caruso—His Capture and Destruction of his Band—Operations against Crocco and Ninco Nanco—Endurance and Perseverance of Italian Soldiers . 219

CHAPTER IX.

Trial of the Brothers La Gala—An Atrocious Deed—Character of the Roman Government—The Army the Emblem of National Unity—Formation of Roads and Railways—Improved Aspect of Southern Italy—Education—Social and Municipal Changes—Revival of Commerce—Italian Ports—Good Qualities of the Neapolitans—State of Rome—The Convention of the 15th of September—Transference of the Capital to Florence—General Cialdini's Speech—The Temporal Supremacy of the Pope—The Progress of Italy—Conclusion of the Work . . 261

APPENDIX 305

CHAPTER I.

BRIGANDAGE AT THE END OF 1862—APPOINTMENT OF A PARLIAMENTARY COMMISSION—VALUE OF THE MORAL SUPPORT OF ENGLAND—THE CHIEF HOME OF BRIGANDAGE—RECEPTION OF THE COMMISSION IN SOUTHERN ITALY—DEPUTATIONS—THE CAUSES OF BRIGANDAGE—INFLUENCE OF THE FEUDAL SYSTEM—BRIGANDAGE IN THE REIGN OF FERDINAND II.—THE ASSERTIONS OF WINSPEARE—RE MARCONE AND ABATE CESARE—HONOURS CONFERRED ON BRIGAND CHIEFS—BRIGANDAGE UNDER THE SPANISH RULE AT NAPLES—REGIONS INFESTED BY THE BRIGANDS—WANT OF MEANS OF COMMUNICATION.

CHAPTER I.

The preceding volume contains the history of the first period of Neapolitan brigandage, a subject which necessarily gives rise to many painful considerations, but which, connected as it is with our great revolution, must be fully understood before the latter can be comprehended in all its phases. In order, therefore, to complete the work which I have undertaken, I now proceed to consider the history of brigandage in its ultimate form—that is to say, during the last two years. While, in the former part of this history, I have been able to avail myself of the labours of a talented predecessor, M. Monnier, in the present I am fortunately able, in a great measure, to avail myself of the results of my own studies. But in order to fulfil my task more conscientiously, in lifting the veil that still clouds these sad episodes of the Bourbonist reaction, I deem it necessary, in the first place, to acquaint the reader with the investigations made on this subject by the parliamentary commission lately appointed at Turin. The natural anxiety felt throughout the country on this painful subject induced the Italian Government to appoint a parliamentary commission with the view of fully inquiring into it, and of satisfying the desire of the public to know the causes that had produced and still maintained in existence that great national calamity, Neapolitan brigandage, notwithstanding the energy with which it had been opposed. From the conscientious investigations of that commission we obtain a more satisfactory idea of the state of the southern portion of the Italian peninsula than is to be obtained from any other source, and they constitute the real philosophical history of the tyranny of the past. In giving a short account of its proceedings, I shall carefully follow the memorial drawn up by my learned friend, the Commendatore Massari, who was the reporter of the commission, availing myself at the same time of other official documents, for the correctness of which I am able fully to vouch. On a subject like this, on which one is so apt to be swayed by a spirit of prejudice, or, at least, to yield too readily to the influence of preconceived opinions, it is of extreme consequence that the writer should be thoroughly impartial. I therefore confine myself mainly to the narrative of well-attested facts, to the authority of which alone I wish the reader to yield assent. I shall endeavour to narrate the events with all the moderation and impartiality of one whose only object is the discovery of truth. Both our friends and adversaries will thus be able to see whether the Holy See and the Bourbonist faction may rightly claim the reputation of that innocence they have always boasted of in their official declarations. From the verdict given by the liberal majority of England, I have no doubt my country will derive new strength to persevere resolutely in that path which must ultimately lead to the complete consolidation of its political unity. The moral support which, after the Treaty of Zurich, England gave to Italy has certainly been, to a very great extent, one of the causes by which the almost entire realisation of our national unity has been most effectively promoted; and it is my object now, by a faithful representation of the present state of Italy, to show that this moral support is still desirable, inasmuch as it would no doubt greatly tend to the settlement of our present difficulties, which, after all, are nothing but the old struggle between nationality and freedom on one side, and reaction and tyranny on the other. To obtain the approval of public opinion in England would be, I think, an act of real patriotism, and should

I succeed in my endeavour, I shall be very proud to have rendered such an important service to my country.

Two years had elapsed since the fall of Gaëta, the last important stronghold of the Bourbons. The country had been constantly though slowly progressing under the guidance of its ablest men, both civil and military. Although the army and the National Militia had both distinguished themselves by their zeal and valour, yet brigandage was still raging in the old kingdom of Naples, apparently drawing new strength and vigour from the efforts which it made to resist the measures by which Government was endeavouring to effect its entire repression. Scenes and names only were changed. Sometimes the theatre of violence and bloodshed was the province of Capitanata, sometimes the Basilicata, and not seldom the very neighbourhood of Naples. The monster of reaction, like the dragon of the fable, seemed to acquire new power at each blow that was inflicted upon him. When, as we have seen, General Lamarmora arrived at Naples in the autumn of 1861, the bands of brigands were, to all appearance, reduced to a few wretched wanderers, hunted like wild beasts. It was soon discovered, however, that the fatal legacy left by the Bourbons to the newly-formed Italian kingdom was not so completely destroyed as many had imagined. Brigandage, in fact, began again, ere long, to show its head in various quarters. The determination was therefore formed to take still more vigorous measures against an enemy so fatal to the peace and prosperity of Italy.

It was with this view that the commission selected among the members belonging to the different sides of the house was formed. They were to investigate on the very spot the causes and extent of that unhappy evil by which the country was kept in a permanent state of agitation, and to report upon the most practical means of its repression. The commission left Turin at the end of January, 1863, and arrived on the 1st of February at Foggia, the capital of the province of Capitanata, and, so far as modern brigandage is concerned, the basis from which the brigands directed their operations. Foggia, indeed, since the revolution, had been the chief home of brigandage; for neither in the Abruzzi nor in Calabria had it, for the last two years, made any appearance worth speaking of. The country infested by this great evil comprised the whole district lying between the high mountains of Marano and Gatello, fifty miles due east of Naples, and Monte Chilone and Auro, about thirty miles due north of the two former. These mountains, forming two joints in the backbone of the Apennines, are connected by a number of intricate cross-ridges with numerous tracks, which may be passed on foot or on horseback at almost any time of the year, but over which there is but one carriage road leading from the Adriatic to the Mediterranean. The western slopes of this range of mountains are abrupt, except where the sources of the eastern branch of the Volturno come out close by the páss of Ariano, and, passing Beneventum, wind their way down to the plain of Capua. The eastern slopes, on the contrary, fall off more gradually, opening out into a number of valleys, which carry off the waters of these mountains to the Mediterranean. The northernmost of these valleys is that of the Fortore, in the province of Molise; then come a number of smaller ones, which end in the plains of Apulia; and, lastly, the wide valley of the Ofanto, forming the northern boundary of the province of Basilicata. These eastern slopes and valleys and the upper valleys of the Eastern Volturno, comprising an area of about 120 square miles, were the district in which alone brigandage, properly speaking, still remained. This district comprises the whole province of Capitanata, a portion of the Basilicata, of Molise, and of Principato Ultra.

At Foggia the parliamentary commission divided. One part of it visited successively the district of Sanseverino, in the province of Capitanata, the woods of Fortore, the district of Larino, in the province of Molise, and then, returning by way of Foggia, went through the well-known district of Melfi, and the wood of Monticchio, proceeding by Rionero and Avigliano to Potenza, the capital of the province of Basilicata. The other part of the commission, after visiting the province of Puglia, the districts of Bari and Lecce, went from Taranto to another district of the province of Basilicata, that of Matera, passing by Gioja, Santeramo, and Altamura on their way. Proceeding, then, by Grottole, Grassano, and Tricarico, they joined the other division of the commission at Potenza, from which, at last, all the members went together to Naples, whence, after a short delay at Salerno, they went to Sora on the Roman frontier. They were all very anxious to complete the mission with which they had been entrusted, by extending their visit to the Abruzzi and Calabria, thus showing the patriotic southern populations that no less interest was taken in their security than had been displayed for the other parts of the kingdom. Many considerations, however, and chiefly the loss of time occasioned by the difficulty of communication, prevented them from going to those distant districts, in which, moreover, brigandage had been already successfully repressed, and chiefly by the brave mountaineers themselves, who, having admirably seconded the national movement, succeeded likewise in driving from Calabria the bands of assassins who attempted to fight in the name of Francis II.

The mission of the representatives of the nation was thus brought to a close. They had been everywhere received with the utmost cordiality, and even enthusiasm. It was something entirely new to the people of the south, so long trodden under foot by the tyranny of the Bourbons, to see the agents of Government, sent specially to inquire into their condition, taking the evidence not only of the rich, but also of the poor, and evidently anxious to promote their welfare. Deputations were spontaneously sent from the neighbouring hamlets and villages, not comprised in the itinerary of the members of the commission, to express the satisfaction with which they welcomed them; and it is certainly gratifying to say that, in those popular demonstrations, the clergy were by no means lacking, many a priest taking the opportunity to express his devotion to the king and to liberal institutions. The venerable Bishop of Larino went in person to meet the representatives of the nation, an example which was followed in a great many bishoprics by the prelates who occupied the places of those who had fled from the country on account of their reactionist opinions. The monks of the celebrated convent of Montecassino, so familiar to everyone who has travelled in the south of Italy, entertained the envoys of Parliament most hospitably, both on their journey south and on their return. I mention these facts as proofs that the Italians of the south, emulous, not envious, of their northern brethren, were second to none in devotion to the principle of national unity, and to the constitutional monarchy which represented and maintained that principle.

Before giving the result of the inquiries instituted by the commission, it will be desirable to cast a retrospective glance on the origin of brigandage in its modern form, and explain the causes of that pertinacity with which it resisted all the exertions made for its destruction. Did it arise from the political changes of the year 1860, or was the overthrow of the old system but the occasion that determined its development? Although the political crisis in 1860, as in 1806 and in other times of political trouble, certainly had a great influence, there were at the same time other causes, and the root of the evil lay elsewhere. Neapolitan brigandage is only the symptom of the decay that for centuries has been constantly undermining that unhappy country. The demoralisation of the lower classes, in the provinces where brigandage has most widely spread, is beyond expression. The peasant there has no interest to bind him to the soil, and even the proprietors, far from being owners of the land, are only vassal tenants of the so called Tavoliere di Puglia.* In those districts there is a part of the population, designated by the name of *Terrazzani*, who have actually nothing to live upon but the proceeds of plunder and theft. To quote a statement used by the tax-collector of the province of Foggia—" These people sometimes eat

* The Tavoliere di Puglia, originally an immense uncultivated moor, many miles in extent, is now partially cultivated. It lies between the provinces of Capitanata, Bari, Basilicata, and Lecce, and since the days of the first Norman kings, it has been ruled by a special legislation, and given on lease to the proprietors of Puglia, on condition that they should let it to the shepherds from the Abruzzi for the pasturage of their numerous herds and flocks during the winter months, when, at the end of October, they were obliged to leave their own mountainous districts and immigrate to the plains. The proprietors, bound by this condition, cannot improve their land by draining and cultivation, because they would thus injure the rights of the nomad population of the Abruzzi, who, even in these modern times, wander from place to place with their families and flocks, like the nomad tribes of whom we read in the Bible. Parliament has now adopted a bill for the disfranchisement of that land. The advantages of such a measure will be considerable, because the proprietors will be free to introduce any improvement they may think proper, and by thus cultivating the land, the deadly malaria which reigns there will be destroyed for ever. In that plain the memorable battles of Cannæ (216 B.C.), and later of Ceriguola (1503), were fought. The peasants still call the place where Hannibal cut to pieces the 80,000 Romans commanded by Terentius Varro and Paulus Æmilius, " Il Campo di Sangue."

such food as dogs would not deign to touch." The misery and destitution of these classes are the direct causes of brigandage. When the poor labourer compares the brigand's life with his own wretched lot, he cannot avoid drawing conclusions far from favourable to the cause of law and order, and we cannot wonder that that romantic existence lures him from the constant labour and misery to which, in his own station, he is hopelessly condemned. The voice of conscience is silenced, and he betakes himself to a course of life which appears to him a legitimate way of obtaining his livelihood.

Such has been for centuries the social state of the country, and multitudes of the poor resorted to brigandage almost as if it were an honourable and lucrative calling, a statement which is confirmed by the fact that of three hundred and seventy-five brigands in the gaols of the province of Capitanata, in the month of April, 1862, two hundred and ninty-three were labourers (*Braccianti*); while, on the contrary, in those districts where the labourers and proprietors stood in a better relation to each other, brigandage attracted only a few of the worst characters, and was easily put down. In the districts on the borders of the Papal States, where it is a foreign importation, bands of brigands are organized without difficulty. Sheltering themselves on the Roman side of the frontier, they make irruptions into the Italian territory, emboldened by the certainty that, at the approach of danger, there is always a safe retreat in their rear. Thus, from different causes, brigandage has sprung up in several provinces of Italy.

The feudal system, though abolished by our civilized age, has left such traces of its long domination, that its pernicious influence is not yet entirely destroyed. Although barons, in the feudal signification of the word, no longer exist, the tradition of their tyrannical privileges still lives in the memory of every one; and in many of the localities I have mentioned, the proprietors are still, in the eyes of the peasants, like the old feudal lords. The miserable labourers know that their toil is not for their own well-being, and the degrading poverty to which they are condemned excites the instinct of vengeance, as a means of gratifying which they often betake themselves to the adventurous existence of the bandit. Brigandage is thus, to a certain extent, a kind of savage protest against their social wrongs.

When, in addition to the unhappy condition of these people, we consider the complete ignorance in which they were kept by their Bourbon rulers, the barbarous superstitions spread among them, and the systematic corruption to which they were exposed, it is no wonder that they should have lost the consciousness of everything just and honourable. Ferdinand II., especially, brought to the achievement of the nefarious work a really diabolical skill. Both the ecclesiastical and civil tribunals he had converted into receptacles of espionage and falsehood; he had transformed his soldiers into abject spies and oppressors; he glorified crime, and punished virtue and heroism as abhorred vices. Thirsty of absolute power, he little cared that he ruled over a desolated country, provided he ruled as a despot. What was it to him that iniquity, falsehood, and venality were the only supporters of his crown, provided he could retain the sovereignty? His long reign was but an uninterrupted protest against the most sacred of all principles, that of honesty, and against the most lofty prerogative of a nation, that of morality. He foresaw that his dynasty could not reign long, and still he was not the less eager in his work of destruction, meaning to leave the kingdom of Naples to the rest of Italy on the day of her rising, not one of the most vital parts of the national body, but a rotten corpse. Ferdinand II. said once, in the beginning of 1849, to the old Prince Dentice, formerly his minister, "If I am compelled some day to abandon the kingdom, I shall leave to my successors an inheritance of fifty years' anarchy." This design he could not realize, thanks to the firmness of the Neapolitans; but such a system must have involved the most fatal consequences, and the display of immorality on the throne could not fail to produce its sad effects on the rude uncivilized mob.

It has been very often said that these populations had lost all sense of morality; but is it to be wondered at when one considers how, for a long series of years, they had been accustomed to behold the ministers of God exchanging their heavenly mission for the base occupation of political spies, magistrates making a trade of justice, and soldiers doing the work of the hangman? Is it surprising if people thus educated have been swelling the ranks of the brigands—if, in the violent change through which from the most unheard of tyranny they have suddenly passed to the pacific rule of freedom and justice, these poor wretches rebel against the new order of things, seeking by violence the reparation of the wrongs inflicted on them throughout a long period of the most brutalizing oppression?

From the Greeks to the Normans, the Suabians, the Angevins, the Aragonians, the French, the history of the Neapolitan provinces is but one long narrative of material conquests, in which no regard has been paid to the great principles of justice. Might has triumphed over right, and, as there is nothing more calculated to destroy the national feeling of a country than an uninterrupted series of foreign dominators, each adding new grievances to those already existing, the people at last were driven into a state of complete political apathy, of which the late Bourbonist rule offered an unparalleled example. Misgovernment, giving new strength to the elements of internecine and social strife, has rendered their action much more pernicious; and this was not the work of mere chance, but the premeditated effect of a long and well-contrived plan. The first impulse given to the present system of brigandage dates from the summer of the year 1860, when the Bourbons, seeing they could not deceive their subjects with the constitution violently wrested from them, came to a perfect understanding of their true position, and became aware that, sooner or later, they would be obliged to flee the country. They remembered how, at the end of the last century, and in the first years of the present, they had in both cases ascended the throne through the help of the brigands. It was thus natural that in 1860 they should prepare their wonted weapons for the same purpose.

To all these causes, finally, must be added another, which we may call an historical and traditional one. There exists a sort of tradition of brigandage, drawing its origin from the earliest periods of the most despotic feudalism, and very widely prevailing in the Neapolitan provinces. These remnants of mediæval tyranny were put down not a very long time ago by the kings. According to that system, might alone was the only arbiter of justice. The barons used to live surrounded by their bravoes, and amongst them the most praiseworthy were those who had committed the greatest and most sanguinary atrocities. The army of the baron was an assemblage of ruffians ready to perpetrate any deed of violence, and the poor vassals had no other way of escape but to enlist among them, or to submit to the most ferocious despotism. In the endless succession of conquests which have desolated the south of Italy, these social conditions and the bad government of the rulers have never failed to produce the same fatal consequences. During the long period known in history under the name of the Spanish "Viceregnato," which lasted more than two hundred and thirty years, brigandage became a natural occurrence, and almost an endemic disease.

"The barons of the kingdom," says Winspeare, the historian, "employed bands of brigands as their regular militia. . . . The equerries and militia of the barons were generally recruited among men who, having polluted themselves with every sort of crime, sought a refuge under their protection. Owing to one of those false principles that had originated and been prevalent in times of feudal anarchy, to be an outlaw was considered as a proof of bravery, and, therefore, greatly contributed to gain for a candidate the favour and the suffrages of the people. With such a title of honour, no one was refused admittance into the ranks of the baronial band. Among the reasons which caused the Prince of Salerno Sanseverino to be exiled, it is to be remembered that he was accused of being not only the protector of the brigands, but actually their leader; and among the principal complaints which the municipality of Naples addressed to the Emperor Charles V., there was that concerning the bravoes every nobleman was in the habit of keeping in his castle, and through whom they used to commit all sorts of excesses, sometimes killing peaceful citizens for the mere sake of private revenge, and then helping the criminals to escape from the hands of justice. The Viceroy Don Pietrantonio d'Aragona in 1668, after having created an extraordinary commission to judge abettors and supporters of bandits, and after he had had some of the more powerful barons in the kingdom arrested and tried, made arrangements with the culprits, through which they were once more restored to liberty on payment of a large sum of money! From that very hall of justice where people believed they had gone to enforce by their presence the respect due to the laws, these miscreants retired gorged with more than 320,000 ducats, the price of an infamous bargain. The Viceroy Count of Castrillo, whilst pursuing the bands of brigands, being suddenly recalled to Castellamare to oppose the landing of the Duke of Guise, was not ashamed to seek the help of that very host of assassins whom he had till then vainly endeavoured to destroy."[*]

The chronicles and histories of that epoch are full of instances which confirm in every particular the assertions of Winspeare, and give an alarming idea of the power, the daring, and effrontery of these bandits. In 1559 a considerable body of them, numbering 1500 men, led by a certain Re Marcone, besieged the town of Cotrone, defeating a strong force of Spanish troops which had been sent against them, and only giving way when a second body of soldiers, stronger than the first, had come up to the rescue of their comrades. Another bandit, known by the name of Abate Cesare, had the audacity, during the viceroyalty of the Count of Penneranda, to besiege Naples itself.

In the year 1644, the Duke of Medina being viceroy, it was considered necessary to appoint a special viceroy for the counties, with the particular object

[*] V. Winspeare—"History of Feudal Abuses"—Introduction.

of keeping the brigands in check. During the viceroyalty of the Count of Castrillo, a certain Carlo Petriello kept the field with such success, that he was able to intercept all communications; so that, as recorded in the histories of the *period, the Cardinal Buoncompagno, Archbishop of Bologna, being once obliged to cross the Papal frontier, on his way to Sora, was compelled to ask a free pass from Petriello, who magnanimously granted it to his eminence. In 1642, the Duke of Maddaloni, having conspired against Masaniello, in order to carry out his intentions, secretly sent to Naples a great number of brigands, who, after the revolution had subsided, continued to infest the country so long, that they were only dispersed when the Count of Conversano, one of their most powerful supporters, was banished to Spain.

In the history of the Spanish rule in those provinces, the deeds of violence committed by the brigands acquired a sad celebrity. The heroes of that time were the bandits Re Marcone, Pietro Mancino, Carlo Rainera, Benedetto Mangone, l'Abate Cesare Riccardo, Marco Sciarra, Carlo Petriello, Buttinello, Verticillo, Angiolo del Duca, and Spicciarelli. The traditions of the Spanish Viceroyalty were continued by the Bourbons. Colletta says that, in the first years of the reign of Ferdinand IV., a royal decree containing the following statement was issued:—

"Robberies in town and in the country are incessant; exactions, plunder, and profligacy are of daily occurrence. All security is gone, trade is destroyed, and the revenues of the land are misappropriated."

In the year 1799, hordes of assassins, instigated by the Bourbons, and commanded by a cardinal of the Holy Church, carried throughout the whole kingdom the most fearful devastations, laying everything waste with sword and fire, and, after exciting the most tremendous social anarchy that ever was known, succeeded in restoring an unworthy dynasty to a throne reeking with human blood. During the ten years of the reigns of Joseph Napoleon and Murat, brigandage, assuming the bearing of a mock national defence, again brought a long series of indescribable miseries upon the unhappy country, especially on Calabria.

If the co-operation of the Austrians had failed in the year 1821, Ferdinand I. would have undoubtedly employed brigandage for the purpose of suppressing the constitutional movement; and had not the liberals been crushed on the 15th of May, 1848, Ferdinand II. was already prepared to take his revenge by once more letting loose numerous bands of assassins upon his helpless subjects. Like the Spanish Viceroy, Don Pietrantonio d'Aragona, the Bourbons, as is testified by Vardarelli and Talarico, were in frequent relation with the brigands. From these facts we may conclude with certainty that in the old kingdom of Naples brigandage was a popular tradition connected with the most important political events of the country. Among the ranks of the infamous host of 1799, the Bourbonist army found its generals, Pronio, Mammone, Sciarpo, Fra Diavolo, and many others. "The scum," as Colletta stigmatises them, " of the most degraded populace" were not only appointed colonels and generals, but also created barons and knights. Guilt, no longer followed by punishment, was rewarded by preferment, wealth, and such honour as it could receive. Crime was the surest means of attaining the highest dignities, and plunder was considered the most legitimate and honourable way of enriching oneself. Poor people have often heard from their fathers or their grandfathers that such and such a family, now so prosperous and wealthy, was once very poor—that in 1799 they were not richer than themselves, and that they owe all their fortune to brigandage. The temptation therefore was great, and many a one, dazzled by the brilliant prospect, gave way to the fascination held out by the hope of being with little trouble rich and powerful in his turn. His cupidity, awakened by example and by popular recollections, was more eloquent in his untutored mind than the voice of conscience; and the attraction of the long caressed dream silenced remorse for the guilty means of attaining its realisation.

Crocco and Caruso, two of the most desperate brigands, had probably dreamt of being some day appointed generals, and, like many of their predecessors in 1799, of being even rewarded with the dignity conferred by such titles as those of baron and marquis. Some of these ruffians, anticipating the future bounties of their royal master, had already assumed high military and aristocratic titles. Chiavone, we know, having dubbed himself general, used to appoint officers in the name of Francis II., and received the title of Excellency. Pilone assumed the knightly dignity and title of Cavaliere, coupled with that of commander-in-chief of a corps of observation. Crocco wore on his breast two decorations, one attached to a yellow riband, the pontifical colour, and, by the bandits of Capitanata and Basilicata, was always addressed as general. In a letter written by Ninco Nanco to the unhappy police delegate of Avigliano, whom he afterwards treacherously murdered, he signed himself, "The Colonel Giuseppe Nicola Somma, *alias* Ninco Nanco."

Such facts as these show by what inducements the southern populations of Italy were tempted to throw themselves into the wild vortex of brigandism, and will explain how, to these poor peasants, with their imperfectly developed moral and intellectual faculties, the brigand appeared a superior sort of being, around whose existence was thrown the halo of romance, and who was rather to be envied than despised or abhorred. The popular legends, which represented him as the vindicator of their wrongs, kept alive this feeling. The people who had been so long oppressed by a government which, without sympathy for their suffering, never attempted to improve their condition, saw in the brigand the type of the highest aspirations which, in their degraded position, they were able to form.

The natural tendency of the people towards brigandage, produced by such moral and historical causes, was further favoured by the peculiar configuration of the country, the want of means of communication, and the impenetrable woods and forests by which it is covered. The points most infested by the brigands were the extreme slopes of the range of the Apennines, gradually declining into the province of Puglia, and all along the rivers Fortore and Ofanto, the banks of which are so thickly wooded, that they offer a safe refuge to banditti of every description. From these slopes one could easily descend into the immense plain of Puglia, where, although there are very few towns, the number of farms is very great.

The Garganic region, so called from Mount Gargano, is bounded by the Adriatic on one side, and extends on the other as far as the immense plain of the Tavoliere di Puglia. With its fortunate position, its delightful climate, and the extraordinary fertility of its soil, it might be reckoned amongst the most happy and smiling countries in the world; but with all these natural gifts there are few places in Italy equally desolate, poor, and degraded. In the whole of that vast plain there is not a road, except the one communicating with the sanctuary of San Michele, and its inhabitants, amounting to several thousands, are therefore entirely separated from their fellow-creatures. Living in a state so isolated that they have no knowledge of the world beyond their narrow valley, they are utter strangers to the refining influences of civilization, and live in a condition little removed from total barbarism.

Another district of Capitanata, which is equally alpine, is that of Bovino, in which also there are no roads. The plain of the Tavoliere begins at the opening of the valley of Bovino, from which it stretches away to a great distance. The brigands haunted such localities as these when they were pursued, finding a safe retreat in the wild passes of the mountains or in the depths of the woods. The wood of Dragonaro, and the forest of Delle Grotte, on the side of the Garganic region, were their favourite haunts—the latter especially, on account not only of its size and position, but also because it communicates with the woods of the province of Molise, where the brigands could safely conceal themselves, and baffle every effort of their pursuers. The whole of the region comprised between the river Fortore and the wood Petacciato, or, in other words, the district of Vasto, in the province of Chieti, is nothing but one long forest, in several parts of which there are extensive tracts overgrown by impenetrable bushes. The country is everywhere intersected by precipices, by masses of rock and horrid caverns, safe and easy places of retreat for the brigands, but to the troops almost inaccessible. At the time of the French occupation, as well as at the present time, these woods were the constant resort of the brigands. In Basilicata, the woods of Monticchio, of Lagopesole, of Ripacandida, of San Cataldo, of Policoro, and of Montemilone, afforded to them the same advantages. From the wood of Monticchio they had the command of the district of Melfi in Basilicata, that of Sant' Angelo dei Lombardi in the Principato Ulteriore, and of the province of Capitanata. From the wood of Montemilone they could invade the mountainous zone known in the province of Bari under the name of Murgia. One cannot enter these dark and gloomy woods without perceiving at once how well adapted they are for the concealment of bandits, who, in their impenetrable recesses, may safely defy the troops sent in pursuit of them. So secure, indeed, did they find themselves in these sanctuaries, that they collected in them their stores and booty, and have been even known to conceal in them their ambulances for the sick and wounded.

With such secure retreats, in a country without roads, the brigands were in reality alsolute masters of the country. The fatal effects of the want of means of communication between the more populous centres of Southern Italy were well known to the Bourbons, but it was the interest of that selfish and degraded Government to take no step by which abuses could be remedied. It is true that they generally took care to keep the splendid roads in the immediate neighbourhood of Naples in a state of perfect repair, in order, by their magnificent appearance, to deceive foreigners into the belief that they spared neither labour nor expense in facilitating communication. They knew that the greater number of strangers confined themselves to the capital, nobody ever thinking of visiting the central provinces, such as Capitanata or Basilicata. At Naples, a mask of mock civilization was thrown over the city, while the provinces, where there was no one to observe the real state of things, were most cynically exposed. Basilicata, a province very nearly equal in extent to the whole of Tuscany, is almost entirely without carriage roads; the only ones being those between Melfi and Potenza, and from these places to Salerno, and thence to Naples. In addition to these, there is a road by Lagonegro, which puts the province of Cosenza in communication with that of Salerno; but beyond that there is no communication whatever with any place on the shore of the Ionian Sea. One may travel for ten or twenty miles over rugged footpaths, and along dangerous precipices, without meeting with a village or a hamlet. The inhabitants have no means of holding intercourse with the distant centres of such civilization as has extended to southern Italy; and as they have no roads, anything that deserves the name of commerce is utterly unknown.

The immense tract of country which separates the Abruzzi from Capitanata is equally destitute of roads. When the numerous proprietors in the Abruzzi, who are greatly interested in the neighbouring province of Foggia, are obliged to go there, they must make a long circuit, proceeding first to Naples, and thence to Foggia. Every year the shepherds who come down from the Abruzzi go across the so-called "tratturo"* on their way to Capitanata; but to them alone such

---

* A shepherd's footpath across the mountains.

a road is practicable, except in winter, when to all it is entirely impassable. Capitanata and the neighbouring province of Beneventum, are likewise without a single carriage road. In England it will scarcely be believed that, of the 1848 communes which formed the old Neapolitan kingdom, there were in 1860 no fewer than 1321 entirely without roads.

Such were the conditions in which the revolution found the Neapolitan provinces in the year 1860, and, notwithstanding the constant efforts of the Italian Government, very little improvement was discernible in them in 1862. Experience showed that it was impossible to destroy in so short a period the bad results of many centuries of corruption.

CHAPTER II.

CONDUCT OF THE DEPOSED DYNASTY—THE BAND OF LAGRANGE—GIORGI—COMPLICITY BETWEEN BOURBONISM AND BRIGANDISM—CROCCO—RENEWAL OF REACTIONARY EFFORTS—CONDUCT OF THE CLERGY—PASQUALE ROMANO—REMARKS ON THE ATTEMPT OF BORJÈS THE SPANIARD—COMPLICATION OF AFFAIRS—BRIGANDAGE STRENGTHENED BY MUNICIPAL DISSENSIONS—THE COMMUNAL ADMINISTRATIONS—DEFECTS IN THE PUBLIC ADMINISTRATION—THE OLD AND NEW MAGISTRACY—THE SYSTEM OF TRIAL BY JURY—THE POLICE ADMINISTRATION—FACILITY IN THE PAYMENT OF RANSOMS—THE ATTRACTIONS OF BRIGANDAGE.

CHAPTER II.

HAVING thus indicated some of the more remote or indirect causes that favoured brigandage in South Italy, I must now speak of those circumstances by which it acquired such strength, that it was able to oppose a bold and stubborn resistance to the utmost efforts of the Italian army. Among its proximate and immediate causes must be mentioned, in the first place, the conduct of the deposed dynasty. When the national movement developed itself in the southern provinces, preparations were already made to oppose it. Foreseeing the fate which awaited him, and faithful to family tradition and paternal dictation, Francis II. deliberately resolved to disturb the peace of those provinces which he had been unable to preserve. The first seeds of brigandage were sown in the latter years of the Bourbon reign. In the months of July and August, 1860, while declaring its wish to protect and promote constitutional liberty, it had prepared in secret the threads of that reaction with which, as in May, 1848, it hoped to suffocate the national movement. With this view the old officials were retained in the prefectures, and in the municipal and judicial courts, the old mayors obtained commissions as officers in the National Guards, the troops were promised indulgence in rapine and plunder, the prisons and hulks were designedly so ill-guarded, that, in less than one week, two hundred galley and prison convicts escaped from Castellamare and Avellino. Before abandoning Naples, Francis II. issued a decree which opened the prison doors immediately to many, to others in a short space of time. These measures were the result of a premeditated reactionary plot, and, in fact, in some localities, as, for example, at Bovino, either through excessive impatience, or because the necessary word was not transmitted at the proper time, attempts at reaction were made even before the departure of Francis II. from Naples. In October, 1860, when the Bourbon standard still floated on the walls of Capua, and Francis II. yet reigned from the right bank of the Volturno to the Roman border, the band of Lagrange was formed, recruited among the most miserable and ragged peasants of that part of the Terra di Lavoro. These bandits carried devastation and pillage wherever they passed, attacking several country places, and among others the town of Arpino, which, being strenuously defended by the citizens, repulsed and dispersed them. The country people were everywhere stirred up, and joined the regular troops. At Castelmorone, Piedimonte, Caiazzo, and Casolla, the volunteers of the southern army had to fight with armed countrymen. The sanguinary deeds of Isernia consisted of fierce conflicts between the soldiers and the lower class. The bands of Giorgi in the Abruzzi, as the reader is already aware, were composed of the most rapacious adventurers, burning only for pillage.

This Giorgi, accompanied by an officer of the Bourbon army, haranguing countrymen at San German, in order to persuade them to join the bands, said, "Francis II. intends to make short work with these *galantuomini*, who do you harm. He charged me to tell you he will give you all their goods and houses. I am also directed by the Pope to bless you in his name, and to absolve you from your sins;" words which indicate the purpose of the Bourbons to effect their restoration by means of social war, stirring up the passions of the poor against the rich, of the proletarian against the proprietor. When Capua fell, the kingdom of Francis II. was bounded by the walls of Gaëta, and Chiavone commenced his career. When he was driven by the regular troops out of Sora, which he had held for some days, he gave himself up to brigandage in the country.

The soldiers of the Bourbon army, on returning to their homes, were informed of what they were to do in the spring; and, in order that no doubts might arise, every one of them received a ring of a particular form, which was to serve as a sign of recognition. So that, from the very first days of the deliverance of the Neapolitan provinces, there is plain evidence of that complicity between Bourbonism and brigandism which still exists, and which, in the course of these pages, will be demonstrated by authentic documents. In the earlier days of the dictatorship of General Garibaldi, also, numerous and desperate efforts at reaction were made at Ariano, Montemiletto, Castiglione, Carbonara (in the province of Avellino), San Marco in Lamio, San Giovanni Rotondo, and almost all the country places in the Garganic district (province of Foggia), and in other localities. The first nucleus of the band of Cipriano La Gala, which afterwards for so long a time made havoc in Terra di Lavoro and the surrounding provinces, appeared also at the same period. While, therefore, a great political change was going on, which of necessity affected and injured many interests, and thus inevitably produced a general perturbation throughout the country, brigandage arose under the auspices of those who alone could promise themselves advantages from it, namely, the Bourbon dynasty. Without ever renouncing its true characteristics—robbery, rapine, and murder—brigandage, at the period of its first manifestation, had so strong a' political tendency as to kindle a civil war.

It is therefore perfectly idle to discuss the question, whether brigandage had an exclusively political origin or not. The party which is not ashamed to seek its proselytes and paladins among assassins and robbers, relieves others of the troublesome task of forming a judgment on it. The Bourbons, for their own political ends, let loose the fury of brigandage upon the Neapolitan provinces. This was in 1860. The ranks of the assassins were not slow in increasing; for recruiting was successful and rapid. The reaction which followed here and there had been repressed, not always without excesses, and of those who had instigated them many fled, and, not finding any other way of escape, took to the field. It must be added that in many cases the measures of repression had overstepped the limits of legitimate defence, and served as an easy pretext for the gratification of private rancour and personal revenge. Hence in many the desire of vengeance in their turn, a gratification which was to be obtained by siding with the brigand. Personal strifes and hatreds singularly ardent and tenacious, especially in little country places, provided in this manner fresh fuel for the flame. At Cervinara, Sansevero, and elsewhere, other reactions took place, and the result was the same. On the other hand, the prisons, carelessly and feebly guarded, furnished a dangerous and not inconsiderable contingent to the brigands. Criminals, escaped from the severity of retributive justice, naturally joined the bandits. The disbandment of the Bourbon army, in which discipline was far from strict, and the soldiers of which were accustomed to theft and falsehood, gave many adherents to the brigands.

The contingent furnished by the disbanded Bourbon soldiers, however, was not so numerous as might reasonably have been feared, though it became considerable enough when they were again summoned to military service. The first levy of brigands was therefore composed mainly of escaped convicts, of those who had taken part in suppressed reactions, of those charged with crimes or misdeeds, but who had not been brought to justice, of such deserters as had evaded the military levy, of disbanded soldiers, and of wretches urged by an insatiable craving for booty and pillage. But more than the dismissal of the disbanded men, their subsequent summons to their colours was the cause of a great revival of reaction, and hence of brigandage.

In the spring of 1861, the bands thus increased were animated by such a spirit of audacity as to attack villages and towns. Crocco, with his band, as we know, overran the neighbourhood of Sant Angelo dei Lombardi, robbing and murdering wherever he went, and giving up to pillage such places as Caliti, Monteverde, Conza, and Teora. The National Militia of the province of Avellino flew to combat with the infamous hordes, which were defeated and pursued as far as Venosa and Melfi. There they committed new atrocities. I have previously described how, entering Melfi amidst rejoicings and acclamations, Crocco hoisted the white flag. The Bourbon authorities were reinstated, and Francis II. proclaimed King of the Two Sicilies. On the approach, however, of such forces as it was possible to get together, the brigands fled, and their attempt at reaction had no result.

This renewal of reactionary efforts was occasioned by the recall of the disbanded soldiery. Some of these had already taken the field, but the majority were apparently living at peace in their homes. The announcement of the recall dissatisfied them exceedingly. The execution of the decree made matters worse, because suitable preparations had been omitted. There were even no established dépôts, so that, when men presented themselves, nothing having been got ready, they were sent back, and afterwards recalled—a process which sometimes took place three times successively. Not a few, to escape the obligations of military service, showed false discharges; while others, profiting by the opportunity, made a regular speculation in this fraud. These false discharges are said to have exceeded 30,000. The recalled disbanded soldiers were the principal instruments in the new reaction, especially in the provinces of Avellino and Bari, in July, 1861. On the seventh of that month thirty-one communes of the first of these two provinces hoisted the white flag, and even the town of Avellino was threatened.

The few disposable troops and the citizen volunteers set off to crush the rebellion. The resistance in some places was stubborn, but it was everywhere overcome; and at Candida, Chiusano, Montemiletto, Montefalcione, and Lapio, this outburst of reaction was suppressed. It was, in a great measure, instigated by the clergy, who were dreadfully exasperated at the promulgation of the law of the 17th of February, relating to the property of the convents. At Gioja, a populous and flourishing town of Terra di Bari, the brigands broke into the dwellings, but after a long conflict they were repulsed by the brave inhabitants and the National Guard.

Among the champions of reaction was one Pasquale Romano, formerly a sergeant in the disbanded Bourbon army, who, having succeeded in placing himself in safety, made himself chief of that company of brigands which, up to January, 1863, infested the greater part of the Puglie, and was named from him the Company of the Sergeant of Gioja. This fact demonstrates the intimate connection existing in the southern provinces between reaction and brigandage. Reaction subdued in towns becomes brigandage in the country; just as in those rare instances in which it has succeeded in establishing itself in the towns, it has immediately fused and assimilated itself with reaction. The same might have happened a few months later, in the year when the Spaniard Borjès attempted a rebellion in favour of the Bourbons. Pursued, first, by the Calabrese, and then contending with the inhabitants of Basilicata, he saw himself so reduced, like Crocco and others of the same stamp, that he was forced to become, not a guerilla leader, but a highway captain— an alternative to which he preferred flight. This was the last time that brigandage could boast important proportions in number and strength. If Borjès had succeeded in effecting his intentions, the horrible events of 1799 would have been repeated, and brigandage would again have recovered the throne for the Bourbon family. It may thus be considered as a settled point that the dynasty which knew not how to govern when it had at its disposal an army of 100,000 men, and a phalanx of officials and hirelings, sought, after having lost the throne, to recover it by subsidizing assassins. To the shame of an inglorious end is now added that of wicked acts to accomplish an impossible return.

Engendered and fostered by the causes we have enumerated, brigandage had, so to speak, encamped itself in the continental provinces of southern Italy, and, although clearly enough on the decline, it had inflicted all the injury it could, and produced a general sense of insecurity and uncertainty among the population. The permanence of brigandage is one of the most singular problems that this history presents. To account for it, we should have to investigate the sources whence it derives support, and enumerate the reasons why all the means adopted for its suppression have proved for a long time ineffectual. Without charging any political party with it, it is evident that a great social disorder, like brigandage, cannot but receive nourishment during such a grand work of political reorganization as that in which Italy is at present engaged.

Italy is going through a period of transition, the example of which is not to be found in the history of past revolutions—a work full of grandeur and glory, but bristling with difficulties, which must necessarily be greatest in those provinces of which the past misfortunes have been most severe. Errors were committed by the Government of the dictator, by that of the four lieutenants, and by the following administrations; and the well-intentioned efforts of each, as it came into office, to correct the mistakes of that which had preceded it, augmented their number. The rapid succession of different men produced uncertainty, and increased the unsteadiness natural to the infancy of any form of Government. To a population accustomed to see everything done swiftly and suddenly, the delays inevitable in the introduction of a different system could not but be alike inexplicable and intolerable. Hence a natural inclination to doubt, suspicion, discontent—all conducive to weakness, and stimulating rather than soothing the social disorder already existing. The state of dependence in which the people had been kept led them to blame the Government for good not done, for evil not repaired—to continue to talk of it as something distinct from the nation, if not antagonistic to it, and even to hold it responsible for its inheritance of past failings and wrongs. The heritage of historical reminiscences strengthened this tendency. The people remembered that when, in 1799, the Bourbons were driven out of the kingdom, they came back; that, again ejected in 1806, they again returned;

that, in 1820, the Government became again liberal, but, in a few months, through fraud and violence, returned to despotism; and that the same thing happened in 1848, in the brief space of three months. These recollections no doubt encountered a great obstacle in the power of the sentiment of nationality, and in the progressive appreciation of the new order of things; but their influence was not to be annihilated at a stroke, and it is not to be wondered at that they afforded support to guilty hopes and gave rise to wretched fears.

From this complication of affairs we see how serious were the difficulties of the period which intervened between the destruction of the old order of things and the commencement of the new—from the abolition of the reign of force to the inauguration, or, rather, the realization, of the rule of law. On the day when the system of Constitutional Government comes into full operation in these provinces, every pretext for distrust will disappear, and all will equally enjoy the protection of just laws.

From the apparent instability of the actual order of things, brigandage for a time derived strength and permanence. Municipal dissensions, too, which are especially injurious to small countries, where private animosities easily assume the appearance of political discord, and where the partisanship of an individual is often determined by his hostility to another, with whom he has had some differences, or against whom he cherishes some resentment—a tendency which is a legacy of the departed system, not to be easily destroyed—had also their due share in the developement of the agitation. That system lived only by encouraging distrust, animosities, discord, among the citizens, which, by a natural reaction, would, on its fall, be developed into vehement hatred, neither easily nor quickly extinguished. This reaction was natural, but not therefore exempt from the defect of all reactions—a tendency to exaggeration. Mutual distrust and jealousy were the natural results of the old system, as appeared plainly enough from the organization of the municipal body and the National Guards. Local ambition became more than usually ardent. The posts of syndics of the officers of the National Guard were eagerly coveted, being recognized as the means of obtaining authority over others, and not unfrequently of gratifying personal revenge. The new electoral system could not, of course, escape the unpropitious effects of such a state of things. From the moment when the dignity of the civil magistracy and the rank of officer in the National Guard were regarded as sources of power which might be applied to personal ends, the privileges of a free people, by a necessary reaction, degenerated into sources of social disorder, of which brigandage was the immediate consequence. The testimony of facts in this matter is direct and positive, and leaves no room for contradiction. The extent of brigandage could always be inferred from the state of the different provinces —it being most prevalent in those which were the most opposed to orderly government.

One of the few districts of the Basilicata free from brigands was the little commune of Vietri, situated on the borders of that province and Salerno—a locality so fortunate as to have no civil animosities. Altina, a fair and fertile village of the province of Terra di Lavoro, inhabited by a quiet and united population, possessing an excellent syndic and a good captain of the National Guard, has never been troubled with brigandage, though it has been busy enough in neighbouring districts. Civil discord is more rife in the Capitanata and the Basilicata, and there brigandage has always been very prevalent.

Two years ago, the brigands entered the large villages in Terra di Otranto, Grottaglie (in the district of Taranto), and Carovigno (in the district of Brindisi). In these places the municipal authorities were criminal, the National Guard unworthy, and they pillaged, destroyed, and murdered without opposition. A short distance from Carovigno, a little place called San Vito opposed a gallant resistance to the bandits, and beat them off. Four citizen volunteers were enough for the protection of Erchia, another place in the same district, from these savage inroads; the brigands, when they were fired upon, immediately taking to flight. In every place agitated by internal dissensions, governed by bad officials, and protected by unworthy National Guards, no effective resistance was offered to the brigands. This unhappy state of things is perhaps to be explained by the fact that the municipal officers had not yet formed an adequate idea of the importance and responsibility of their office.

At one time a syndic, a decurion, profited by his post to persecute his private enemies, anathematising them as liberals. In their turn the officials of the new government merely altered the word, and called their enemies Bourbonists. Besides it was difficult at first to accomplish a radical change, and many of the old municipal officers aided the machinations of the Bourbons, conspiring with the brigands. The communal administrations were generally not very active in their attention to the interests of the people. In Basilicata four or five councillors had even dared to declare publicly that it was not necessary to provide rudimentary instruction. In the municipality of Bisaccia, in the province of Avellino, which had an annual income of twenty thousand ducats, the only boys' school was a miserable place which hardly deserved the name. The National Guard was organized without the desirable precautions, the lists being so numerous, that even poor labourers were called to active service, losing, thereby, the wages on which they depended for their subsistence. From this circumstance, as discipline could not be attended to, great disorder arose, and one of the best guarantees of liberty was changed into an element of disturbance. Another cause of disorder was the fact that every municipality included an element which, adopting the term sanctioned by custom, we may call bureaucratic, which, although dependent on the orders of those representing the commune, was yet by no means without power in municipal affairs. In many places this bureaucratic power proceeded from the former state of things, or, rather, was simply a continuance of it, the old Bourbon opinions and traditions being preserved in such harmony with the new laws as could be maintained between them.

In many of the Neapolitan communes the secretariate of the municipal council, the same as in the time of the Bourbon decurion, not unfrequently exercised greater influence than it had ever arrogated before. The new syndics, either through indolence or lack of experience, allowed the old chancellerie of the commune, notwithstanding the new ordinances, still to exist upon the ancient model, a shoot of an old stock grafted on a new stem, which it certainly did not invigorate. It was only in such a state of things that, in a commune of the province of Terra di Lavoro, the communal secretary could agree for a given sum of money not to include the citizens in the list for the conscription, though this commune was called upon by the laws to provide thirteen recruits. Such facts as this produced in the minds of the population that unfortunate feeling of distrust which entailed such destructive results; for with them the most powerful argument in favour of the new state of things was their confidence in that justice which had no respect of persons.

The influence of good government and of just laws is seen in the working of the levy. In 1860 this operation proceeded in conformity with the ancient system, with all its concomitant abuses, and the result was by no means encouraging. In 1862 it proceeded according to the new laws, and the result has surpassed the greatest expectations. The people, seeing that justice was done to rich and poor alike, no exemption being granted merely on account of superior wealth, the levy came to a conclusion which, without exaggeration, might be called under such circumstances very satisfactory. Suffice it to say that even throughout the Garganic region, so much saddened by reaction, the number of the recalcitrant was exceedingly small. The operations of the levy of 1862 have not only provided for the necessities of military service, but, as one of the presidents of the council of the levy appropriately remarked, they have, by the way in which they were conducted, promoted the cause of liberty and morality. The eloquence of such facts as these will awaken in the southern people a feeling of faith in the stability and permanence of the new order of things.

The success of the levy of 1862 removed a cause of discontent and disorder, and therein a powerful source of brigandage itself. Provincial as well as municipal adminstration has suffered from the decay inherent in the old system. The same bureaucratic abuses with which the municipal administrations were visited existed also in the prefectures and subprefectures. The ancient employés encouraged the miserable notion that the changes made in the laws and institutions had not had the power to destroy the old evil customs. The despatch of public business suffered long delays, from which arose incalculable evils. There was so much corruption and venality that the administrative machine could not work with due regularity. Even in provinces where good and industrious prefects had been introduced, the evil could be cured only in one way—by extirpating the causes whence it took its rise. "You wish to destroy brigandage," said a wise Neapolitan to the commissioners of parliament; "well, strike at once the evil which grows out of the civil *camorra* existing among all the officers of our municipal administration, and you will have done half the work —from brigandage will be taken away one of its chief and constant supports."

As regularity and justice in public administration are the best guarantees of public safety, so their absence was the most powerful support to brigandage. Bureaucratic antagonism was not one of the least oppressive of the legacies which the Bourbons left to the National Government. This evil could be removed only by an entire transformation, for, while things remained in so unsatisfactory a state the Neapolitan provinces were deprived of the advantages of good administration. Many improvements, however, have taken place since 1860. Still, even in 1862, the administrative machine was not yet altogether renewed, nor did all its parts work in conformity with the new laws. So long as the administration worked imperfectly, there was, to a greater or less degree, the foundation of social disorder, and thence a support to brigandage. Many grave complaints regarding the administration of justice having been made, great changes have been effected in the judicial department in regard both to persons and things. From the 1st of May, 1862, the law of judicial organization has been applied in the southern provinces, but magistrates for the most part inexperienced have been charged with its execution. It was certain, too, that the administration of justice did not proceed with such expedition, nor was it so efficacious as was desirable. The trial of those accused of brigandage was carried on in three processes, and, generally speaking, without vigour. *Instructions* were slow and halting, and criminals were too frequently set at liberty.

The magistracy, like everything in the southern provinces, was going through a process of transformation from the old to the new, and it could not be reasonably hoped that, at the period of a crisis, affairs should proceed with the regularity of ordinary times. The procedure was novel, customs new, the code unknown, trial by jury, with all its benefits, necessarily subject to delays, the processes overwhelming, the prisons crowded with culprits, legal proof difficult in many cases, information often impossible of attainment, the sessions few and far between, on account of the extent of the ground to be gone over, the magistrates prevented by hostile interests, by the continual danger of life and property, from compelling witnesses to depose to the truth, the people prone to unjust accusations, and public opinion too exacting. All these are well-founded reasons, but none of them justify the severe censures lavished upon the magistracy, and the parliamentary commission strictly fulfilled the duty of impartiality by asking the House to take these circumstances into consideration. It could not conceal the fact, however, that in some things, apparently, at least, these censures were just; as, for instance, in the alleged negligence of too hastily acquitting on the ground of attenuating circumstances so much complained of, especially in the case of that famous verdict pronounced by the Tribunal of Potenza, in favour of some proprietors of Basilicata charged with complicity with Crocco and his hordes, who, in April, 1861, notoriously welcomed the entrance of the brigands into Melfi. The announcement of the sentence in this case greatly excited men's minds in the Basilicata. This affair was brought specially under the notice of government, as it was felt to be of the greatest importance to secure to the magistracy the greatest possible amount of public confidence.

In the judicial administration, too, there was a bureaucratic element, which infected every office. Like the municipal and administrative institutions, it still retained some of those elements of decay left by the Bourbons in everything. This corrupted bureaucracy could not, of course, find much favour with the populations, to whose minds the chancellors and their deputies recalled those who had been their terror in the old iniquitous criminal courts. The fact that the government was compelled to place under the surveillance of the police the chancellor and the deputy of the tribunal of one district, will in some measure account for and palliate the popular aversion and distrust.

In considering penal justice, we must make some remarks on trial by jury. It is satisfactory to know that the testimony everywhere given to this precious institution, since its first experimental introduction into the Neapolitan provinces, has been most favourable. The introduction of this system helped to restore that confidence in justice which, necessary in every civil community, is specially indispensable in the present condition of the south of Italy, as the want of confidence in the action of retributive justice tended greatly to the permanence of brigandage.

Another circumstance which was greatly in favour of the brigands was the want of a good police. The constant and well-directed action of a watchful and judicious police must be a great obstacle to the progress of brigandage, which could not exist in the country if it had not accomplices in the towns, who could be detected and convicted only by its agents. Hence it was that the brigands scoured the country, and secured an uninterrupted correspondence with their accomplices in cities and villages. Troops cannot supply the place of an active police. Brigands and soldiers have been found in the same house, the former entirely unsuspected by the latter. Frequently, when the brigands saw the soldiers coming, they hid their arms in a furrow behind a hedge, taking the pickaxe in their hand, and, by a sudden metamorphosis, became peaceful countrymen engaged in the labours of the field. These bandits so carefully avoid meeting the troops, that our military, speaking of encounters with them, are in the habit of saying, "We have had the rare fortune to meet them." By chance the troops learned the retreat of the band of Palliacello, which infested the neighbourhood of Cerignola, and captured the whole; by chance the lancers of Montebello have several times fought and routed the band of Caruso. The brigands, when they entered cities and villages to provide themselves with food and ammunition, and to procure medical aid, were not harmed in any way. They used to enter into and depart from large towns unobserved, no police whatever being on their track. When they sent notice to the landowners to pay ransoms there were no police to watch the bearers of such messages. If the authorities occasionally prevented their receiving food in the villages, they easily obtained it from the larger towns, without the knowledge of the authorities. If the syndics did not always exercise their functions as police, it was because they did not dare to do so. The fulfilment of their official obligations would have exposed them to musket balls or to the burning of their houses. The public security was neglected, not so much from bad intention as through fear and want of ability; most of those to whom, at the commencement of the revolution, the task of providing for the public safety was confided, possessing no great capacity for municipal duties. The brigands, on the other hand, were well organized, and had faithful agents at their command. Through these they were enabled to obtain precise information of the movements of the troops, of the places through which they were to pass, of the arrangements made by the authorities, and even of what was said in the towns about them. They had arranged a system of signs which never deceived them. In Capitanata, for instance, it was said, a peasant, riding off on an ass in a certain direction, gave intimation to the brigands who saw him, that the troops were about to march in the same direction. Hence the ease with which they eluded search, and the fatal success with which they prepared ambuscades for our soldiers.

When General Franzini devised the destruction of the

band of Cipriano della Gala, in order to ensure success he preserved the most scrupulous secrecy, and thus baffled the spies of the brigands. One of the most considerable of the proprietors of Foggia stated that, having one day had a long conversation with the prefect of the province, the next day the brigands proved to him that they had been accurately informed of all that had passed. From a farm in Capitanata, belonging to the family of the deputy Emidio Capelli, there were one day stolen a hundred and twenty-five brood mares. This whole booty was so skilfully concealed by the brigands that all efforts to recover it were in vain. They had information even of the decisions that were come to regarding themselves, and knew how to profit by it when the occasion presented itself.

A major in the army one day, in the neighbourhood of Martina, in Terra di Otranto, met several brigands, who, seeing themselves overmatched, threw down their arms. On being taken to the judge of Martina, they declared that they had so acted because they knew that they should thus escape being shot. The condition of the southern part of Italy was thus very favourable to the development of brigandage. Incredible as it may appear, these bandits had their bankers, their recruiting agents, and their dépôts. They found their recruits among the idle, the wretched, the reckless, and the lawless. The galleys and the prisons, both by reason of the numbers of their occupants, and from being badly guarded, constantly kept up the strength of their bands. The prison police was even unable to prevent communication between those within and those outside. In accordance with an old abuse, unfortunately still prevailing, entrance into the jails was seldom prohibited with the inexorable rigour which ought to have been observed; nor were the guards always persons inaccessible to corruption. In some places, notably at Brindisi, it was said that, as often as the brigands came into the neighbourhood, indications of excitement appeared among the convicts, and the attempts at escape were redoubled. Nor were these attempts isolated. The escape of prisoners or galley-slaves from one place of detention was often simultaneous with similar evasions from another at a considerable distance. The bagni and the prisons were the dépôts from which the brigands preferred to receive accessions to their numbers. From every arrival of criminals and convicts might be expected a fresh contingent to brigandage, which had its indefatigable supporters, who were ever ready to recruit men for its ranks. There were agents who forewarned the robbers of the movements of the troops and of the designs of the authorities, and who kept the country in a constant state of agitation by their assurances of the speedy return of Francis II. Many of them even pointed out to the brigands the richest houses to despoil, the wealthiest families to plunder, the most hostile proprietors to murder. Others, through fear, performed similar offices for them, dreading, if they should manifest any opposition or display any hesitation, the conflagration of their homes, the plunder of their property, and the slaughter of their cattle and horses.

The ransoms paid for the deliverance of captives, and the sums exacted for protection from injury, tended greatly to the support and spread of brigandage. With such an imperfect system of police it was rarely that the demands of these unscrupulous robbers were refused. Instances of such daring, however, were not wanting. The Prince of Sansevero, at the cost of much injury, has always prevented his agents from paying a single ransom to the band of Caruso. The brothers Domenico and Carlo del Sordo, of the city of Sansevero, have always refused to take the least notice of the threatening summons of the bandits. The syndic of Anzano, when the brigands threatened, if he did not pay a ransom, to burn his house and devastate his farm, replied by sending them a box of lucifers. Such instances prove that those who paid so readily the ransoms demanded were guilty of an amount of submissiveness which cannot be sufficiently condemned. The facility with which such impositions were paid, especially in the beginning, was in itself a painful indication that but little confidence was placed in the protection of the law. The fear manifested by the landowners was greater than their confidence in the power and justice of Government.

Such was the state of things, that, in the midst of surrounding poverty, the brigands were rich and abundantly supplied, not only with the necessaries, but with the luxuries of life. They were even provided with newspapers. Among the papers found on the body of Sergeant Romano, was the number of the 13th December, 1862, of the journal *La Stampa* of Naples, which contained an article called "Il Nuovo Ministero," overflowing with insults against Farini, Manna, and Pisanelli.* Caruso had, at Selva delle Grotte, an infirmary well provided with every necessary. In the asylum of Crocco, in the forest of Monticchio, there was plenty of victuals, wine, and provisions of every kind. In the forest of Lagopesole, the retreat of Ninco Nanco, the troops who, in January, 1863, were exploring the country, found many military greatcoats, and clean linen in large quantites, hidden in the hollows of the trunks of trees. Even musical instruments have been occasionally found. In the environs of Foggia, the best white bread, with the mark of the municipality of the city, has been seen on their tables. Brigandage was thus in a position to attract both the needy and the adventurous to its banners.

* All three members of the new Cabinet at that time.

CHAPTER III.

BRIGANDAGE AND THE CATHOLIC PRIESTHOOD—THE BRIGANDS' MASS—SUPERSTITION OF THE BRIGANDS—THE INFLUENCE OF RELIGIOUS FEAR—SERVICES RENDERED BY THE PRIESTS TO BRIGANDAGE—COMPLICITY OF THE BOURBON COMMITTEES WITH BRIGANDAGE—PILONE—GIUSEPPE TARDIO'S PROCLAMATION TO THE PEOPLE OF THE TWO SICILIES—ILLUSTRATION OF ADMINISTRATIVE CORRUPTION—TRISTANY—ENCOURAGEMENT OF BRIGANDAGE BY FRANCIS II.—ARRANGEMENT OF EXPEDITIONS FROM THE PONTIFICAL TERRITORY—PREDICTED RETURN OF FRANCIS II. TO NAPLES—TENACITY OF BRIGANDAGE IN THE NEAPOLITAN PROVINCES—FORMATION OF BRIGAND BANDS AT ROME—THEIR MILITARY EQUIPMENT AND ORGANIZATION.

CHAPTER III.

EVEN the rudest and most depraved human creature experiences from time to time the necessity of being supported by something which is neither food nor any other mere material gratification. However thick the darkness in which ignorance and crime may have wrapped the mind, it still feels itself occasionally swayed by aspirations which it cannot understand, but which it is unable to resist. Nor is the brigand exempted from the empire of this necessity. The gloomy atmosphere of murder and rapine has not the power of closing his eyes even to a feeble ray of light; and hence he is instinctively compelled to seek elsewhere that solace which he cannot find in the serene consciousness of innocence. Who holds out to him this consolation? The minister of that religion which especially abhors blood and crime, and unceasingly pours forth humane and charitable counsels. Yes, it is a melancholy truth, a great portion of the

Catholic priesthood has, in this sad affair of brigandage, proved false to its mission of peace and charity. We are not of course speaking of all the clergy, but of those members of the body who, sacrificing religious principles to worldly interests, and identifying the cause of the Church with that of a power essentially human and perishable, have ignored the magnitude of their duties, and have formed an alliance with all the enemies, open and concealed, of the peace and unity of the Italian nation. Goaded and provoked by the law on the suppression of convents, of February, 1861—alarmed at the prospect of the fall of ecclesiastical domination—these members of the Neapolitan clergy first sought to favour the reactionary movements, and then, when these were baffled and overthrown, instead of repenting their past course of action, they lent their aid to the natural heir of the reactionary movements—to brigandage. A single word spoken by them from the pulpit, a single hint uttered in the confessional, would have sufficed to remove, or, at least, to mitigate the scourge. But that word was not spoken; that hint was not given. It has been said, and the statement has been repeated in all the districts which were visited by the members of the Parliamentary commission, that from the confessional proceeded the incitements to brigandage. There is a difficulty in producing legal proofs of this assertion, but it does not the less express a universal moral conviction. Certain it is that a single word spoken in the confessional, addressed to the female relatives of the brigands, would have had an immediate salutary efficacy. Now, is it hazarding too much to infer, from the absence of the effect, the absence of the cause? The pulpits in the Neapolitan provinces have generally remained dumb; or, when they spoke, it was to brave the rigours of human justice, by advocating an iniquitous cause, by sacrilegiously seeking to raise the malefactor stained with infamy and blood to the dignity of a martyr. In December, 1862, in the pulpit of one of the most crowded churches of Naples, the preacher said, "Our brethren, the brigands, are obtaining victories in different provinces of Italy, and will always obtain them, because they are fighting against a usurping king; the Virgin cannot but perform the miracle of driving the usurpers from the kingdom." And another priest, when preaching in another church of the same city, in honour of the Immaculate Conception, broke out into the following apostrophe: "Oh! Immaculate Virgin, I will cease to believe that thou art a virgin, if thou dost not immediately restore to us our adored sovereigns, Francis and Maria Sophia." And if the pulpits had only remained dumb their silence respecting brigandage would have been a crime. Formerly it was the custom of the ministers of the sanctuary to implore from heaven the cessation of a public calamity. On this occasion nothing of the kind has been done. Sergeant Romano, the chief of the brigand band of Gioja, in the province of Bari, was in the habit of having a mass celebrated by priests, whom he paid for their services, in the chapel of the Masseria dei Monaci, which was commonly known as "the brigand's mass," thus attempting to make heaven the accomplice of their crimes. At Minervino, in the very same province, a corporal of our army was lying on his death-bed, and the priest, when called to administer the consolations and sacraments of religion to the brave man who had fought against the brigands, heartlessly refused them. At Viesti, in the Garganic district, merely because a priest, after performing mass before the troops, had chanted "Domine, salvum fac regem," the church was laid under an interdict. In another locality, on the contrary, a brigand entered the church on horseback, and, in that fashion, heard mass; nor, so far as we are aware, was any interdict ever pronounced. One of the Gargano brigands, nicknamed Prince Luigi, having succeeded, in an encounter with the lancers of Montebello, in saving his life by flight, chose to celebrate his escape as a miracle wrought by the blessed Virgin, and had a picture painted in which he was represented as protected from danger by the Vergine del Carmine. The picture was placed, with due religious solemnity, in the church of Monte Sant' Angelo. It is but justice to add, that the prefect of the province of Capitanata placed under arrest both the artist who had executed the picture and the priest who had lent himself to that act of profanation.

The brigands are extremely superstitious. On certain days they eat no butcher meat, although they never refrain from murder and robbery. In order to make themselves invulnerable, that they may be able to brave death with courage when about to enter on their bloody enterprises, they get themselves consecrated by a priest, who delivers to them the wafer of the Holy Sacrament, which, by means of an incision in the flesh, is inserted into the root of the thumb. Several brigands who, not long ago, fell into the hands of justice, deposed to having received from the priests little figures of saints, which, if kept in their mouths, they were assured would protect them from all harm in their encounters. Other brigands, captured in the neighbourhood of Zungoli, in the district of Ariano, wore on their breasts the Papal star. "The brigands," said once General Villarey, "whenever they can, have litanies chanted in the woods, and they wear on their persons little images of the Virgin and horns to protect them against the influence of the evil eye." When the brigand Sergeant Romano was out on his raids, he used to write sentences full of pious ejaculations, and he called the assassins who depended on his orders "the sworn soldiers of the Catholic faith."

Into minds thus ignorant and degraded by the constant habit of crime, religion can only penetrate in the form of fear. Remove this influence, and every restraint is destroyed. The brigand is not afraid of the criminal code, because he has been assured that, with the return of Francis II., he shall enjoy impunity. He is not afraid of the punishment of a future life, because the minister of religion has assured him that even by his crimes he is serving a righteous cause. It is sad to think of the clergy thus morally abetting the brigands—a work far worse than the mere abetting them by material means, for the help given by the latter must soon come to an end, whereas moral aid leaves its indelible marks in fanatical and superstitious minds. The spirit of murder remains implanted in the assassin's heart after the weapons of murder have been wrested from his hands. In the province of Salerno, five Capuchin monks were arrested in March 1862, because they had given every kind of assistance to the bandits. In order to convict them, some of our soldiers, disguising themselves as brigands, received from the monks the kindest reception, and were presented with a quantity of provisions, with the assurance that the convent was victualled for four hundred brigands. The convent of the Liguorini Fathers at Pagani, in the province of Salerno, was a regular recruiting station for the bandits. In the city of Andria, in Terra di Bari, many placards were circulated in August, 1862, with the following words :—"The brigands are blessed by the Pope, and as often as they fight, they charge in the name of God, and are sure of victory. A deputation, therefore, must be formed to go out and meet them with a white flag and bring them into the town, and then everything will be finished." In this city, with a population of more than 20,000 souls, there are about 300 priests and monks; and there have been cases—as was verified after the defeat which, in the beginning of November, 1862, a large brigand band sustained at the hands of the Montebello lancers, in the neighbourhood of Lucera—in which the priests actually belonged to the bands. One is therefore compelled to arrive at the painful conclusion that, in the southern provinces, brigandage received from a portion of the clergy encouragements of every kind.

Nor did less encouragement proceed from the Bourbon party. That party, which, in 1860, allowed its own flag to be covered with obloquy, which could defend neither its principles nor its king, which knew neither how to surrender with dignity nor to fall with glory, has been able to find no other expedient for revenge, but that of allying itself with assassins; of assisting, by advice, direction, and money, in the promotion of crime. The participation with brigandage of the Bourbon committees is a fact which cannot be contradicted, the trials of Monsignor Cenatiempo and the Bishop of Cosenza placing it in the fullest light. Other trials, for instance, that relating to the accomplices of the so called sergeant of Gioja, already mentioned, and that of the Princess Sciarra, confirm this fact in an indisputable way. But in a following chapter these trials will be fully placed under the eyes of the reader. The inquiries made in consequence of the detention of the Marquis Avitabile, and the capture of several followers of Pilone, produced the same result. Pilone called himself commander of the corps of operation in the neighbourhood of Naples, in the name of Francis II., and on his brigand's clothes bore the marks of a Bourbon knight. The other malefactor, Pizzichicchio, entered Grottaglie, flying the white flag on the trees, and shouting " Viva Francesco II. !" A Bourbonist, not long since arrested, declared that the Bourbon committee at Naples had sent orders to Crocco to capture the members of the Parliamentary Commission of Inquiry on their passage through the Puglie—orders which must have been sent also to his subordinates, or to people with whom they were in correspondence. One, Giuseppe Tardio, of Centola, province of Salerno, a youth of twenty-five, a civilian, formerly a student of law at the Salernitan Lyceum, made a journey to Rome, whence he marched off to his district, where he put himself at the head of a band of wrong-doers who infested the commune of Vallo. Without the least attempt at concealing the name of him who was disturbing the public peace, there appeared in July, 1862, the following proclamation :—

"*To the People of the Two Sicilies.*

"CITIZENS!—The factious despotism of the Piedmontese government seduced you, at the conquest of the kingdom, by deceiving promises. You have reaped bitter fruits therefrom. This fair country is reduced to a province, you are oppressed with taxes, loaded with misery and desolation. They have inaugurated among you a system of shooting for reasons of State. (What a Re Galantuomo for you!) They are the more violent now that they have brandished their arms for a year. Delay not to arm and array yourselves under the standard of your legitimate sovereign Francis II., the only symbol and bulwark of right, of humanity, of citizenship, and of the commercial prosperity and wealth of the people. Will you hesitate to encounter fearlessly the hateful Piedmontese soldiers, and thus compel them to pass over the Liri?

"Published in . . . . and by confirmed copy in this commune July 2, 1863.

  (Signed)   "GIUSEPPE TARDIO,
    "Captain Commanding the Bourbon Army."

Near the confirmation was a seal with the Bourbon arms.

Tardio also exacted ransom in the name of Francis II. The following is one of his documents:

"*Francis II., King of the Two Sicilies.*

"Don Raffaele Salerno, of the commune of Camerota, is desired to pay the bearer without delay the sum of 120 ducats, to serve for payment of the individuals comprising the column under my command. This is therefore brought to his knowledge.

  (Signed) "GIUSEPPE TARDIO,
    "Captain Commanding the Bourbon Forces."

As an illustration of what has been previously said regarding the administrative corruption prevailing in many districts, this adventurer, as appears by the following letter, found accomplices in the municipals of Camerota:—

"Camerota, July 4th, 1863.
"*Administration of the Commune of Camerota to the Delegate Don Paolo Ambrosano.*

"SIR,—We send you two women, to whom you shall give, with all possible haste, as much bread as they can carry, to serve for the armed force about to join in this district, and the expenses will be paid by this commune.

(Signed) "THE MUNICIPAL COUNCIL."

An officer who, for several months, was in command of the military district of Vasti, in Abruzzo Citeriore, stated that a brigand, who was sentenced to death, declared that his captain, named Pizzolungo, had read to him and to his comrades an order of the day, issued from Rome by Francis II., in which that deposed monarch announced his speedy return to his states, and exhorted the brigands to persevere in their hostility to the new government. In another letter, found on the persons of the wretches who had formed part of the band of Chiavone, it was plainly intimated that some of the malefactors had direct personal relations with Francis II., and kept him informed of all that the brigands were doing.

Francis II. is said to have entertained very bitter feelings towards Tristany, by whose orders Chiavone and some of the most faithful members of his band were shot,* believing that in him he had lost one of his most faithful and affectionate servants. In the beginning of the year 1863, a youth, who had been detained by the band of Crocco in the district of Sant' Angelo dei Lombardi, being questioned by the Delegate of Public Security, deposed that, while among the brigands, he had seen them joined by one Teodoro, with his band, who said to Crocco—"Two days ago one of our friends came to tell me that our King Francis will send us, in the spring, reinforcements of men, with foreign officers, ammunition, and money. And he will soon be able to put himself at

---

* According to another version, this was only a fiction, and Chiavone was not shot, but safely concealed in the recesses of the eternal city. Curiously enough, I was once in communication with a man who was connected with the Bourbonist conspiracies, and it is from him that I received the above information. He said to me that at Rome he had seen repeatedly this chief brigand at the palace of His Royal Highness the Count of Trapani, uncle of Francis II., and had afterwards met him again in the mountains of St. Angelo, where he had brought him a sum of money he had received from the well-known Bourbonist, General Vial, which was to pay the daily expenses of his brigands. Abiding by such a statement, this velvet-clad bandit was in direct correspondence with the aforesaid Royal Highness, and, in recompense of his services, was created captain by King Francis. I was then told that at last, seeing that life in the mountains was getting dangerous, he secretly repaired with his anything but honestly earned savings, represented to be very considerable, to Rome, where he lived retired in a convent of monks—strange but instructive metamorphosis!

the head of the soldiers of the Pope and of Austria, in order to return to his kingdom." A peasant who had been sent to redeem this young man confirmed his statement. One of Crocco's comrades, by name Sacchitiello, also confessed that he had joined this band because he had been asked on the part of the king to do so. "Now," continued he, "we were told yesterday by Teodoro, the captain of the band which came to join us, that he had had notice from the king that in the spring he would certainly send a large force with foreign officers and money, and that he would also himself join us. We therefore await the fulfilment of this promise. Then I should find myself, my dear fellow, quite in another position! Enough for the present—we shall meet again!"

On the first of February in the same year, a brigand named Francesco Gambaro, who was in Sant' Angelo dei Lombardi, being asked with what object he had joined the brigands, replied—" I attached myself to the band, of which Andreotti and Sacchitiello were chiefs, about the sixteenth of August last year, the day of Saint Rocco. The band was then about forty in number. Being a shepherd, frequently in contact with the brigands, they persuaded me that they were protected by Francis II., who sent them money, ammunition, and arms, and that he would soon re-enter his kingdom, and give us much land in the commune. They also told me that the king was the son of a saint, who protected him and us."

All the incursions of brigands from the pontifical territory are arranged by the Bourbon committees scattered here and there beyond the limits of the kingdom of Italy, acting in concert with those within its limits. These foreign committees are found at Marseilles, at Paris, and at Malta; they abound in Rome and at places nearer to our frontier. The committee of Alatri was presided over by the bishop of the diocese. The heads of these committees resident in Rome notoriously form part of the court of Francis II., and the communication, by means of couriers, between them and the Neapolitan provinces is incessant. The prince, who, cognizant of all their machinations, does not hesitate, under the shelter of a foreign flag, to let loose hordes of miscreants, to carry desolation into those provinces which he was unable by his valour to preserve, has surely forfeited all claim to that respect which men are always ready to pay to unmerited misfortune. He appears no longer as the dethroned monarch, but as the accomplice of such men as Crocco or Ninco Nanco.

The material assistance which the residence of Francis II. in the eternal city affords to brigandage is not its worst consequence. Its moral and political effects are a great deal more injurious, disturbing the peace and interfering with the progress of the southern provinces. In the same way as, during the ten years of the French military occupation at the beginning of this century, the sojourn of Ferdinand I. and his court in Sicily kept alive the hopes of the partisans of the Bourbon dynasty, so the actual residence of Francis II. in Rome keeps alive to this day the hopes of his adherents. Those who, during the last ten years, have never lost their faith in the ultimate return of the Bourbons, have been christened by the populace "speranzuoli." Relying upon the ignorance and credulity of the multitude, they spread the most absurd reports, by which they sometimes succeed in producing a certain amount of agitation in the public mind. Yesterday the Austrians are said to have occupied part of the old state; to-day the French have compelled King Victor Emmanuel to throw down the crown of Italy and agree to the confederation. Then the return of Francis II. to Naples is confidently predicted, a prophecy which obtains credence from the presence of that monarch at Rome, the guest of the Pope, unharmed by the French, and surrounded by a Court, with ambassadors accredited to him as though he were in the full exercise of the functions of sovereignty. There, free to do what best suits his own purpose, he plots against the welfare of Italy, and seems to this imaginative people scarcely less powerful than if he were on the throne at Naples. Serious doubts as to the stability of the new Government are thus generated, and men of unsettled character are easily drawn into the vortex of brigandage, believing that to them it will be a source of honour, renown, and wealth. The judge of the district of Cerignola stated that he had been informed, by a brigand in one of the prisons of that city, that Crocco had declared he should hasten to place himself in the hands of justice whenever he was assured that Victor Emmanuel had entered Rome. The same brigand is also stated to have twice gone to Rome, disguised as a monk, to confer with Francis II.

The stay of Francis II. in Rome points also to another great cause of the duration and tenacity of brigandage in the Neapolitan provinces —that is to say, the connivance, and complicity of the Pontifical Government. It will be said, perhaps, that hospitality does not imply perfect unity between him who gives and him who accepts; that a benefit does not confer on the benefactor the right of fettering the liberty of action of the benefited, and that, therefore, he who gives hospitality may repudiate all responsibility for the conduct of him who receives it. But it is, above all, important to reflect that the hospitality bestowed by the Pontifical

Government is not a consequence of the principle of the right of asylum, sacred and inviolable among free nations, but simply a spontaneous and revocable concession of that Government. The wishes and acts of the Pontifical Government and the Bourbon Court are so nearly identical as to afford full evidence of their common responsibility. The inhabitants of the Vatican are not ignorant of the conduct and acts of the occupiers of the Farnese Palace, and therefore are as accountable for them as though they were their own. And it is a truth which needs no demonstration, that the means by which brigandage is maintained in the Neapolitan provinces by Francis II. and his cosmopolitan followers in Rome, must in the future annals of Italy condemn him to eternal infamy.

It is said that the asylum conceded in Rome to Francis II. was prompted by gratitude, Pius IX. wishing to repay the son for the hospitality shown by the father in the year 1848 and 1849. But, considering the peculiar circumstances of his residence in Rome, Francis II. must be regarded as abusing the hospitality bestowed on him by the Pope, from whose tolerance of an evil of which we cannot conceive him ignorant, we are compelled to infer his complicity. " Francis II.," said an inhabitant of Sora, " is the pivot of brigandage, and the Pontifical Government is its open protector."

"The root of brigandage," said the senator Ferrigni, advocate-general before the Court of Appeal, "is at Rome, and, until it is pulled up, brigandage cannot be extirpated." "From Rome," said the senator Niutta, president of the same Court, "comes the chief support of brigandage." "Its principal inducement," said the illustrious Luigi Settembrini, "comes from Rome, whence is circulated, even more than money, the idea that the king of the Two Sicilies is there, and that he is able to return at any time."

The opinions thus authoritatively pronounced are supported by facts. At Rome there is a regular organization for the formation of brigand bands. The convents of Trisulti and of Casamari were notable receptacles for these outlaws. In 1861, Monsignor Montieri, bishop of the diocese of Sora, now dead, establishing himself at the convent of Casamari, organized, with the assistance of the father abbot of the monastery and of several foreign supporters of legitimacy, that band of brigands, commanded by De Christen, which was defeated by the troops under the gallant General Count Maurice de Sonnaz. Although the Pontifical police has employed all its ingenuity to conceal its complicity with the brigands, yet the truth was betrayed by various circumstances. The bands were permitted to organize themselves without molestation or restraint. Tristany always made provision of bread and victuals within St. Peter's patrimony, and the Pontifical authorities found no cause for complaint. In March, 1862, one hundred and twenty-one rations of bread were daily sent from Veroli to the brigands assembled at the convent of Trisulti. Two native highwaymen of Selva di Sora, who lived at Veroli, acted as guides both to Tristany and to the Papal gendarmes.

None of the peasantry of the provinces of Frosinone and Velletri, in which the bands were organized, joined them—they were composed chiefly of foreign adventurers, many, probably, criminals and vagabonds escaped from the Neapolitan provinces. The members of the band of Tristany were, for the most part, clothed in military uniform, their officers bearing the distinctive marks of their respective grades. The Pontifical police, apparently unconscious of these hostile preparations, allowed them, as they do still, to be completed without the slightest interference.*

* At the end of the summer, 1861, the band commanded by Chiavone, which, as has been seen in the first volume, was so many times destroyed and again organized, had at one period attained, as far as regards numbers, considerable importance. It was composed of eight companies, of fifty men each, its chiefs bearing grades and titles borrowed from the military hierarchy. The members of this band, and especially the chiefs, were nearly all foreign adventurers—Spanish, French, Swiss, Irish, and notably the Belgian Marquis de Trazigny. The band used to take up its quarters with impunity near the

Although the brigands, on crossing the frontier, were met and dispersed by our troops, they were always able to reorganize themselves, by returning into the Roman territory. At Campo di Fiori, and at the Piazza Montanara in Rome, there were agents who enlisted recruits for the brigand ranks, obtaining them among the peasants of the Abruzzo Aquilano, who, on account of their crimes, were at enmity with the law. The Pontifical Government aided them with arms and with money, employing all manner of artifices in order to avoid discovery. Having provided, for instance, several hundred military cloaks, it announced its intention to dispose of them by a public sale. A French priest, who presented himself, made a show of buying them; and, as soon as they were in his power, they were at once consigned to those for whom they were destined. The Bourbon committees of Alatri, Frosinone, Ceccano, Velletri, and Pratica, employed themselves incessantly in assisting the brigands in every way. On the committee of Frosinone was a judge, the episcopal chancellor, two canons, and a curate; on that of Ceccano, a person attached to the household of Cardinal Antonelli; on that of Alatri

frontier of Sora, between Santa Francesca and Casamari; it even had its regular vedettes and vanguards. It was never molested by the Papal authorities until the 11th of November, 1861, when the bandits resolved to cross over to the Italian territory—it is known with what result.

included two canons ; and on that of Pratica the curate, who sometimes used to accompany the brigands in person. At the abbey of the Passionisti, in Ceccano, resided a pontifical gendarme and two pensioned gendarmes, who acted as guides to the robbers.

Tristany never attempted to conceal his object, openly assuming the title of field-marshal commanding the royal troops of the kingdom of the Two Sicilies, as will be seen from the following original document :—

"*The Supreme Commandant of the Royal Troops of the Kingdom of the Two Sicilies.*

"No. 41.

" I despatch with great haste my quartermaster, with instructions to exact sums of money from certain people whom you know, and to whom are directed the enclosed papers. On the receipt of the money the said quartermaster will give to the interested parties the regular receipt. I engage you to employ all his energies in this affair, assuring him of my entire consideration.

"From the head-quarters of Rendinara, July 15th, 1862.

(Signed) " R. TRISTANY, *Field-Marshal.*
" To Signor Isidoro Borselli, Captain in Ceprano."

Near the signature of Tristany is the impression of

the Bourbon seal, identical with that which has been mentioned in speaking of the letter of the brigand Tardio, in the province of Salerno. It even appears, from the depositions given on the 27th of January, 1862, by the two brothers Colafella, ex-Bourbon soldiers, before the president of the great criminal court of Chieti, that the enrolled Bourbonists, volunteers, and veterans were quartered, some without, some within Rome, the latter at San Sisto; that their officers were partly Neapolitans and partly strangers; that among them there were Calabrese, Abruzzese, Sicilians, and Neapolitans, who received direct orders from Francis II.; that before they were billeted they had from him a daily allowance; that, besides a full military accoutrement, they were provided with guns, bayonets, and daggers; and that they were even obliged to go through the regular military drill.

On the night of the fifth or sixth of April, 1862, two hundred brigands, who, as usual, had been recruited and drilled on the Pontifical territory, crossed the Liri, and at ten in the forenoon of the sixth fell unexpectedly on Luco, a small place on the banks of Lake Fucino, in the district of Avezzano. The garrison was composed of a detachment of twenty men of the 44th regiment of Italian infantry, five of whom were absent on service. The brigands, whose courage was inspired by their overwhelming number, occupied in a few moments the whole village. The sergeant who commanded the detachment shut himself up in the barracks, resolved to sell his life dearly. The fight was long and deadly. As the brigands were unable to force the door of the barrack, they climbed on to the roof, through holes in which some of them threw down tiles, while the rest collected faggots, which they set on fire, the soldiers meanwhile firing through the windows and the openings in the roof. When the fight had lasted three hours, the roof being already on fire, and threatening to bury the heroic band under its smoking ruins, a patrol of five men and a corporal, who had come from the neighbouring village of Trasacco, hearing the noise of musketry, rushed to the aid of their besieged comrades. The brave corporal advanced fearlessly upon Luco, shouting the war-cry of the Piedmontese regiments, "Savoia! Savoia!" * The brigands, who were on the watch on the outskirts of the village, supposing that these few soldiers were the advance guard of a column of troops about to attack them, gave the signal which warned their comrades of the supposed danger, and the whole band took to flight.

* "Savoia! Savoia!" was the old war-cry of the Dukes of Savoy, and from the scanty but stubborn ranks of the Piedmontese army it has been adopted as a glorious tradition by the young legions of united Italy.

Their chief was one Pasquale Mancini, of Pacentro, lieutenant of Chiavone; he was taken and shot, and the band decimated and dispersed. Among those arrested was a certain Paduli, once a Bourbon sergeant, who, when asked, declared that their dépôt was at Rome, in Campo di Fiori, in the vicinity of which arms had been distributed by a priest named Don Luigi, who bestowed his benediction upon them, and then directed them to Anticolo, on their way to which they found at a farmhouse military clothes, including cloaks and knapsacks.

CHAPTER IV.

IMPORTANT DOCUMENTS—REPARATION FOR AN INSULT TO THE ITALIAN FLAG—CUCITTO—THE MURDER OF SPINA—NECESSITY OF ROME TO ITALY—THE FRENCH PROTECTORATE AN ENCOURAGEMENT TO BRIGANDAGE—SYMPATHY BETWEEN ITALIAN AND FRENCH SOLDIERS—FURTIVE LANDINGS ON THE COAST—PATIENT HEROISM OF THE ITALIAN ARMY—ITS SUFFERINGS FROM THE CLIMATE, SICKNESS, AND PRIVATIONS—GENERAL LAMARMORA—INFERIOR MORALE OF THE BRIGANDS—ORIGIN OF THEIR CHIEFS—RELIGIOUS EXPERIENCE OF A BRIGAND—THE FOREIGN BANDITS—HAUNTS OF THE BRIGANDS—ERADICATION OF BRIGANDAGE.

* Vol. II.

CHAPTER IV.

THE Papal Government, as is evident from the facts mentioned in the preceding chapter, showed its complicity in every way with the brigands. Not only were they allowed to enroll and drill recruits, but the bands had full permission to overrun the Roman territory without molestation, seeking shelter from the just punishment which the Italian troops would certainly have inflicted on them if they could have passed the frontiers. Full power, moreover, was given to the chiefs of the expeditions to obtain provisions in the country, and gendarmes were given to them as guides. What more could the Pontifical Government have done to show its ceaseless complicity with brigandage ?

In spite of the astuteness of the Pontifical police, there are not wanting authentic documents which further corroborate this important fact. The two letters subjoined were written by a brigadier of the Pontifical Gendarmes, who certainly could have had no correspondence with the brigands if he had not had the permission or connivance of his superiors. This brigadier, in correspondence with Chiavone, styles him His Excellency. At this time reinforcements in men and arms were coming from Rome and from Velletri to Chiavone, who was in the mountains between Veroli and Sora; but, in order to save appearances, these men avoided the principal roads, and, leaving Terracina on the right, reached the residence of the brigand chief, where the band had been summoned to assemble. At Sezze, one Gallozzi, a servant and neighbour of the house of Antonelli, was nominated by Chiavone first lieutenant and then captain, with the duty of collecting, directing, and providing for the brigands. Some similar duty seems to have been entrusted to the gendarme who wrote the letter, and to him who, in answering it, accepted the offer. The following is the letter:—

"September 5th, 1861.
"Pontifical Gendarmerie,
"Bureau of the brigade of Vallecorsa.

"EXCELLENCY,—Quite undeservedly I have received from two of your couriers your despatch of yesterday. From the said two couriers I have been informed of all that your Excellency desires me to do. On my part, I assure your Excellency that I will do everything, even at the cost of my life, to satisfy your wishes ; and I pray you to rest assured that all will be provided with the greatest promptitude and secresy. Meanwhile, with sentiments of the highest esteem and most profound respect of your Excellency's most humble servant,

(Signed) "GAETANO BOLOGNESI,
"Commander of the brigade.
"To his Excellency, the General-in-chief Chiavone."

Under the signature is the stamp of the Pontifical Gendarmerie. The other letter was addressed to Galozzi :—

"ESTEEMED AND EXCELLENT SIGNOR LIEUTENANT GALLOZZI,—Quite undeservedly, Signor Lieutenant, I have at this moment received, by means of two couriers, a despatch of his Excellency the General-in-chief, Luigi Chiavone, commanding all the royal Neapolitan troops, which desires me to endeavour to assist in every possible way, and carry in safety beyond my jurisdiction the men and the weapons they have with them, who are joining him from this quarter. Whereby, Signor Lieutenant, I pray you to assure the worthy General that I will do all I can, even at the risk of my life, to gratify his wishes, which are enjoined upon me in the said dispatch.

" And I also inform you, Signor Lieutenant, that your excellent family are in perfect health, and I go almost every day to your dwelling, to exhort your worthy wife to remain in the most perfect tranquillity in all respects while we are on the track of the iniquitous and assassin-like Piedmontese, who have even dared to make an attempt against the rights of the Holy Church. In this juncture I beg you, Signor Lieutenant, to inform his Majesty, by means of his Excellency, General Chiavone, of the faithfulness with which I have served his troops; and even should we find ourselves at more critical periods, I would never cease my co-operation. But very soon success will be ours.

"Counting on your tried goodness that you will attend to the above, I beg you at the same time to pardon the liberty which I take. Meanwhile, with sentiments of the highest esteem and most profound respect, I have the honour to subscribe myself,

"GAETANO BOLOGNESI, *Brigadier.*
"From Vallecorsa, September 5th, 1861."

The stamp of the Pontifical Gendarmerie is appended to this second letter also. Another brigadier of the Pontifical Gendarmerie, by name Fontini, commanding the station of Torretreponti, wrote to his captain, Chevalier Fabbo, at Velletri, a letter, in which he informed him that he had recovered ten Spanish officers intended to join an the mountains the troops of Francis II., *i.e.*, the brigands; that he had kept them out of the way of the French troops, and then sent them, with two guides, on to the place where they were to present themselves.

On the 16th of July, 1861, four Italian carabineers, exploring the mountain of Sora, saw a man dressed as a peasant, who said to them (thus revealing the password): "Well, are you looking for our general?" The carabineers, perceiving immediately that there was a mistake, answered in the affirmative. "Well, then," he replied, "I'll take you to him, but wait a moment." After saying this, he approached a tree, climbed up into it, took from it a gun hidden among the branches, and then set off towards the top of the mountain as if to guide the carabineers, who, however, did not permit him to continue his journey, but arrested him, and took him to Sora. This man, who belonged to the band of Chiavone, had imagined that our carabineers were Pontifical gendarmes.

The Pontifical gendarmes insulted the Italian flag whenever they had an opportunity. At the bridge of Isoletta, they fired upon it from the opposite bank of the Liri. As soon as Major Freyre, commandant of the 4th battalion of the 59th infantry, was informed of the outrage, he hastened to send to the captain commanding one of the companies of the battalion stationed at Isoletta a telegram, complaining of the manner in which the Italian flag had been insulted by the Pontifical gendarmes. The same officer also sent a telegram to the commander of the French troops in Ceprano, declaring that he had a right to look to him for some reparation of the wrong that had been done. In accordance with the orders of General de Montebello, commander of the French troops in Rome, the reparation demanded was made. On the morning of the 14th September, the French and Italian troops being present, the Pontifical gendarmes, with uncovered heads, advanced, supporting the edges of the outraged flag to the middle of the bridge of Isoletta, where, being met by Major Freyre, the flag was restored by the French commander with an ample apology for the conduct of the Pontifical troops. The Major replied in suitable terms, at the same time assuring the Pontifical gendarmes that if they transgressed by a single step the line assigned to them, they should assuredly suffer for their rashness, as the gallant hands to whose custody the Italian flag was entrusted, would never allow it to be insulted with impunity.

When the brigands find it impossible to keep the field, they do all they can to gain the Papal frontier, sure of finding there shelter, aid, and protection. And when the guilty do fall into the hands of justice, this is owing rather to the French than to the Papal authorities. When the brigand Cucitto barbarously murdered the syndic of Mola di Gaëta, by name Spina, he took refuge in the Papal territory. At Rome he boasted in public of the murder he had committed, and showed the watch he had taken from his victim. The homicide stayed some time in Terracina, unnoticed by the Papal police, and for several months went about the country, until, in consequence of the extradition requested by the commander of the Italian troops in Gaëta, he was taken by the French, and consigned to our authority. The murder of Spina was a deed of the most barbarous character. He had, in Frosinone, a brother, who was the Abbot of the monks of the "Sangue Sparso." This relative having been captured by Chiavone, Spina sought the influence of the Papal authorities to obtain his deliverance. A non-commissioned officer of the Papal gendarmes was accordingly sent, by desire of the delegate of Frosinone, requesting Chiavone to order the liberation of Spina's brother. Chiavone, having asked Galozzi for information as to the circumstances of the case, the latter wrote the following letter in reply :—

" EXCELLENT DON LUIGI,—Francesco Spina, syndic and commissary of the Italian Government, in the commune of Mola, has already had his head cut off, and the 'moustache' of the deceased has been brought to Rome by Cucitto. Francesco Piazza, *alias* Cucitto, has, in my opinion, done well, and rendered a service in taking the life of a celebrated revolutionary enemy of our own master, the king. The defunct syndic had summoned Cucitto, and wished to force him to form a volunteer band by promising him a large sum of money. This band was to have marched against us, to destroy us, and he wished, also, to induce him to murder even you; but Cucitto, instead of turning traitor, killed him, and, thereby, I think, has fulfilled the sacred duty in which we are all engaged.

"Your most devoted, humble servant,
  (Signed)   "GIUSEPPE GALLOZZI.
"December 16th, 1861."

But for the intervention of the French, we may conclude that, as far as the Papal authorities are concerned, Cucitto would have been at this moment at liberty to commit new atrocities with impunity. All the brigands who have been arrested by the French, and handed over to the Pontifical authorities, have invariably been set at liberty, and have again joined these bands of malefactors.

The Pontifical authorities take charge of the prisoners made by the brigands, when—a very rare thing—any of our troops are captured by them. A case of this kind, however, happened in the month of July, 1862. A portion of a detachment composed of carabineers and of soldiers of the 11th infantry, exploring the mountain of Fossa della Neve, fell into the hands of the murderer Crocco, by whom they were consigned to the Pontifical gendarmes, passed on by them to Rome, and from thence to Civita Vecchia, where was the dépôt of the Papal mercenaries. Although great efforts were made to induce them to desert the Italian flag, and take service with the brigands or in the army of the Pope, only two of them, soldiers of the disbanded Bourbon army, allowed themselves to be seduced. All attempts to gain over the others having failed, they were embarked and taken to Genoa. A few days afterwards an official periodical of Rome, giving an account of the affair in its own way, took the opportunity of praising the generosity of the Papal government, attributing to its magnanimity a resolve which was the natural consequence of the faithfulness of these soldiers.

Many instances might be added of the united action of the brigands and the Pontifical troops, a complicity which is apparent on many occasions; the Papal Government assisting in every way the work of brigandage, even protecting in Rome the recruiting agents of the brigands. This they did out of hostility to the new order of things. The instructions to the Neapolitan episcopate, also, as proved by the proceedings against the bishop of the diocese of Foggia, were undoubtedly prompted by a sentiment of undisguised aversion towards the Italian Government, whose consolidation Rome has in every way attempted to prevent. The instinct of self-preservation would be enough to make Italians desire the recovery of Rome, because by this means the chief support of brigandage would be taken away. The alliance between that nefarious system and the temporal power of the Popes has placed in relief, more than anything else, the necessity of the restitution of Rome to Italy.

In the meanwhile, the generous protection of France has been extended to this territory. It is not my intention to consider either the motives by which the French were induced to occupy Rome, or those by which the Emperor was prompted to prolong the occupation after the peace of Villafranca. From that unfortunate circumstance, however, brigandage derived great moral and material support. The presence of the French troops in that central part of the Italian peninsula has always afforded a pretext to the enemies of Italy and of the French alliance for the expression of a want of faith in the destinies of the one, and in the sincerity of the other. The Bourbonists have constantly asserted that France was averse to Italian unity, and wished at all costs to revert to the treaty of Villafranca. The Emperor Napoleon was said to keep his soldiers in Rome because he did not wish that Italy should be one, an assertion to which he owes that mistrust with which he is regarded by so many Italians. The presence of the French has consequently been a great encouragement to the brigands, who, when pursued by our troops, have always found safety as soon as they stepped on ground protected by the flag of France. Chiavone and Tristany have thus availed themselves of the protection which the French arms only meant to bestow upon the Pope.

It is true that the French troops always treated the Italian soldiers as brothers-in-arms, and that the French generals have always shown the utmost respect to the illustrious conqueror of Traktyr, General Lamarmora and his lieutenants, and whenever they have encountered the brigands they have invariably dispersed them or made them prisoners; but it is equally true that the French have to do with a government which, in return for their protection, seeks every means of compromising them. In the opinion of the French the complicity of the Pontifical Government with brigandage has been much exaggerated. Brigandage, they say, might be effectually combated by a local police, whose duty it would be to keep a constant watch on the proceedings of the brigands; but whenever the troops are set in movement against them they are straightway informed by the ever-active Pontifical police. There have even been sometimes French commanders who have taken such an exaggerated view of their military duty, as to be alarmed by the appearance in the waters of Terracina of an Italian ship on cruise, when her only object was to watch any possible attempt to disembark brigands on the shores of Gaëta. The operations of the Italian troops must have been very much obstructed by these causes. The brigands, restrained by no laws of honour, pass the frontier, easily eluding the vigilance of the French; whereas our soldiers, faithful to their instructions, stop as soon as they arrive at the frontier, leaving to the brigands complete liberty of offence, while the Italian soldiers are deprived of the opportunity of defence.

It is, however, gratifying to say that, notwithstanding these circumstances, certainly arising from no bad intentions on the part of the French, but only from the difficulty of the position created on both sides by an abnormal state of things, the most friendly relations have always prevailed between the soldiers of the two nations, old comrades of the Crimea, of Palestro, and of Solferino. The chain of fraternal sympathy which was riveted in glorious battles and in common danger has not been loosened, both armies having understood that, though for political reasons they could not unite their efforts, they were contending against the same enemy, and that it was not only against Italy the reactionist was conspiring with impunity, but also against France, for, under the very protection of its powerful flag, Rome has constantly been the chief centre of brigandage in every sense, morally and materially—morally, because brigandage, indigenous to the Neapolitan provinces, drew from it continued and effective encouragement—materially, because there was its dépôt and chief recruiting quarter.

Among the causes of this pernicious system, we have not yet mentioned the landings on the coast, because, if we except that of Borjès on the coast of Calabria, there seems to have been no other. There had been uneasy anticipations of such landings in the neighbourhood of Taranto, on the shore of the Ionian Sea, and at some parts on the Adriatic, but these appear not to have taken place. Some barque perhaps, with a few men, coming from Corfu, may have succeeded in furtively approaching the shore at some point of the Adriatic or the Ionian Sea, but this was a matter of little moment. It was supposed, however, at one time, that the increase of brigandage observable in Terra d'Otranto, was due to the landing of some adventurers, but there was no evidence that this impression was founded on facts. From Barcelona, men have sometimes sailed to swell the band of Tristany, but they have disembarked at Civita Vecchia. The active vigilance of our ships along the shores of the Mediterranean, from that port downwards, has no doubt hindered attempts at disembarkation in the neighbourhood of Gaëta; and the brigands have always preferred to throw themselves into Terra di Lavoro from the land side. It is clear that the adventurers who addict themselves to this calling make their head-quarters at Rome and Civita Vecchia, and from them, in preference to any other places, set off to prosecute their infamous career.

Such is a succinct view of the various causes from which brigandage, in 1860, proceeded, and by which it has been supported in subsequent years. It has been a vast conspiracy, fatal to the security of the provinces of the south, and to the power of Italy. The mere enunciation of the causes which have produced the evil, suffices to make manifest the reason of its duration, and to show the inefficacy of the remedies by which it has been sought to check it. As brigandage was considered for a long time a question of strength, it was resisted by opposing force to force, and the task was consequently entirely entrusted to the army. But the knot of brigandage could not be cut by the sword alone. If it had had no support but its own strength, a fourth of the troops which have been contending with it, would have been enough to accomplish the object. But without a good and prudent administration, without a police, without prompt and impartial justice—in fact, without an entire change from the old system, which could not be obtained in a short time—the military action must have been paralyzed. In such a condition of things, the military intervention was an energetic palliative, which, however, did not prevent the rapid and prompt renovation of the evil, and therefore other remedies were to be applied.

In expressing this opinion, which is that of the chiefs and officers of the army, the Parliamentary Commission, in laying its report before the House, could not omit to pay to our army an ample tribute of admiration. In this inglorious and unhappy war against brigandage, the Italian soldier has heeded neither danger nor fatigue in the fulfilment of his duty; and neither the discouragement caused by failure, nor the perpetual renewal of the evil, has shaken his fortitude. Our army has given proof of that patient heroism which transcends even valour, and which, being difficult to maintain, is so much the more worthy of admiration. The battlefield abounds in attractions for brave men; the love of glory is a natural and powerful incentive to acts of heroism; but such attractions have been lacking in this war with the brigands. They are enemies who do not fight except when they are unable to avoid it, or when they have a large excess of numbers. Our soldiers know this, and when they come to the trial are not consoled by the idea of meeting death at the hands of gallant enemies, but have reason rather to dread the risk of falling victims to some ambuscade, and of being miserably insulted and butchered. The consciousness of being endowed in a supreme degree with the heroism of duty and self-abnegation, is the strength and greatness of the Italian troops. Well might it have been feared, without any disrespect to the army, that in such a war of guerillas and ambuscades, which renders it necessary to disperse and scatter our forces, discipline would have been extinguished. There are companies which for months and months have not seen the colonel of the regiment to which they belonged; and regiments of cavalry, which, from the exigencies of the service, have been stationed in detachments in three or four provinces.

Notwithstanding, however, the perils to which discipline was thus exposed in an army containing many new soldiers, the trying circumstances in which it was placed, instead of weakening discipline, has strengthened it. Between the old soldiers, whose breasts are

SKILL IN WARFARE.

covered with medals commemorative of so many battles, and the young ones animated by the hope of winning similar marks of honour in memory of battles yet to be fought, there is no difference, each having been an example and an encouragement to the other. The new Italian army, modelled on that old stock of Piedmontese soldiers, traditionally brave and faithful to their king and country, could not fail to be animated by the same spirit and act accordingly. Difficulties, instead of discouraging their spirits, have rather spurred them on, and afforded them the opportunity of displaying their tact and ingenuity in this awful war of artifices, in which audacity and coolness are required as well as valour and discipline.

The following facts, which may serve as examples of their skill in warfare, have been reported to the Parliamentary Commission by General Reccagni, commander-in-chief of the military division of the Abruzzi. A sergeant of the 42nd regiment of infantry, about dusk on the 7th of August 1862, was going at the head of a few men from Lanciano to Atessa, in the province of Chieti. He and the soldiers being in their campaign clothes, some peasants took them for brigands and joined them. The serjeant perceived their mistake, but taking care not to correct it, he heard from the rascals an account of the devastation and rapine they had committed, and of more which they intended to commit, a design which they were happily prevented from fulfilling, as he arrested them in the neighbourhood of Atessa. On the 16th of September, in the same year, an officer of the 6th regiment of infantry, hearing that a band of brigands was infesting the hills adjoining the city of Sulmona, disguised himself and a few soldiers as brigands, pretending himself to be the captain of the gang. By this artifice he succeeded in obtaining an interview with the chief of the real band, accompanied by whom and one of his men, he visited the hiding-places of the bandits, and assured himself of the connivance of two syndics. A little way from the scene of this event the other soldiers met him, as had been pre-arranged, and, displaying themselves in their true character, attacked the brigands, the chief of whom they killed, the rest of the bandits being either killed, wounded, or dispersed. The troop was thus completely destroyed.

The climate, which is particularly baneful in the summer season, in Capitanata has been very injurious to our soldiers. Fevers, more cruel than the brigands, cut short several noble lives, and, with the fatigue and privations to which they were exposed, rendered many unfit for longer military service. Colonel Migliara, commander of the 8th regiment of the line, stationed for several months in Capitanata, has related the following particulars regarding the sufferings of that regiment from fatigue and sickness. Of 1800 men there were sometimes 560 sick, and in each company of 100 men there were often only 35 fit for service. In the month of January, 1863, the regiment was transferred to Nocera to recover from such fatigues, and then, of 1,200 effectives, 293 were laid up. In one single month eighty men and three officers perished from exhaustion. The extent of territory they had to guard, a hundred miles in circumference, rendered necessary the exercise of their utmost energy. For months the soldiers had no resting-place but the cold, hard ground. One column guarded from Cerignola as far as Troia and Sarracapriola, another had charge of the Garganic district. The regiment had to furnish for the custody of the prisons of Lucera, sixty men a-day, who alternated with another sixty, with the rest of only a single night. One day the number of the sick increased to such an extent, that it was necessary to place on guard at the prisons the bandmen of the regiment. It had to furnish a detachment to Manfredonia, and to provide escorts between Lucera and Troia, between Lucera and Foggia, between Lucera and Torre, Maggiore, and all along the "Via Sannitica." Men were continually needed for exploring expeditions and ambuscades. At harvest time, in order to prevent the brigands from burning the crops, the soldiers had to pass the night in the fields. At seed-time they had to do the same. It was thus impossible to hold even one company in reserve. These particulars of the sufferings of one regiment are enough to give an idea of what the army suffered, for the history of the other regiments is not very different.

The four battalions of the 21st and 28th infantry, which spent some months in the valley of Bovino, were sadly tried by sickness and privation. The difficulties of the cavalry were no less. In three squadrons of the Lancers of Montebello, in garrison at Capitanata, there were, in January 1863, ninety-two sick, and fifty-two in the course of convalescence. But even such sufferings as these had no injurious effect on the discipline of the Italian soldier, nor did they diminish his energy and zeal in the fulfilment of his duties. The experiment was a most difficult one, and the successful result a satisfactory proof of the capability of the Italians for military organization, a fact which affords a great guarantee for the national unity. The war against brigandage has placed in the most striking relief the virtue of the Italian soldier, and the priceless treasure of moral strength derived from the glorious military traditions which, for eight centuries, the Piedmontese have handed down to the Italian army. The obscure war against brigandage might well have proved a terrible injury to the military organization of Italy. It has been, however, the reverse, and, instead of weakening our army, has given it new strength and vigour.

Among the many favourable testimonies to the conduct of the troops it will be enough to note here that of the Commendatore Antonio Spinelli, president of the council of the ministers of Francis II., in July, 1860. "The troops," he said not long ago, "have been truly heroic in their contest with brigandage. They have rendered immense services; they have effected prodigies of valour. Were it not for them there would now be twenty thousand brigands. They have displayed a self-abnegation without parallel, and these qualities belong to every branch of the army."

In speaking of the merits of the army, it would be unfair to pass over in silence the name of General Lamarmora, the illustrious soldier who commanded the troops in the Neapolitan provinces. It was he by whom the nucleus of that army was formed, and by whom it was so perfectly organized that it obtained those triumphs on the distant fields of the Crimea and in the south of Italy, which have given it so many claims upon the gratitude of the nation. In General Lamarmora, Italy possesses one of those rare personifications of valour and nobility of character, that so well represent the national army, the safeguard of Italian unity.

The numerical condition of the force which composed the sixth *corps d'armée*, stationed in the south of Italy, in 1863, was as follows. The active force of the corps, including the mobilised portions of them and the dépôts, comprised altogether nearly eighty-six thousand men. The mobilised force amounted to sixty-five thousand eight hundred and seventy-five, of whom, in the 3d of March of that year, four thousand eight hundred and fifty-five were ill. These forces were divided into several military divisions and subdivisions, the commanders of which had full freedom of action against the brigands. This active force included seven regiments of cavalry, the lancers of Montebello, the lancers of Aosta, the light horse of Lucca, the hussars of Piacenza, the light horse of Saluzzo, the lancers of Milan, and the light horse of Lodi. The first four were stationed in Capitanata, the fifth in the province of Salerno, Potenza, Bari, and Lecce, the sixth was at Caserta, in the province of Beneventum, and in the environs of Naples.

The enumeration of these forces is undoubtedly a valid ground for confidence in the contest carried on by our troops against brigandage. The brigands assuredly can compete neither in numbers nor in valour with such soldiers as ours. Their tactics are extremely simple. They rarely unite in large bands, because they know that if they did it would be easy enough for our soldiers to destroy them. They never attack, and if attacked they always run away. They lay ambuscades when they have the certainty of escape and superiority of numbers, in the proportion, probably, of five or more to one. There is not one single instance, even when brigandism was at its very worst, in which they have been known to attack a company of soldiers. When they fire at the troops, it is from a position where they are safe themselves. They have vedettes, and, when on horseback, some of them are disposed as "flanqueurs." They wield their arms with little skill, and their volleys of musketry seldom do any harm. They rarely have the courage to fight hand to hand, and they always profit skilfully, by their knowledge of the slightest advantage offered to them by the configuration of the ground, to choose positions where they can easily attack, but where it is hardly possible to assail them. It is not true, as has been alleged, that they all meet death with courage. This is the case sometimes, but is by no means the general rule, unless stupidity be confounded with stoicism, and a brave contempt of death with a brutish indifference to it. Cowardly, for the most part, they possess all the attributes of cowardice, ferocity being their most striking characteristic. I do not wish to horrify the reader with details of the cruelties which the brigands inflict on the unfortunates who fall into their hands. The inhumanity of some of them has occasionally been enough even to horrify their own comrades. An instance is on record of one Cerritacchio who was put to death by order of Caruso for having barbarously tortured an unfortunate child. The most cruel among them were such as Coppa, who had been with Crocco, and a certain Varanelli, who was with Caruso. While some of them are not so bloodthirsty as others, they all bear more or less distinctly the dye of crime, and some of them eat human flesh and drink human blood. They all are superstitious and ignorant. In destroying the telegraph wires, however, they made a shrewd distinction, cutting only those they imagined might be useful to Victor Emmanuel; such as might be serviceable to Francis II., they allowed to remain. Their chiefs have always been for the most part fugitives from the prisons and the galleys. Caruso, of Torre Maggiore, was one of the shepherds of the Prince of Sansevero. Imprisoned for commonplace delinquencies, he managed to escape, and took to the field. Ninco Nanco was a miserable peasant of Avigliano, who was employed as a keeper in the forest of Lagopesole. Condemned in 1856 for murder, he escaped from the prison in 1860, and going to Naples to present himself to General Garibaldi, was ordered to return home, instead of which he took to the field. Crocco, a native of Rionero, was a cowkeeper, belonging to the Bourbon army. Being prosecuted by justice early in 1860, he was one of those who had fallen by mistake into the ranks of the cause of liberty. In doing so, he hoped for impunity, but when he heard of a warrant for his capture, he turned reactionary and brigand. Apprehended and consigned to the prisons of Cerignola, he found means of effecting his escape. Coppa, of San Fele, in Basilicata, was one of the disbanded soldiers of the Bourbonist army. Paolo Serravalle, of Marcone in Calabria Citeriore, was a homicide, twice escaped from the galleys. Tortora, of Rapacandida, was one of the disbanded; as was also Marsino, of Marsico Vetere. Pilone was a master carpenter, of Bosco Tre Case, who, on account of a quarrel with the civil chief of the district, had been put into prison, but was liberated through the protection of Captain Caracciolo. In 1860 he followed the Bourbon army to Sicily, and then returning to his country, entered into communication, through the Bourbon committee, with Francis II., and organised the troops which, for months, infested the neighbourhood of Vesuvius and of Naples. Nicandruccio, Nicandrone, the Prince Luigi, Mangiacavallo, Orecchiomozzo, Bruciapaese, were the chiefs of smaller but equally sanguinary bands. These ruffians are the Mammone, the Pronio, the Di Cesare, the Fra Diavolo of our age; worthy in every respect of their antecessors; generals "*in pectore*" of Francis II.; the worst scum of a degraded populace.

The aspect of one of these bands has been described by a witness whose testimony cannot be doubted, one of their own chiefs. The sergeant of Gioja, the same who caused an oath of fidelity to be administered to his bandits, and who styled them the sworn defenders of the Catholic faith, was in the habit of writing from time to time some account of his proceedings, which was afterwards found in his pocketbook, and, as will be seen, has formed part of the documents of the process against his accomplices. This brigand exhibited a strange mixture of infamous fanaticism and a certain rough piety, nor had a long course of crime extinguished in his breast all sense of honour. Some ray of light occasionally illumined the obscurity of his conscience, and awakened an agonizing feeling of remorse. In these moments of self-abandonment he wrote the diary, entitled "My Misfortunes." Listen to the judgments wrested from him on the subject of his own companions in the following passage—a curious illustration of the religious experience of a pious brigand, translated from the original:

"A year since, within the solitude of the forests, one day there presented themselves to me thirteen highwaymen, poorly armed, announcing themselves as defenders of Francis II., and of the Holy Roman Catholic Church. I, wishing to promote these objects, to defend these rights, to which I had long been well disposed, as is known to everyone, welcomed these men, and with great zeal began directly to busy myself with all that I had to do. Those who accepted me as their chief were bound to render obedience to all the commands which proceeded from me, with the object of advancing the cause of our legitimate king. As these men, however, had no desire but that of robbery, they began to agitate against me, saying among themselves—'We have taken the field and were called robbers, so we must plunder; and if our chief does not act as we wish, he will come to a bad end, or remain alone.' This state of feeling in the troop was entirely unknown to me.

"Notwithstanding my orders to the contrary, they committed several acts of theft on the people with whom they were brought into contact. But God, who has never sanctioned deceit, has frequently shown that the deceiver may be himself deceived. They contrived to betray me, although I was only prompted by one wish, that of obeying the laws of honour; and by so doing they became an easy prey to the treacherous invading usurpers who were pursuing us, and were thus sadly defeated, many of them, to my great sorrow, being barbarously slain. But the ever blessed Almighty who allowed me to be left alone in that cruel and atrocious conflict, has yet saved my life through His holy protection. . . . . . .

"I am painfully grieved for the few men collected by me. After the thirteen had arrived, who made up with the others a total of five-and-twenty, many of them, if not all, partly innocent and deceived, like myself, met with death. But God, if not in this world, will recompense them in the other. For myself, I firmly believe that he who dies in innocence dies a martyr, and has laid up much treasure for the eternal life. Their souls are now with Him."

The foreign brigands, who professed to be the champions of legitimacy, were in reality adventurers in search of riches. Such, for instance, was the Spaniard Tristany, who boasted to be at the head of regular troops, and paraded the title of general in the service of Francis II. To the bands of foreign adventurers belonged De Christen, Lagrange, Langlois, Zimmerman, and the Spaniard Borjès, who perceived too late that the vaunted phalanxes of Francis II. were but hordes of low assassins.

The localities preferred by these modern brigands have always been the wooded banks of the Ofanto and the Fortore. From the first they could infest the district of Melfi in Basilicata, and that of Sant' Angelo dei Lombardi in Principato Ulteriore; those of Altamura and Barletta in Terra di Bari, those of Foggia and Bovino in Capitanata. From the second, they made incursions into the neighbourhood of Sansevero and the Garganic region in Capitanata, the province of Beneventum and the district of Larino in the province of Molise. Crocco, with Coppa and Sacchitiello, were on the Ofanto; and there sometimes Ninco Nanco, whose station was at the forest of Lagopesole, used to join them. Chiavone scoured the valley of Bovino, in the commune of Ariano, and Beneventum. Caruso, with Varanelli, was on the Fortore, and from thence, sometimes alone, sometimes with other bands, scoured the plains of Capitanata, the outskirts of the Gargano, Molise, and Beneventum. Coppolone and Serravalle, from the district of Matera in Basilicata, extended their depredations along the Ionian coast as far as the wood of Ginosa. Tortora resorted to the forest of Ripacandida. The woods of San Cataldo, of Montemilone, and other forests in Basilicata, were also the usual rendezvous of brigands; and the little wood of the Incoronata, between Foggia and Cerignola, has long been their basis of operations. They drew their provisions from Foggia, and from Manfredonia, in the forests of which they concealed men and property. Pizzichicchio hid himself in the forest of Marsano, in Terra d'Otranto, and from thence made irruptions into the surrounding country. In the province of Salerno was the band of Tardio, in the district of Vallo that of Ricci, and Marcantonio's in that of Campagna. In Vasti, in the province of Chieti, there was the band of Pizzolungo, whose usual hiding-place was in the forest of Petacciato. In the province of Terra di Lavoro were the remnants of the band of Maccarone. In the mountainous parts of this province, which borders on that of Avellino, was a small band, at whose head was one Piccocchi, who sometimes showed himself in the neighbourhood of Montefall in Avellino; and in the Abruzzi the brigands were scattered here and there, not in large bands, but in bodies of some importance, making incursions from the Roman frontier. In the province of Reggio, in Calabria, there was no brigandage of any kind, and in the rest of Calabria—the provinces of Cosenza and Catanzaro—it has always been very insignificant. In the Gargano, likewise, there used to be a great many brigands, divided into small bands of two, three, or six together. The centre of brigandage was thus on the banks of the Ofanto and of the Fortore, which were the rendezvous of those formidable bands mounted on horseback. An exact calculation of their numbers would be impossible. Each of the principal bands had a nucleus of from fifteen to twenty men, to whom others "unattached" could be joined at need in various numbers, so that a band of twenty could sometimes in a very short time be increased to a hundred. When, in March, 1862, an ambuscade was prepared for a detachment of the light horse of Saluzzo, the brigands, amounting to a hundred, consisted of the united bands of Crocco, Gioseffo da Barile, Coppa, Ninco Nanco, and probably others also. Some of these chiefs have been at times so reduced as to have only ten, seven, or even three followers. In forming an approximate estimate of the numerical strength of brigandage, occasional brigands and common thieves, whose number was very great, must not be forgotten; for in the localities most troubled with the scourge of Southern Italy, every offence assumed more or less the aspect of the great crime of the country.

"Among the crimes of brigandage," says Pietro Colletta, "and those which take their rise from it, the judicial censor of the kingdom enumerates in this year (1809) thirty-three thousand violations of the laws!"* The same historian relates that Joseph Napoleon, while on the throne of Naples, did not dare to "set on foot the conscription, because the repugnance of the people to military service, and the ease with which recruits could escape into Sicily, made him fear that the men levied for the military service would

* See Colletta, vol. iii., p. 120.

join the ranks of the enemy." The Italian Government has, however, already had the courage to raise two levies in these very provinces—the first time according to the Neapolitan law, the second according to the Sicilian; and the result, as already stated, has justified the most thorough confidence.

Brigandage is one of those evils, however, which cannot be estimated by its external proportions or its numerical strength. On the contrary, it becomes more difficult to eradicate· in proportion as its strength diminishes. Every germ of infection must be eliminated, at any cost, from society, because the evil, which has been apparently subdued, may at any moment assume gigantic proportions, and become the cause of profound perturbation. The Government and the Parliament have thus been bound to consider all the remedies by which such a plague might be cured In fulfilling this duty they have revived the confidence of the southern population, who can now look forward with hope to the future. As it had been insinuated that the Government desired the duration of brigandage, with the object of inducing the French to desist from their occupation of Rome, it was, therefore, the more necessary to use every effort to root out this scourge. The people needed to be shown that the liberty they had invoked possessed the power of securing their prosperity, and that in becoming citizens of the kingdom of Italy, instead of subjects of a government despotic and hostile to the nation, they had obtained all the advantages of a free and civilized life. The question of brigandage being extraneous to all political controversies, every honourable man earnestly desired that the provisions for its extinction should be energetic and effectual ; and such was the view with which the Parliamentary commission was specially appointed.

CHAPTER V.

CONNECTION OF THE ROMAN GOVERNMENT AND OF THE BOURBON COMMITTEES WITH BRIGANDAGE—THE REVELATIONS OF ETTORE NOLI—TRAITORS AMONG THE EMPLOYÉS OF THE ITALIAN GOVERNMENT—CARACCIOLO'S INTERVIEW WITH FRANCIS II.—DE GOTTEDON, DE LUPÉ, AND DE CHRISTEN—PECUNIARY AID FROM THE EX-KING FRANCIS—DE LUCA—INSTRUCTIONS FROM ROME—THE DEPOSITIONS OF PASQUALE SCUOTTO—TESTIMONY AS TO THE INVASION OF GENERAL BORJÈS—THE ADVENTURES OF MR. BISHOP—THE PROCESS AGAINST THE BARON ACHILLE COSENZA—REVELATIONS MADE BY EUSEBIO CAPITANEO—THE CASE OF THE MARQUIS AVITABILE.

CHAPTER V.

A LINK would be wanting in the chain of those sad events that have desolated the south of Italy if no mention were made of the celebrated trials that have taken place at Naples, showing the complicity of Francis II., of the Bourbonist committees residing in Rome, and of the Roman Government itself, in that reaction which has plunged the fairest part of Italy into all the horrors of the worst of wars. A rapid glance at these trials will prove interesting in the highest degree, as most of them concern persons of repute, standing high in social position.

Those who have followed the course of events in Italy will very likely recollect the dark revelations which were made in that judicial drama which was developed in consequence of the discovery of the Bourbonist committee of Naples, known under the designation of Frisa, or Posilipo, after the name of the "villa" where the conspirators used to meet. The master-key to it is found in the revelations of Ettore Noli, one of the conspirators, who gave to retributive justice an account of these dark plots. The facts which he revealed are known to be perfectly in conformity with truth, as has been proved by the judicial proceedings, and fully confirmed by the verdict of popular justice.

From the various documents sequestrated at the villa of Frisa and secured for the trial, combined with the above mentioned revelations, the complicity of Francis II. was clearly established. This process included the draught of a memorandum addressed to Francis II. in Rome, written by Noli, by order of General Nuists and Cavaliere Tortora, in which he informed the ex-king of the growth of the Bourbon party, of the discouragement of the Liberals, and of the earnest endeavours of the committee; and also two papers, written by the same individual, by order of the above-named persons, containing the names of the most important partisans of the Bourbon cause, in respect of which Noli declared that, "in consequence of orders received from Rome from Francis II., the General had proposed the promotions, remunerations, and future appointments to be given to the conspirators, in order to submit them to the royal sanction in Rome." In a letter addressed to D. Cesare Firrao, expeditionary at the Roman Court, by Monsignor

Cenatiempo, he recommends the bearer, Captain del Paranzello, with whom the "other friends" came, and "who is now returned by command of the General, as known personally *by our principal*. If, on his return, you have anything to send, you can entrust it to him." To this information about the committees is subjoined the remark, "All is here arranged and well disposed, and I assure you that the delay does us a great deal of harm." There are also replies from Firrao and a letter of the Baroness Teresa Federici, addressed to Monsignor Cenatiempo. The latter, when asked who was "the friend" to whom he was to recommend the husband of the baroness, answered that it was Francis II.; that the "other friends" spoken of in the letter to Firrao " were two gentlemen of the names of Besio and Sarti, both of Rome, come thence to Naples for the purpose of conspiracy."

With regard to another document, containing some names marked in pencil, Noli declared that two days before his arrest a letter came from Rome to Signor de Gottedon, in which he was enjoined to despatch a messenger to Roccamorfina, in Terra di Lavoro, to summon several persons of the family of Pippo, to induce them to recruit Bourbon troops, and send them into the country to reinforce the bands of Chiavone. Nor will it be useless to note here that Noli, being asked about the other names written on the same piece of paper, replied, among other things, "that Diego Terlizzi, as ex-chief of the electric telegraph office in Naples, received daily from the present employés all the telegraphic messages which interested the present government—both those which concerned the provinces and other parts—and that he circulated these among the various Bourbon committees, and sent them even to Rome," by means of couriers, to Francis II.—two or three times a week, as he repeats in his examination.

It must be observed that during the search there were found three telegrams, in which the governors of the provinces demanded reinforcements, and gave information about reactionary movements. This shows that among the employés of the Italian Government there were still to be found some of the old Bourbonists, who continually betrayed it. The cipher used by General de Gottedon in writing to Francis II., to whom he addressed his letters under the name of the Count Mayel, Via Poli, No. 50, Rome, was also found. A report made by the police, under the date of 7th September, 1861, states that, in consequence of the discovery of the reactionary committee of Frisa, Don Dominico de Luca, head of the "Compagnia della Morte," who had been authorised to form that company by Francis the Bourbon, being arrested among the others, it came to light that De Luca had commissioned an artist to make the sketch of a uniform according to instructions received from Rome from the ex-king, to the effect that the company was to be attired in a fashion that should inspire terror. And, in fact, in the course of the search made in the painter's house, a picture was found representing the figure of a soldier with black tunic, black waist-belts, and a black cap, with a death's-head. The painter declared that this picture had been ordered by Don Domenico de Luca, who had been thus instructed by Francis II. himself, and who was to have gone into Avellino to organize the bands, which were to have taken the ill-omened name of "Compagnia della Morte!"

It was here noted by the public prosecutor that "Francis Bourbon gave de Luca money, and three letters of introduction, for a Father Pepe, for a certain Sansone, and for the Bourbonist committee." But a still greater light is thrown upon the matter in the revelations of Noli, from which it appears that the arms which were to be distributed among the partisans of the factions were to be embarked at Marseilles for Civita Vecchia, where General Bosco was expecting them. Marino Caracciolo, he then states, who had been a naval officer in the time of the Bourbons, had told him that "a few days before" (the deposition is dated the 21st of August, 1861), "he had gone to Rome, taking with him Salvatore and Giuseppe Cardinali, and Antonio Monteforte, who were sought for by justice as fellow-accomplices in the same conspiracy of Frisa; that they had scarcely arrived in Rome when, by means of Major Torrenteros, one of the most staunch supporters of reaction, he was admitted to an audience of Francis II., in the Palace of the Quirinal, an hour after midnight." This Caracciolo explained the means which he would advise for promoting the restoration. "Then Francis urged him to set out at once for Naples and Sicily, giving him authority to promise in his name higher ranks and decorations to all who should remain faithful to his cause, and deny the new Government; and as Caracciolo had shown that he intended principally to avail himself of the assistance and influence of a Garibaldian major, named Pagani, who lived at Palermo, the ex-king, Francis, empowered him to promise to Pagani the rank of general, if he really exerted himself to procure him the adhesion of a large number of Garibaldians." He then gives further proof of the conspiracy, and adds: "With regard to the correspondence, they informed the same Caracciolo that the address, for communication between Torrenteros and the other Bourbonists at Rome, was that of Robert

Smirne or Adelaide Smirne, and that they had charged Captain Legaldano to send some one each day to the post to take the letters which bore such an address for the whole time that he remained in Palermo to carry out the reactionary movements concerted with Major Pagani."

And here it is well to observe how these statements concerning the revelations of Caracciolo are confirmed by Captain Legaldano, who adduced arguments to prove that the former really went to Rome and offered himself to Francis Bourbon; and, besides, that in pursuance of his instructions, he appropriated at the post a letter addressed to Robert Smirne, which evidently related to the conspiracy. According to the statements of Noli, this must have been written in Rome by Major Torrenteros, and addressed to Marino Caracciolo, indicated under the pseudonym of "*Mio caro Fra Diavolo,*" a name but too well-known in the annals of brigandage! It also speaks of Luisella, a name arranged by Torrenteros, with the committee of Frisa, to signify the ex-King of Naples.

In another examination Noli deposed that one Giuseppe Cardinale, belonging, with his father and his brothers, to the committee of Frisa, was sent to Rome, and was there during the Holy Week of the year 1861, where he was joined by his father, and whence they returned together. " They said that they had seen Francis Bourbon several times; that he had encouraged them to keep the reaction alive by inspiring confidence in its complete success, by promising large rewards, and by bestowing honours. In fact, Salvatore Cardinale smuggled out of Rome six or seven brevets of knighthood for some of the adherents of the ex-king."

In speaking of the money collected by General de Gottedon, who was sent to Naples by Francis Bourbon, in company with Signor de Christen and the Viscount de Lupé, he says, "The money which Girlando Boccadoro and his son Antonio received upon undertaking to murder General Cialdini, was sent to them by Gerolamo Tortora, to the amount of 120 ducats, more being promised when the deed was done." He next proceeded to state that he was again in Rome early in July, 1861, and that then, as has already been said, de Luca was put under his care. De Luca confessed to him "that he had gone to Rome to see the ex-king Francis, and his reactionary adherents, in order to obtain information of the revolution in the Neapolitan provinces."

Equally important were the revelations made by him in another examination. He repeated that the three Frenchmen, de Gottedon, de Lupé, and de Christen, went to Rome to receive directions of the committee. He confirmed the account of the charge given to assassinate Cialdini, an event which was to have taken place between the 24th and 25th of July, 1861. "I was present," he said, "when Girolamo Tortora, to whom in such matters everything was trusted, gave this order to the two Saladini, and to the Boccadori, in the villa of Frisa, and handed to them the weapons. Among the agents of the committee," he said, "was reckoned also Captain Fusco, of the National Guard of Pianura, who had at his disposal a band of brigands—collected through the efforts of his brother, chaplain of a regiment—which dissolved itself after his arrest." He went on to say that "he received pecuniary aid from the committee, but that other money he could not have, because there was none except for splendid dinner-parties, on which they lavished forty to fifty ducats a day; and he expected that I should go to Rome to get two hundred thousand ducats, and thirteen thousand muskets, which were sent from Marseilles, and were to be brought to Naples, and make the final arrangements for the designed reactionary movement. But in this they failed, having been arrested, and the committee dispersed."

He repeated what he had said of his stay at Rome, and of de Luca being placed under his charge by General Vial, and continued, "In my presence he gave also some instructions as to the direction of the undertaking. They were to attack when there was a probability of conquering, to retire from the presence of superior force, to break into the post-offices, to burn the letters, to attack collectors and appropriate their moneys. On entering districts, they were to sack and burn everything, to take from the public chests whatever money they found there, leaving appropriate receipts, that account might be taken of it on the return of King Francis to his kingdom." Monsignor Lettiero admitted that he had gone to Rome with letters from Madame Lalon, in whose house was held a Bourbon committee, which was in close relation with that of Frisa, which might well have been called the central committee, since on it depended the smaller committees scattered about the city of Naples. The said letters, addressed to Francis II., requested him to send to Naples some one with authority, who would be able to reunite the various threads of the conspiracy, and carry it into execution. It was upon this and other similar demands that he decided to send the three Frenchmen above mentioned.

One "Salvatore Viola, an ex-sergeant of gendarmes, went as a courier to Chiavone, in the Abruzzi, to arrange the way in which his band should be joined by that of Cipriano La Gala, which was in the mountains above Maddaloni, and that of Viscusi, which was spreading terror in the mountains of Somma, and the adjacent places. Salvatore Viola having been to Rome, where he had taken letters from a monk, Father Apreda, had there received a round piece of bone of deep pink colour, which was to serve him as a mark of recognition, a similar piece of bone being in the possession of all the chiefs, who, when they desired to recognise Bourbonist adherents, laid the bones upon each other to see if they corresponded in size and colour." He adds that when he was at Rome in May, 1861, on behalf of the committee, he saw Francis II., who said to him, " It is not yet time." It was about the end of June the three Frenchmen were sent.

What a light is thus thrown by these revelations on Bourbonist machinations! It is well said in the act of accusation: "The spontaneity and constancy of Noli's statements, the minute details into which he enters, his consistency with the documents found and with information obtained from other sources, and, lastly, the fact that, while revealing criminal and guilty acts, he does not excuse himself, give to his declarations the complete impress of truth." His testimony was also confirmed by the depositions of one Pasquale Scuotto, ex-cabman, from which it appears that he was in communication with a certain Capobianco, sergeant of artillery under the previous government, who one day asked him for four or five carriages to facilitate the disembarking of a quantity of arms which were to serve the cause of Bourbon reaction. He urged him further to collect men, and told him he expected money from Rome. "He said to me that the time was come when there would be as much money to be had as was wanted, for a good sum would arrive that day from Rome, and he invited me to go to the house of the general to ascertain the fact with my own eyes. I went there one Thursday, in the evening, as Capobianco had told me to do, and I saw a man come up in a little carriage, carrying a black leather portmanteau studded with brass-headed nails. This man left the portmanteau in front of the house, and it was taken up to the general. . . . . I remained for a while before the house, expecting Capobianco would come out and speak to me about the money. Capobianco did come out, but only to tell me to drive up the next day with my carriage at a particular time, and that then I should receive a good sum. . . . . The next day I drove up with my carriage, as I had been desired, but, perhaps through being too late, I found no one there—the house was deserted! Remembering that Capobianco had told me the day before that all the people whom I had seen at the house of the general were to leave for different points, to take the money to the brigands who infest the country on behalf of Francis II., I ran off at once to the railway, and there I found the general, with all the Swiss officers whom I had seen at his house. They went off by the last train, by way of Salerno, and carried the portmanteau, which I had previously seen, with them."

Many letters sequestrated in the villa of Frisa, belonging to some of the Frenchmen who were staying there, from the legitimists sent by Francis II. to Naples to head the conspiracy, likewise formed part of these proceedings. Some passages contain expressions of regret that Francis II. should be unable to reward his faithful servants in a measure commensurate with their devoted labours in his cause. "If," it is added, "he has had enough up·to this time to maintain his party and support the insurrection in his favour made by his partisans, he will certainly have enough to enable him at least to acknowledge the services which your devotion has rendered to his cause."

A letter of the 23rd of March, 1861, says :— "Your last letter has irritated us all, as it ought to do, against the imbeciles who surround Francis II. If you had not the French volunteers, you would have not only nothing to say, but also nothing to do with such people. Borjès has said as much as yourselves, and his Spaniards declare that in the whole kingdom of the Two Sicilies there is not an·officer fit for war."

This voluminous process comprised even some documents relating to the invasion of Borjès. Signor Achille Caracciolo,* also involved in the conspiracy of Frisa, formerly lieutenant in the Bourbon army, and who formed part of this expedition, says, in his examination of the 15th of October, 1861: "Being in Rome about a month ago, I was ordered by General Clary to proceed to Malta' and place myself at the disposal of the Spanish General Borjès. Arrived in that island, I found, in fact, General Borjès with other foreign officers, and not long after a vessel was provided by the chancellerie of the Neapolitan consulate-general, in which we, to the number of twenty, embarked for Calabria. As the captain, Merenda, aide-de-camp of General Clary at Rome, had declared to me that General Borjès would command a regular expedition, I saw the deceit which had been practised on me, and that instead of being a member of a *corps d'armée*, I was, in fact, only assisting in the command of a band of brigands who were plundering Calabria and infesting the country. I pretty soon resolved to abandon Borjès, not being anxious to distinguish myself in such a capacity." . . . . .

Giuseppe Coriba, formerly captain of the fourth company of the 4th Chasseurs of the Neapolitan army, who, with Caracciolo had followed Borjès, stated, in

---

* This is the same Caracciolo mentioned in Borjès's journal.

his examination on the 24th of October, 1861, that when he reached Malta, General Borjès had been there for a month or more, to receive men sent him by the committee of Marseilles. He further stated that, "in going to Malta and putting himself in correspondence with Captain Merenda, he certainly intended to take service in favour of the Bourbons, but in a regular corps; since, if he had wished to make himself an accomplice of brigandage, he would have profited by the facilities which existed in Rome to throw himself into the Abruzzi, as so many did who found a return to Rome so easily practicable."

In speaking of past events, I feel bound to give here an account of the adventures of Mr. Bishop, who was probably guilty of imprudence more than anything else, entrapped as he was by the brilliant inducements offered by the Bourbonist party. At all events, it was no business of his to enter into a conspiracy against a nation with which his own interests were in no way connected. Why did he not perceive that his employers were glad to make use of him only on account of the safety which his nationality was likely to afford in a country where Englishmen, I am happy to say, are considered as the staunchest supporters of liberty? Our able statesman Signor Peruzzi, the late home minister, said two years ago in Parliament, in one of his eloquent speeches: "Mr. Bishop, according to what has been stated by the enemies of the Government, was an Englishman, who had come to Italy for the benefit of weak health. This I do not deny; there are many who come to Italy for a like purpose, or to admire our artistic treasures; and generally those who love Italy only under this point of view, are displeased on finding that, instead of being now a *terra dei Morti*, the tranquil home of the relics of the past, it is a country in which a new life is unfolding itself, and where that *dolce far niente* so much sought after by foreign visitors, is no longer to be found." Now, Mr. Bishop did not, perhaps, go to Italy with any intention of conspiring against the Italian Government; but that he did conspire against it, is a fact which can by no means be explained away, and here are the proofs of it. On the 2nd of April, 1862, in Mola di Gaëta, an examination, made on the part of the authorities of public security, of the person and effects of Mr. James Bishop, a British subject, journeying from Naples direct to Rome, resulted in his arrest, and the sequestration of many of his papers, among which was found a letter addressed to Father Serafino Torquato, general of the Minorites at Rome, signed 'Carlo Lillo,' the contents of which were as follows:—"Venerable friend, having, according to the royal command, put myself in communication with Mr. Bishop, I have openly revealed to him the whole number of my forces, giving him an abstract of them, to the effect of acquainting this new·acolyte of ours of their importance, and thus enabling him to present the truth to the king, since he, full of enthusiasm for what I have said, has decided to proceed to Rome at once. We are in consequence ready to act, but are unable to do so for want of means. I pray you, therefore, to use every effort to have money sent me, for it is imperatively necessary for our action. Make our lord aware also that, among all my friends who have distinguished themselves by their labours in his cause and their love towards his throne, Signor d'Agostino is indefatigable, and is never for a moment absent from any operations. Beg of the clemency of his Majesty to grant me the privilege of holding brevets of knighthood, that I may be able thereby to win over those who are desirous of possessing them."

Who this Carlo Lillo was, Bishop refused to say, nor could he be prevailed on to give any information about him. He was also bearer of a paper divided into two columns, annotated on the margin with numerical ciphers corresponding to the names of various cities of the Neapolitan provinces, and bearing the title of "Abstract of the entire force of 80,702 men—that is to say, 16,353 armed, and 64,349 unarmed, and distributed among the above-mentioned towns. The paper concluded with the following statement : " In the foregoing abstract are not included twenty-two districts of Beneventum, the districts bordering on Naples. The brigand bands of Giuseppe il Caporale, of Cipriano La Gala, of Pilone, of Romano, and of Major Procella, which makes part of Baron Cosenza's band, and also another, will take position on the territory of Camaldoli, with the old officers and brigand chiefs to take the command."

The importance of this document will not escape observation, inasmuch as it makes manifest the relation of Francis II. and the Bourbon committees with such men as Giuseppe il Caporale, Cipriano La Gala, Pilone, and Romano, who have distinguished themselves even among the vilest of the brigands by their unparalleled atrocities. In a letter signed C. N., which was also found, occurred the following passage: "This is in reply to yours received by post, and which has been punctually read by the *master*. By the same post, and at the express desire of the *master*, a certain person is ordered to present himself to our friend, the Duchess of M. C., and to concert measures with her, and put her in accord with her brother. Therefore, on receipt of this, give notice to the duchess of the expected arrival of this person, who enjoys all the *master's* confidence. The five persons sent here by you are altogether useless."

Although Mr. Bishop altogether refused to give explanations on the point, it will not be difficult to identify the *master* mysteriously referred to in the above letter. In the draught of a letter, which he admitted he had addressed to Prince Torella, he says, "Signor Principe, I forward you a letter which I have lately received from Rome, in answer to a proposal made by me to the king. His Majesty would pray you to assist the forces which are being raised to accomplish his return. This proposal is made in consequence of the repeated assurances of the Duchess of M. C., that you would receive with pleasure such a mark of your sovereign's esteem." Prince Torella, however, not only refused to act the part suggested, but sent back the letter to Mr. Bishop, as the latter admits, and as is proved by the reply of the prince, found among his papers. Principally on acconnt of these documents, Bishop was declared, by the voice of popular justice, guilty of conspiracy and condemned, but afterwards, by a royal amnesty, was set at liberty.

The existence of a central Bourbon committee in Naples, dependent on that of Rome, from which came the orders and instructions for the affiliated committees of the southern provinces, is further manifested by the process instituted against Baron Achille Cosenza, Michele Gallo, and other companions in crime. A conscientious analysis of the evidence collected in the case of Baron Cosenza and others removes all doubt of the actual existence of a conspiracy in Naples, carried on by the most seditious and violent means, with the object of destroying the new form of Government. The letter found on Cosenza, the papers taken from the hands of a Signor Troise, the proclamations discovered in the house of Signor Tancredi, and of Signor Gallo, the testimony of Signor Potenza and others, plainly showed that a reactionary committee was organised there to promote the restoration of the Bourbons to the throne, by inducing the soldiers to desert, by promoting brigandage, by inciting terror among the people, and by exciting civil war. One of the most strange and effectual measures adopted by the conspirators in the prosecution of their infamous attempt, was the opening of a public-house under the direction of Tancredi, in the Vico Quercia, where many of our soldiers went and were supplied with wine gratis, as well as with promises to incite them to sympathy with the Bourbon, and to persuade them to desert. With the same object, using freely the name of Francis II., they spent money in recruiting for the armed bands, in assisting the more needy, and in rewarding the boldest, giving account of all they had done to the head committee of Rome.

The body thus constituted at Naples had all the characteristics of a central committee in communication with the other committees of the province—with that of Caserta, for instance—and depended on that of Rome. Carlo Poli was the organ of the secret communications, and his servant, Tobia Troise, the confidential messenger, who carried the packets in a little boat. The latter, who at first hesitated and denied the fact, afterwards revealed all the secrets of his clandestine expedition.

These documents, which have been collected by thoroughly lawful and honourable means, exclude all suspicion of party spirit or of exaggerated zeal, either on the part of the police or of the judicial authorities. The most severe and fastidious of critics could not fail to recognise in their proceedings that dignity and delicacy which commend their actions to the fullest confidence. Among the papers thus secured by justice, is a letter addressed to a parish priest in Rome, signed " Giulio Nemes," which says, " The central committee here is divided, because some of them, not being overzealous for the cause of their sovereign, opposed energetically the resolution to act immediately on the receipt of orders from there." And further, "Make the sovereign reflect that the liberals are discouraged by the brigand bands, and these can save us if their present number is increased. I can supply four hundred men, and even more, and this is a propitious moment for favouring desertions from the army."

A great deal of light is thrown upon the subject of brigandage by this process, which has made such a stir in Italy. Eusebio Capitaneo, once a superior officer of the Bourbon troops, and imprisoned since upon a charge of conspiracy, declared that the ex-general Fabio Sergardi, of the Bourbon army, with whom, against his will, he had certain relations, imposed secrecy on him as to the fact of his being at the head of a Bourbon committee, whose rendezvous was the parish church of San Matteo at Naples and a neighbouring chapel. Many times he had to accompany him thither. He knew also that the ex-major Torrenteros, a refugee at Rome, "brought the most important correspondence from that city for this general, and that the committee of which he was a member, suggested the movements of the brigands, especially those of the band of Pilone, which was always supplied with money and other similar assistance. That this is true," he added, "I know of my own personal knowledge; because, when the commission of inquiry into the causes of brigandage was here in Naples, a report being current that energetic measures were to be undertaken against this band, and that, among other things, certain persons were to make a pretence of joining the gang of Pilone, in order to conspire against his life,* Signor X——, who at the moment acted as the agent of the committee which corresponded with Pilone, undertook the commission, and executed it by means of one Scudieri, formerly a soldier in the Bourbon army, to whom Pilone sent word that he wished for a private interview with him." Scudieri was urged to remain firm in the cause of the Bourbons, to enlist men for them, and to be ready for any movement. " Thus," he said, " on the morning in which, by order of the police, the monks of San Severino were to be turned out of their convent at Naples—an event which gave rise to a reactionist demonstration among the mob of the district—the moment he saw me he urged me to betake myself to the place and to take part in the affray, saying, 'Go, help your king.' At Naples, he made the acquaintance of Brother Y——, of the monastery of ——, who was a furious promoter of reaction in the town, in which he went about begging for the convent to which he belonged. As far as I remember, I, together with Scudieri, had four or five interviews with him in a cell of his convent. In one of these interviews, I learned from the lips of Brother Y—— that he had sent to Francis II., at Rome, a present of a gold pin, as a mark of his devo-

* The reader can see by this that the Bourbonists were judging the Italian Government after themselves.

tion; that he was in communication with a seaman of Sorrento, named Giuseppe Atanasio, who was employed in taking to Rome the reactionary correspondence, and in secretly conveying across the disbanded and refractory men who were enlisted in that city." On his arrival in Rome, he was admitted to an audience of Francis II. at the Palazzo Farnese, " who," he says, "told me that he wished me to remain in Rome, as he proposed either to introduce me into the Pontifical army, or to send me with a military division to swell the ranks of the brigands." On the occasion of this audience, he made acquaintance, in the ante-chamber of the palace, with Salvadore, a peasant of Caserta, " who, while we were waiting together, informed me that he was the regular messenger of the committee of Caserta." Brother Y——, when in the hands of justice, did not deny any of these particulars, the truth of which is beyond doubt.

Meanwhile, the National Guard of Magnano arrested a Frenchman, the president of the reactionary committee at Bari, on account of seditious words and exclamations which had escaped him. On this man were found not only arms, but also various photographic portraits of Francis Bourbon, of Maria Sophia, of Count Trapani, of Monsignore Gallo, and of Pio IX. Subjected to examination by Nicolo de Luca, prefect of the province of Avellino, he said that the portraits had been given to him in Rome by Francis II., in November, 1862. An ex-vice-admiral, he added, told him that the moment had come to excite a popular insurrection, and invited him to put himself at the head of this movement in Calabria, where many conspirators would be disembarked from Sicily and Malta, with the view of effecting a revolution. He also stated that in Naples a very dangerous Bourbon committee was incessantly at work, which corresponded with all the provinces by means of emissaries, who were continually in motion. Two pensioned Swiss colonels had tried to induce him to take command of the movement. An old general of Francis II., to whom he was taken, said he was prepared for any excesses, and assured him that he had incited the Lazzaroni to cut the throats of all the Piedmontese. Indignant at such proposals, he answered that he was not a brigand. The principal instigators of such excesses were the ex-Swiss officers and the Bourbon generals in Rome. He admitted that he knew the members of the committee of Bari, but that " honour forbade him to name them." A similar committee, he said, existed in Foggia, which had instigated the brigands to prepare an ambuscade for the Parliamentary Commission, from which they had escaped only by miracle, through some mistake as to time. In reply to a question, he declared that he estimated the number of men collected in Rome from different European countries, for the invasion of Naples in the interest of Francis II., at about ten thousand, among whom were Spaniards, Bavarians, Irish, a few French legitimists, and many Neapolitans, completely armed, but without a capable chief, and in a very imperfect state of discipline. He added, of his own accord, that Francis II. had told him that, in the lawless bands in the provinces, were many men devoted to him, and that the brigands had offered him (Francis II.) 16,000 ducats, which he had properly refused. What admirable self-denial!

Anyone who has followed with some attention the course of events in Italy, must remember the excitement produced throughout the country by the ransom of the Marquis Avitabile from the band of Pilone, at the very gates of Naples. Having obtained his liberty by the payment of an enormous sum, he laid a complaint before the police with regard to this most audacious attempt. From that document, which is to be trusted on account of the high standing of the person from whom it proceeded, I extract some important statements regarding this capture.

On the morning of the 30th of January, 1863, having left his home in Torre del Greco, to shoot over one of his properties, he found himself suddenly surrounded by armed men, who, after making him lay down his gun, told him he must accompany them to their chief, the Cavaliere Pilone. "We proceeded," he said, "towards Vesuvius, and, when arrived at the lower corner of the pine forest on the estate of Signor Califano, were met by an armed man with a Calabrese hat, adorned with a red and white feather, with blue jacket and red breeches, a silk scarf round the waist, on his breast a medal, and several ribbons, the decoration of knightly rank." This was Pilone, by whose order a letter was written by a secretary, which the Marquis himself was forced to sign, desiring his family to send 20,000 ducats (£4,000) as ransom, with the intimation that if it was not paid by evening, he should be put to death. "Pilone," reported the Marquis Avitabile, "avowed that he acted on instructions from Rome, the *padrone* (the king) permitting him, when the Bourbonist committees had spent the 2,000 ducats which Francis II. had sent them, to use such means as these to obtain money, when it was wanted for the maintenance of the band. In a long letter from Rome, which he made me read, the *padrone* said that he wished to hear of the glorious contest, and hoped he would not expose his valuable life too much; that the signora (his wife) had better come to Rome, where she should be well provided for. The *padrone* also said that he permitted him, in order to raise money

'to . . . . . you understand me,' a broken phrase which, Pilone explained, implied a permission to exact ransoms. The bandit then showed me a diploma, but I do not remember its contents, for, at that moment, seeing eight or ten persons who looked like a detachment of bersaglieri coming down Mount Vesuvius, I was alarmed for my life. Pilone immediately sent forward some men to reconnoitre, and said, 'Don't he afraid. If these are the d—— Piedmontese,' alluding to the soldiers, 'there are others who will look after them. They passed this morning a little before us, and I know will not return again to-day.'

"After this conversation, almost all the brigands began to tell me that, though I might not like to have to part with such a heavy sum for my ransom, it would secure me henceforth the protection of the 'illustrissimo Cavaliere Pilone,' which I might implore at the return of Francis II. in the spring. The Austrians, meanwhile, they assured me, had made Victor Emmanuel aware that if in March he had not succeeded in advancing to Venice, they should come to Turin; adding that, as there would not be at that time in these provinces more than thirty thousand Piedmontese soldiers (robbers they called them), their throats would be cut by the people, and by the Neapolitan recruits, who would be forced to join them."

Such, in fact, were the tales by which the reactionary leaders kept up the imagination and hopes of these conspirators! Those, however, who have seen with what ardour the young Neapolitan soldiers are drawn to the banner of Italian unity, can say whether it is likely that they will ever use those arms, which their country has entrusted to them, in such a fratricidal war!

CHAPTER VI.

TRIALS CONTINUED—ARREST OF THE PRINCESS BARBERINI SCIARRA—OPPOSITION OF THE CLERGY TO THE NEW ITALIAN GOVERNMENT—THE REACTIONARY PRESS—LETTERS IN CIPHER TO FATHER CLARENZIO—CORRESPONDENCE BETWEEN THE CONSPIRATORS OF NAPLES AND OF ROME—IMPORTANT DEPOSITIONS—RELIGION AND POLICY—EXAMINATION OF PASQUALE FORGIONE—THE OATH OF FEALTY TAKEN BY THE BRIGANDS.

CHAPTER VI.

THE arrest of a lady of high rank and noble birth, the Princess Barberini Sciarra, made a great sensation, not only in Italy, but in every part of Europe. I do not wish to discuss the question of her culpability, nor should I be inclined, on any account, to be more severe than the jury, who, taking into consideration the time she was detained in captivity awaiting the commencement of her trial, deemed it an adequate punishment for her complicity in a conspiracy against the kingdom, and accordingly acquitted her. It was, perhaps, natural to expect that, after the severe lesson she had had, indulgence should be extended to a woman of her rank. Still, as at the time our enemies availed themselves of the opportunity to abuse the Italian Government, accusing it of blind tyranny and despotism, I think it right to make the reader acquainted with the nature of the documents found upon her, from which it will be seen whether the Italian authorities were not justified in placing her under arrest. Moreover, immense responsibility rested upon the government, which had so many interests at stake, and which would have been accused of partiality if it had released her without settling the question of her complicity. It is probable, too, that even if she had been condemned, the sentence would never have been carried out upon her, any more that was that of her more guilty accomplice, the Cavaliere Quattromani, who had been sentenced to ten years' confinement, but was released immediately by the general amnesty granted by the king.

When, by means of the watchful police of Naples, the Princess Barberini Sciarra was arrested at the station of Isoletta, among the various papers found on her were three letters in cipher, the key to which being discovered, their meaning was explained, and they were made public. Obviously addressed from Naples to Rome, they contained several particulars regarding the organization of the Bourbon committees, which, as a measure of precaution, were composed only of three persons, and also as to the collection of money for the reaction, the despatches to the Bourbons, and the concealment of the reactionists. One of them was from Cardinal Riario,[*] who, it was

[*] Cardinal Riario, it must be remembered, was Archbishop of

said, ought to "remove all the scruples of the priests!"

On the 11th of June, 1862, in the section of accusation in the Court of Appeal of Naples, the Princess Barberini Sciarra, the Marchioness Sophia de' Medici, the Cavaliere Quattromani, and six others, were formally accused of conspiring to destroy the form of government, and to excite the people to revolt against the powers of the State; of having concerted among themselves the restoration of the Bourbon ex-King Francis II.; and of having, by means of brigandage, stirred up civil war.

The elaborate requisition presented by the royal procurator, in the tribunal of the district, contains some passages which are worth preserving. "The *instructions* for this trial," it says, "have revealed a new conspiracy, or, to speak with greater precision, another phase of that conspiracy which, for three years, has been going on at Rome against the Government of Italy. On the morning of the 9th of January, at Isoletta, on the person of the Princess Barberini Sciarra, while going from Naples to Rome, there were taken several letters, among which was a packet addressed to the Duke Caracciolo di Brienza. In this packet was a letter addressed to Monsignor Don Gaetano de Ruggiero, which contained another in cipher, dated the 6th of January, addressed to Father

Naples, but, like many other Reactionist prelates, resided in Rome.

Clarenzio da Viterbo, and a second, dated the 2nd, for the same person." . . . .

"There can be no doubt that the conspirators were many in number, because from these two letters we learn the feigned names of several—Palamede, Enfrasso, Aronne, Adamo, Abramo, of 7, 91, 93, 96, &c." And all these, as the system of their organization proves, were associated with one common view. They were arranged by sects; they had a council, which decided all their operations; and a hierarchy, in which they were all affiliated in various grades; nor could any one take part in the conspiracy without being accepted by the council. "This morning," it was said in the letter of the 2nd of January, "the council met, and a considerable number of brethren were proposed and accepted. Aronne, Adamo, and Abramo have paid for the last two degrees of initiation."

That the object of this secret society was conspiracy, is clearly shown by its programme, which declared that an attempt was to be made to destroy the present form of government, and to restore the Bourbon. Let us recall to mind the agitation of the time when these letters were written, the plots of the clergy, the opposition of the reactionary press, and the seditious proclamations, facts which were all known to the council of the conspirators, and it will be evident that this association has been the centre and the soul of the whole reactionary movement of the time. At the close of the autumn of the year 1863, brigandage, instead of declining in the number of its adherents, and, in consequence of the severity of the season, displaying less activity than usual, rather became more formidable through the increase of its bands, and the determination with which, unaffected by any touch of pity, they carried out their atrocious measures; and the Bourbonists, having raised their head in the towns, continued to conspire against Victor Emmanuel, and to labour for the restoration of that old state of things which the nation had for ever discarded. The clergy, too, both secretly and openly, made war against the Government. Some of the most audacious, as the curates of Santa Lucia, Acciardi, Borghi, Mancinello, and Trama, were arrested ; and all these circumstances were so far connected with the action of the conspiracy, that, in the said letter of the 6th of January, the person represented by number 95 informed Father Clarenzio of these arrests, and said significantly, " This has been a very hard blow for us." Can it be denied, then, that these machinations formed part of a widely-spread conspiracy against the Government and the liberties of Italy ? " Besides," continued the letter, " this morning I have received a communication from Cardinal Riario, which ought to remove all the scruples of the priests to whom I have spoken." What could have been the work for which they wanted the priests, and which only a letter from Cardinal Riario could induce them to perform, but something beyond their sacred duties? As the letter was written by one reactionist to another, the work in which they wished to enlist the clergy could only have been political, and not in accordance with the holy mission of peace entrusted to the ministers of God. The clergy, at all events, must have been fully aware of these intrigues, and of the danger with which the country and the National Government were threatened.

It was at that time that the reactionary press at Naples trespassed the bounds of law, morality, and decency by publishing *Il Ciabattino* and *Il Papa Giuseppe*, which were the savage expression of a fanatical, ignorant, and bloodthirsty revolution. *Il Napoli*, also published by them, represented, so to speak, the intelligence and the aristocracy of the reactionary party, advocating the principle of federation and the restoration of the Bourbons. The so-called religious periodicals, throwing aside all restraint, began to advocate revolution with the most barefaced cynicism, mixing, in a strange and sacrilegious way, religion and the Bourbons, the cross and the dagger, the priest and the brigand, reviving in the nineteenth century the image of Cardinal Ruffo—

blessing with one hand and assassinating with the other. All these papers were published while the conspirators were meeting in council, while partisans were assembing, while money was being obtained, and while the clergy were provoked to sedition. Can we doubt, in these circumstances, that between the conspirators and the writers of these periodicals there must have been a secret correspondence? "Here," said the letter in cipher of the 2nd January, "the police every day seize some of our papers;" emphatically adding, "They are, however, all the more obstinate when they reappear!" That the chiefs of the conspiracy either themselves wrote in the reactionist papers of Naples, or inspired the writings of others, is manifest from another letter, written by Scotorio, in which he says: "Tell A—— that he must keep to what 91, 93, 94, and ourselves have expressed in the periodicals of last week." A proclamation bearing the date of the 31st of December, 1862, in which the citizens were invited to rise in favour of Francis II., ended with the words, "Viva Francesco II.! Viva la Costituzione! Viva l'autonomia delle Due Sicilie!" And on the 16th of January, bills containing similar expressions of party-feeling were posted in the city and the adjoining districts: "Viva Francesco II.! I Napolitani, spogliati da un assassino, hanno ancora la lena di gridare, Viva Francesco II.!"

It is beyond question that the chiefs of the conspiracy collected money, which they sent to Francis II. at Rome. We find in the correspondence such acknowledgments as these, "As received through 7 from 91" (in cipher), the names of contributors. "Through Filippo Ferri, Palamede received besides one thousand francs for the king." Why was that money sent to Francis II.? That deposed monarch, residing in Rome after he lost his kingdom, protected by the Papal Government, and assisted by the reactionary priests and monks, had put himself at the head of a permanent conspiracy against the unity of Italy. During all this time he had been enrolling brigands and letting them loose upon the southern provinces. The co-operation of Francis II. with the bandits, from his asylum at Rome, is a notorious fact, of which there can be no doubt, after the solemn declaration made by the Italian Parliament. With what other view did the reactionists of Naples send this money to him? Their only object was to aid him in the desperate and unhallowed work which he had undertaken. Several persons associate themselves together in Naples; with the most profound secrecy they organize departments; they have their chiefs, their subordinates, their contributors; they ally themselves with the reactionary clergy, urge them to revolutionary measures, publish and circulate proclamations which excite men to revolt, put up seditious placards, write or direct journals which favour brigandage and vaunt the heroism of the brigands, collect money and send it to Francis II. in Rome, make themselves, in a word, the centre and soul of that reactionary movement which manifested itself in Naples during many months, and was ended, in January, 1863, by the capture of these letters, the arrest of some of the conspirators, and the flight of the others—who could credit their assertion when they pretended that they knew nothing of the conspiracy?

The letters of which we have spoken were those addressed to Father Clarenzio in Rome. One of them was enclosed in another directed to Monsignore D. Gaetano de Ruggiero, an intimate friend of Father Modesto dei Riformati, the confessor to the Bourbon family, and both of the most violent reactionary opinions. The letters in cipher were, in reality, intended for the confessor of the king. Although, therefore, as a measure of precaution, not addressed to the Bourbons themselves, they bore the superscription of priests who were domesticated with them. The council at Naples wrote to Rome to give an account of its operations, to ask for advice and instruction, to send the names and numbers of partisans and contributors, and to forward the money to the king—the real head of the permanent conspiracy at

Rome, and of the hordes of brigands sent into those unfortunate provinces with a political object. How dependent the Neapolitan and other committees were on Rome, can be proved from these letters. Sertorio writes to Clarenzio :—" The council met, and a good number of brethren were proposed and accepted. Aronne, Adamo, Abramo, have paid the last two calls—A. will receive the names of the contributors. Approve if you trust the council." With the information that Adamo demurred to remaining at the Monte della Misericordia, and that it would be useless for him to linger there, the Neapolitan correspondent finally asks instructions from Rome, and concludes with the words, " Decide and reply." The charge of conspiracy, therefore, supported by the most satisfactory documentary evidence against the committee at Rome, must be regarded as equally well-founded against the council at Naples, which in its most important operations, looked to the former for advice and direction, which received from agents in the Eternal City money to assist it in the execution of its designs, and which looked to the same quarter for the necessary supply of men to fill up the ranks of the brigands who so worthily maintained the cause of Francis II.

The continual correspondence between the conspirators of Naples and those of Rome was kept up by means of special messengers. Filippo Ferri, who belonged to a family which owed everything to the Bourbons, was one of these. When the Bourbons were expelled from the kingdom he retired to Portici, to mourn their departure, while he eagerly anticipated their return. By his means, according to the letter of the 2nd January, the Neapolitan conspirators sent a thousand francs to Palamede for the king. A warrant was issued for his capture, but he could not be apprehended, as, conscious of his guilt, and knowing his danger, he had taken refuge under the broad wing of the Pope.

We now come to the point upon which these facts have an important bearing. The Princess Barberini Sciarra also lent her assistance in facilitating the correspondence of the conspirators. At Isoletta she was arrested. When the threat was held out that it would be necessary to search her, she produced the letters which she carried, among which were those in cipher, containing all the necessary instructions for carrying out the conspiracy, and directions for continuing the atrocious war which for three years had been desolating the south of Italy. That the Princess Barberini was a voluntary messenger for the Bourbons, there can be no doubt. Although thus professing Bourbon sentiments, she is reported to have said that she should prefer *a republic of demagogues to the infamous Victor Emmanuel.* She had for some time made her house the point of reunion for so many reactionists, as to have brought upon herself the surveillance of the police. She was known, on her journeys from Rome, to have been the bearer of many letters from Bourbon emigrants; and, on her return to that city, to have taken others from reactionists to the king, and from persons who wished to see the triumphal march of the army of the Pope into Naples! She was also the bearer of letters and petitions to the princes of the house of Bourbon, with many other communications of a very compromising character, expressing hopeful auguries that the year 1863 would bring better times, dry all tears, and end this state of tribulation; and last, not least, of a parcel of letters to the Cardinal Riario Sforza. She, who carried so many documents of such a nature, written by such persons, could only have been a Bourbonist messenger; and one who could not have conveyed the letters in cipher without knowing it. But it is said she carried also three portraits of Mazzini! Why not? These portraits might have given pleasure to the reactionists, for *omnia munda mundis!* On her journey to Rome with the above-mentioned letters, which she professed were perfectly harmless, she took the precaution of travelling with three passports—a fact which was satisfactorily proved by the judicial investigations.

Very modest indeed, if the vastness and importance of the conspiracy be taken into consideration; but highly satisfactory, when it is remembered that the seat of the conspiracy was in a hostile country, where evidence could not be procured, and where the trial was got up with the greatest impartiality.

During all this time, whilst priests and monks, princes and generals, prompted by the Bourbons, and actuated by a desire of vengeance, did not recoil from keeping up the agitation of the South by every means in their power, there were people, foreigners especially, who, not taking these circumstances into consideration, judged the Neapolitans in a manner little to their advantage, so far as regarded their relation to the Italian monarchy! The indefatigable questor of Naples, in a memorandum "upon the reactionary conspiracies lately discovered by the political authorities of Naples," says very wisely: "It is not fair to draw from these new machinations of the fallen dynasty any conclusions unfavourable to the inhabitants of these districts, for it is always from the same class of persons, the officials and employés of the late régime, that the conspirators and the brigands recruit their numbers. And in this place the aforesaid processes seem to include a general principle already enunciated by the public conscience, and which all the various discussions about brigandage take for granted. I mean that at Rome, and this can never be repeated too mnch, is the cause of all those snares which beset the Italian Government, and that the peace of this part of Italy cannot be secured except when, with the expulsion from Rome of the last of the Bourbons, the principal centre of the reactionary conspiracies shall be broken up."

But on this subject I wish to mention another fact. The reader must recollect the attack made upon Luco*, in the month of April, 1862, by a band of two hundred brigands, and their defeat by a very small detachment of our troops. Among the prisoners captured on that occasion, there was one Raffaele Brandoli, who said, when examined by the judge of Civitella Roveto, that the band which came from Rome, *by direction of Francis II.*, was to have joined that commanded by Chiavone, and that each was to have received, besides provisions, a daily pay of twenty baiocchi. He stated they had made him firmly believe that the band was composed of old soldiers, and commanded by Neapolitan ex-officers. Instead of that he was by no means proud to find himself in the midst of a gang of assassins. The

* See page 84.

enrolments were made at Rome, and the individuals enlisted were despatched in little troops of ten or fifteen, towards a given point, for conveyance to their destination, after being provided with arms and a complete military equipment. Another of those arrested was Antonio Jugaro, aged sixteen, the son of a cavalry captain of the Bourbon army. His account was that, at Rome, where enrolments were made in the name of Francis II., at two paoli a day, he enlisted in the ranks of the brigands. When his party left that city, on the 2nd of April, they numbered only a score, but others joined them continually along the road. When about half-way, they were met by a priest, an ex-chaplain of the Bourbon lancers, who gave them muskets, knapsacks, and cloaks, bearing yellow facings, as used in the Pontifical army, a distinguishing mark which clearly betrayed their origin.

The importance of these depositions should not be overlooked. The brigands pass the frontiers, capture our soldiers, and then repass. To whom do they consign their prisoners? Undoubtedly to the agents or representatives of the Pontifical Government. The Pontifical gendarmes treat on equal terms with the brigands, and consider them as their allies. The Government of the Pope regards the capture of our troops as perfectly legitimate, and urges our soldiers to break the oath which binds them to their king. What a depth of infamy is revealed by such conduct!

If certain documents show that *political* Rome is the enemy of the Italian Government, encouraging conspiracies set on foot by Francis II. and his Court, and that it lends effectual aid to brigandage, it may also be proved, alas! that *theocratic* Rome is equally hostile. To show this, nothing more is necessary than to call to mind the answers given in December, 1861, by the "Sacra Penitenzieria" at Rome, when some doubts were submitted to them by certain Italian bishops, the publication of which answers was considered criminal by the Court of Assize at Lucera, which inflicted on Monsignor Frapolla, bishop of Foggia, a punishment of two years' imprisonment. The clergy were forbidden to take the oath of fealty and obedience to Victor Emmanuel and his successors, as required by the constitution and the laws of the state. They were obliged to refuse the sacraments, funeral rites, and ecclesiastical burial to those who were specially obnoxious for political causes! But when the pecuniary interests of the clergy were at stake, the Sacra Penitenzieria at Rome did not refuse an unaccustomed indulgence; for it conceded to the curates and the other ecclesiastics, who were deprived of their tithes through their abolition. by the State, permission to accept the compensation offered to them by the same Government. This monstrous confusion of religion and policy bears its sad fruits in the southern provinces, where the clergy are for the most part averse to the new order of things, and the population more superstitious than devout. Their journey through these provinces gave the members of our Parliament ample opportunity to convince themselves that the hostile attitude of Rome and the clergy is a fruitful source of brigandage; a fact the truth of which is proved by every document which has been collected, and is made particularly prominent in the following communication from the Commendatore de Luca, prefect of the province of Avellino, containing the examination undergone the 23rd February, 1863, in Geraldo, by the brigand chief Pasquale Forgione, before the commission of Frigento, a production in every way remarkable, as will be seen by the following quotation from it:—

"*Judge.*—Having this conviction, why did not you and your companions give yourselves up? You must have known that, being hated by the whole population, your life was every moment in danger? You know that the village of Sturno,[*] which was frightened by exaggerated reports of the number of

[*] This place had been invaded by the band commanded by Pasquale Forgione.

brigands surrounding it, no sooner got rid of the two ruffians who had entered, than it again set up the arms of Victor Emmanuel and blessed his name and Italian unity.

"*Brigand.*—We were fighting for the faith.

"*Judge.*—What do you mean by the faith?

"*Brigand.*—The holy faith of our religion.

"*Judge.*—But you surely know that our religion condemns the thefts, the setting fire to houses, the murders, the cruelties, and all the impious and barbarous misdeeds by which brigandage every day is marked, and which you yourself and your companions have perpetrated.

"*Brigand.*—We were fighting for the faith, and we were blessed by the Pope, and if I had not lost a paper which came from Rome you should be convinced that we were fighting for the faith.

"*Judge.*—What kind of paper was it?

"*Brigand.*—It was a printed paper, that came from Rome.

"*Judge.*—But what were the contents of the paper?

"*Brigand.*—It said that whoever fights for the holy cause of the Pope and of Francis II., does not commit sin.

"*Judge.*—Do you recollect anything else in the paper?

"*Brigand.*—It said that the real brigands are the Piedmontese, who have taken away from Francis II. his kingdom; that they were excommunicated, and that we are blessed by the Pope.

"*Judge.*—In whose name was the paper written, and what signatures were attached to it?

"*Brigand.*—The paper was a commission in the name of Francis II., and was signed by a general, who had another title, which I don't recollect, any more than his name. There was a piece of ribbon attached to it, with a seal.

"*Judge.*—Of what colour were the ribbon and the seal, and what impression was on the seal?

"*Brigand.*—The ribbon was white, like linen, and the seal was white, with the impression of Francis II., and letters which spoke of Rome. . . .

"*Judge.*—As it is impossible to admit, or suppose, that the Pope could bless such iniquities, or that Francis II. could degrade his dignity as King, by commanding homicides, extortions, and burnings, even though by means so dishonouring to humanity he could hope to recover his crown, what you have asserted must be false.

"*Brigand.*—Well, as you have brought the Bersaglieri, and I am to be shot—as I know that I am to die—I tell you that I had that paper, and that all contained in it was just as I told you; and if any of my companions have been arrested, like myself, you will then be convinced that I have not lied.

"*Judge.*—That you should keep tied on your breast with a string a crown-piece of Francis II., as a medal, is not surprising, because you believe that when you murder, and exact ransoms, and rob, you are combating for him. But that in perpetrating such wickedness you should keep, as the witness, and I might even say, if the words were not impious, as the accomplice of your crimes, the blessed Virgin, by wearing, attached to your breast, that dirty figure of the Madonna del Carmine, is astonishing. It is enough to make me believe that your religion is more impious and wicked than the religion of the devils themselves, if the devils have any religion. Is not this the most infernal mockery that can be offered to God!

"*Brigand.*—I and my companions have the Virgin as our protectress, and if I had kept the commission with the benediction, I should certainly not have been betrayed.

"On being told that the hour of execution was at hand, he answered, 'I will confirm all the things I have said to the confessor, who, I hope, will be granted to me.''

A very curious discovery was made when the band commanded by Sergeant Romano, to whom reference has been frequently made in this work, and who was the terror of the district of Gioja, was defeated on the 5th January, 1863, by the gallant regiment of Saluzzo's light horse, effectually aided in this exploit by the brave National Guard of Gioja. Twenty-two brigands remained dead on the field, only two being made prisoners. On the body of Sergeant Pasquale Romano was found his portfolio, containing many important papers. One was the oath of fidelity administered to the brigands on the incorporation of the band, a document which I give here entire, observing that it is followed by the names of eighty brigands, styled "*giurati della fede cattolica.*"

"*Oath of Fealty.*—At the present moment, in compliance with supreme orders, in this year, month, and day, we all unanimously take the present oath of fealty, under the following conditions, as established by us in the present articles:—We promise and swear always to defend, even with the shedding of our blood, God, the Supreme Pontiff Pius the IX., Francis the Second, King of the Kingdom of the Two Sicilies, and the commander of our column, worthily entrusted to him, and to obey all the orders of the latter, always to give effect to the articles aforesaid, so that God may aid and assist us always in combating against the rebels to our Holy Church. We likewise promise and swear to defend the standards of our

King, Francis the II., with all our blood, and to make those standards respected and honoured by all the communes now in favour of the liberal party. We further promise and swear not to belong to any sect contrary to the pledge unanimously sworn to by us, and to be willing to incur the penalty of death for violating the said article. We promise and swear that, so long as we remain under the command of our aforesaid commander, we will destroy the party of our opponents who have followed the tricolor flags, always tearing down those emblems of revolution with the zeal and devotion which our whole column has above expressed—to be, as we have shown, and shall show always, under arms, and to be ever ready to defend, in all ways, our legitimate King, Francis II."

From our rapid analysis of the judicial proceedings, every one will see that Rome has been made the true focus of all the foreign reactionists ambitious of power and riches, the centre of the dark plots which are perpetually carried on and renewed against the Italian Government, the head-quarters of the brigands, where they prepare their arms for the assassination of our soldiers, and whence issue the plundering bands that spread revolution, bloodshed, and ruin over some of the fairest regions of Italy. And all this is done under the shadow and protection of the flag of that nation which shed its noble blood on the plains of Lombardy in the cause of Italy, the new government of which was at once recognized by that of Victor Emmanuel. What a gain it would be to Italy if the Emperor of the French could force the Pontifical Government to banish Francis II. from Rome! No one can sympathise with misfortunes better than Italian patriots, who, banished from one foreign land to another, know by experience all the sorrows of exile. But if this young man will not be instructed by the stern lesson of Providence, which in him punishes the crimes of his forefathers—if he is not ashamed, by practising the traditional system of his family, to bring upon his former subjects all the miseries of an ignominious and disgraceful war, in the hope of reconquering a throne for ever lost—then it were well he should be banished from that Italy whose lot he would fain make so sad.

CHAPTER VII.

MEASURES FOR THE REPRESSION OF BRIGANDAGE—GRADUAL IMPROVEMENT OF THE COUNTRY—BENEFICIAL INFLUENCE OF WORKS OF PUBLIC UTILITY—ORGANIZATION OF A VIGILANT POLICE—IMPROVED ADMINISTRATION OF JUSTICE—NECESSITY OF THE REMOVAL OF FRANCIS II. FROM ROME—VIGOROUS MILITARY ACTION—LOSSES OF THE ITALIAN ARMY AND OF THE BRIGANDS—THE NATIONAL GUARD IN THE SOUTHERN PROVINCES—CAVALRY VOLUNTEERS—RESPECT FOR THE LAWS—OFFICIAL CONNIVANCE WITH BRIGANDAGE—LOCAL EXILE—CAPITAL PUNISHMENT—HONOUR AMONG BRIGANDS.

CHAPTER VII.

THE substance of the report of the commissioners of Parliament, on their investigations into the causes which produced Neapolitan brigandage, and gave it a tenacity and persistence so remarkable, is included in the preceding chapters. Every detail had been most scrupulously inquired into, in order that the real truth, however unpleasant, might be laid before the nation. From it we learn that, however great was the influence of the enemies of Italy in the protraction of the struggle between reaction and liberty, yet, on the other hand, much was to be ascribed to the peculiar conditions of that part of the country, and the cessation of brigandage could be anticipated only by pursuing a path entirely different from that which had been followed at the beginning, when, after the fall of the Bourbons, the armed bands made their first appearance. Till then, in the excitement of the first moments of reaction, violence had been opposed by violence. During the changes of the various lieutenancies, in the state of transition in which the country was placed, whilst a great many of the old abuses were still prevailing, it was impossible to do otherwise. But, as soon as things became more settled, the eyes of every one were anxiously turned towards the south, in which public opinion was alarmed by the persistence of brigandage, notwithstanding all that had been done for its destruction, and the country therefore asked that the careful inquiry which had been made should be followed, if the evil was to be effectively encountered, by energetic measures, which might restore at last to peace and prosperity the districts which had suffered so long from one of the most dreadful calamities that could afflict a nation.

The question how an evil so gigantic was to be eradicated, was the last part of the task left to the Parliamentary Commission. The consideration of the causes suggested the precautions and remedies which ought to be adopted. In order successfully to meet the evil, the first thing to be done was to remove its predisposing causes, to combat vigorously those which had determined its recent manifestations. These predisposing causes were so clearly indicated by the very nature of things, that there could be no difference of opinion as to them. The remedies by which they were to be removed were the diffusion of public instruction, the enfranchisement of the people from those old baronial privileges which in many places still bound the possession of land, the construction of roads, the drainage and cultivation of marsh lands, the encouragement of public works, the destruction of certain forests—all calculated to give a vigorous impulse to social amelioration, to transform the condition of the whole state, and to benefit the country. The enfranchisement of the Tavoliere of Puglia, especially was pointed out as an indispensable precaution, which would deliver the inhabitants of all the districts of Cerignola, Foggia, and of San Marco in Lamis, from that life of rapine in which they had so long been plunged. The emancipation of the land would be a source of benefit to the owners of property and to agriculture, and would produce, at the same time, the wholesome effect of changing the condition of the peasant, and of destroying that savage proletariate, which, under the influence of want and wretchedness, and in the belief that any change would effect some improvement in its condition, furnished an ample contingent to brigandage.

In general all the provisions which aimed at freeing the land, at stimulating the circulation of wealth and securing general prosperity, were indicated by the very nature of things, and their execution was a necessity, the beneficial effects of which it is needless to describe. Although it was not suggested to root out or to burn up the immense forests, with which, in many parts, the ex-kingdom of Naples is covered, yet unquestionably it was necessary to make them in some way accessible; for by this means alone would evil-doers be deprived of their secret and often unapproachable hiding-places. The results already produced by railways amply confirm all the views that had been formed of the salutary influence which they would exercise on the material as well as the moral condition of the population. In Terra di Lavoro, in the province of Salerno, of Chieti, and of Molise, wherever these works have been undertaken, the people have had before their eyes an obvious proof of the power of civilization. The thousands thus employed in honest work, and well paid for it, are so much strength taken away from brigandage; and the civilization thus introduced into the country has the most beneficial effects. At Termoli, for instance, there is established a veritable colony of Northern Italian workmen, who, by their orderly habits, their decorous aspect, their civilized customs, exhibit to the wretched population a practical demonstration of the moral and material advantages which men derive from their own toil. The brigands have everywhere done their best to prevent the progress of railway works, and, in many cases, have been too successful in causing them to be delayed, a prophetic instinct, no doubt, warning them that the locomotive would prove more destructive to them than the weapons of the gendarmes. But in that country, placed in the most smiling and favoured conditions that Nature can bestow, how many things were to be accomplished before the light of civilization could reach its abandoned and wretched inhabitants! Ordinary roads had first to be constructed, without which it was not to be hoped that railroads would produce the effect which might reasonably be expected from them. The railways could be made useful only by cutting carriage roads through the valleys of the Ofanto, of the Fortore, of the Sangro, of the Vomano, of the Bradano, which are the natural *embouchures* of many provinces on the lines already in course of construction. After the union of Scotland with England, something very like brigandage prevailed, while the former country was yet without means of communication; but as soon as Scotland was furrowed with roads from one end to the other, the evil ceased. That which happened in this island, then so wretched, but now so prosperous, will surely yet come to pass in our southern provinces.

The most effectual means recommended for benefitting the country was the diffusion of public instruction. Unfortunately the municipalities of the Neapolitan provinces had, with some praiseworthy exceptions, neglected this important part of their duties, and therefore it was necessary for the Government to take into consideration whether it was not advisable, by means of compulsory enactments, with corresponding penalties, to impose upon the municipalities the necessity of fulfilling the obligation which till then they had neglected. With an effective system of popular instruction, the greater number of those who now supported brigandage might be transformed into active agents of its destruction.

It was further argued that as the want of a well-organized and watchful police, and of the prompt and regular administration of justice, were undoubted sources from which brigandage drew strength and tenacity, so the organization of a well-ordered and vigilant police, and the speedy and regular administration of justice, would prove the most efficient means by which its powers might be diminished, and the causes of its prolonged existence destroyed. By giving to the general administration a vigorous impulse, and by re-organising all parts of the administrative machine, confidence must be inspired in the power of Government to place the country in a better position than it could ever have attained under the old system of things. The organization, then, of an energetic police was a fundamental point. Of all the means of repression employed against brigandage this would assuredly be the most effective. The heroism and the self-abnegation of our soldiery could not have the influence which might be expected from such an efficient body, far superior in its action to any military organization, as might be proved by many facts like the following.

For many months the sides of Vesuvius and the neighbourhood of Naples were harassed by the incursions of the brigand band commanded by Pilone. Our soldiers, with their usual perseverance, did all in their power to come in contact with them, but in vain. The capture and the ransom of the Marquis Avitabile, however, suggested the plan of establishing in Torre dell' Annunziata a good system of police, which, as soon as it was fully at work, discovered and defeated the band, most of those who composed it falling into the hands of justice. In this way, an enterprise which had been unsuccessful for many months, was successfully accomplished in a few days. Unfortunately at that time this branch of the public service was greatly neglected. The commissioners of Parliament, in calling the attention of Government to the subject, expressed the hope that the police might be organized after that model of perfection which exists in England.

The necessity of carefully watching the prisons and the galleys, and of providing for the safe custody of culprits, was also pointed out. The English public has little idea of the system prevailing in the prisons of the kingdom of Naples at the fall of the Bourbons. Not to speak of the horrors of the dungeons where political prisoners suffered in silence, such was the disorder which reigned in the prisons where criminals stained with the darkest crimes were kept, that every facility of escape was afforded them. Between prisoners and gaolers there often existed a mutual understanding; the latter being generally as bad as the former. On this point the commissioners insisted with all their power for an immediate reform. All the prisons they had occasion to visit in those districts most infested with brigandage, as Potenza, Foggia, Avellino, Taranto, were in 1863 still in the same wretched condition. The facility of escape from places of confinement was known to have been one of the greatest aids to the formation of brigand bands. The rigorous custody of the gaols was consequently called for in the interests of justice and humanity, no less than in those of public security; and that the gaolers should be kept strictly under the eye of the authorities, many among them being still bound to the old customs, and anything but faithful.

One reform particularly required was the speedy trial of accused persons. At the beginning of 1863 there were many arrested about the close of the dictatorship, in the autumn, that is to say, of the year 1860, still untried. A case has been mentioned of a man accused of the exportation of prohibited weapons, for which he could have been sentenced to at most four months imprisonment, being detained six months ere he was brought before a court of justice. This irregular state of things certainly did not result from premeditated neglect, but rather from the extraordinary political contingencies which had been encountered. Nor was there much ground for the accusation made at the time against the Italian Government by some English philanthropists, "who," as Signor Massari said before Parliament, "must have either not read, or have, probably, forgotten the history of Macaulay, and have judged the present state of things in Italy by a standard derived from a comparison of it with that of England of to-day, not with that of England as it was at the period of the transformation related by the illustrious historian." However, the necessity of doing as much as possible was evident, because in this way alone a perfect legal regularity could be established in the general administration of affairs.

That part of the clergy which had become the blind, submissive instruments of the worldly passions of the Roman Court, interfering constantly with the progress and well-being of the country, required also to be checked in their proceedings. If the clergy had been allowed full licence, they would have availed themselves of their power simply to abuse it; and if such freedom had been denied them they would have cried out that they were persecuted, and would have lamented their martyrdom. In either case they would have kept up a constant agitation, and Government would have been powerless before such enemies. In what way could the power of the law reach those who in the confessional encouraged and glorified brigandage, seeing that, although there was a universal conviction of their guilt, no legal proof could be obtained It was considered necessary to give the Government authority to exercise the most assiduous vigilance over the conduct of such clergy, and to provide for the inexorable application of the laws whenever their proceedings rendered such an appeal necessary. The condition of the poor and liberal clergy was also made known to the authorities, with the view of making better provision for them—a measure which shows that the Liberal Government which rules in Italy is not, as it is pertinaciously represented to be, a persecutor of religion. In fact, when the Government can count on the sympathy of the truly Liberal part of the Catholic priesthood, it will be greatly strengthened against the base machinations of the bad clergy, and the extinction of the moral disorder which has so much aided the production of brigandage will be certain.

The influence of the clergy hostile to the national cause received an additional impulse from the residence of Francis II. at Rome, which, by means of some high dignitaries of the Church, is employed to

A REASONABLE DEMAND. 193

favour their own interests and designs. On this point the commission dwelt principally in proposing to Parliament the measures which would more efficiently contribute to put an end to brigandage. The removal of Francis II. from Rome was urged as one of the most important among them. "The persevering and active complicity of the dethroned prince," said Signor Massari, in impressive words, in his address to Parliament on the 3rd of May, 1864, "with the machinations and the incursions of the brigands, affords a right to the Italian Government to ask the removal of Francis II. from his present abode. This right would be indisputable, even if it only related to a mere pretender, who profited by his proximity to his former dominions to raise disturbances and stir up civil war; but it becomes imperious, and not to be refused, when it relates, as in the present case, to a prince who, trampling on the dignity of misfortune, openly allies himself with criminals of the deepest dye, and employs himself perpetually in kindling, in the provinces revolted from him by the free-will of the people, the bloody torch of social strife. There is no civilized and humane government which could refuse to another the extradition of meaner delinquents, and therefore by what right is the Italian Government refused, not the extradition, but the expulsion of a prince in whose

VOL. II. O

name are committed so many crimes and such atrocities? Not being the aggressor, but the aggrieved, the Italian Government is placed, with regard to Francis II., in the condition of one who exercises the right of legitimate defence. With what justice could the aggrieved be denied the satisfaction of seeing the aggressor banished from a safe asylum, where he plots with impunity? Why should Francis II. invoke the protection of the French standard, which, accustomed to shield misfortune nobly borne, cannot now be sullied by protecting those who favour brigandage? If the French Government does not think that the time is yet come for it to withdraw from the person of the Pope the protection which it has hitherto extended to him, no one, surely, will pretend that this protection confers on the Pontifical Government the preposterous privilege of conspiring with Francis II. and his followers, to the advantage of social anarchy. In every way the Italian Government fulfils its duty towards the nation by making Europe aware of this intolerable state of things, and by renewing its request to its powerful ally that the removal from Rome of Francis II. and his adherents may not be long delayed."

Though we have not yet succeeded in obtaining this desirable object, the conscience of civilized nations has certainly recognised our right to put a stop to the perpetual immigration of assassins and adventurers, which has been going on for more than four years, along that frontier line which divides the territory of the Italian kingdom from the Pontifical provinces. In questions like this it is already a great thing to have public opinion on our side. The greatest and noblest principles have generally taken a long while to make their way. Let us hope that the time is not far distant when the cause of justice will ultimately triumph.

Now, resuming my subject, by means of the provisions which have been indicated, the causes which prepared the way for brigandage, as well as those which supported it, were encountered; but the task of the Government and of Parliament was not at an end with this. It was not enough to meet brigandage at its source, it was especially necessary to endeavour to combat it in its matured manifestations, and to inflict on those who rendered themselves liable to it a just, prompt, and exemplary punishment. And here one is naturally led to the consideration of the last series of remedies which the Parliamentary Commission had suggested, and which resolved themselves into military action and legislative provisions. The military action was to be applied to the immediate suppression of the brigandage which actually existed in the country, the legislative enactments to the punishment of the guilty according to the dictates of justice. While there were still a great number of bands roving about the country, the service of the gendarmes not being increased, nor that of the National Guards improved, military action was indispensable. The presence of troops in those provinces had also the advantage of producing a salutary moral effect, that, namely, of raising the spirits of the population, and inspiring confidence, so that military action added to the advantages of its material results those of its moral effect. It is hardly necessary to record that there has never been anything wanting on the score of valour, and, if anything, our officers and soldiers can be charged only with unnecessary rashness. As regards the command of the troops, the mere names of the experienced officers to whom it was entrusted are a sufficient guarantee that it was vigorous and prudent. The absence of decisive results was by no means due to want of bravery, sagacity, or patience; the causes have been already mentioned. A war against brigandage has a purely special tendency, and is not carried on according to the rules of military strategy—our soldiers fought these bandits in too chivalrous, too loyal a fashion. Between an enemy who never avoids fighting and one whose only resource is flight and safe concealment, regular warfare is not practicable. To meet the brigand effectually, it is necessary to adopt his arts, ambushes, surprises, continual movement; and this is why of all the arms of our service that which is most fit to make war against the bandits is the one composed of our celebrated Bersaglieri, who are trained to act independently, and endure best this kind of fatigue. The accumulation of troops in the cities and villages, so often indispensable for hygienic reasons, was therefore pointed out as dangerous, and to be avoided as much as possible, both because the brigands then could most easily overrun the country, knowing positively the movements of our soldiers, and also because the inhabitants became accustomed to the non-fulfilment of one of their first duties —that of being able to defend themselves. When in 1800 brigandage infested the south of France, the first Consul wrote to Berthier, the minister of war: " Je suis mécontent de voir tant de troupes à Lyon et à Marseilles. Dans des circonstances pareilles les troupes doivent être sans cesse sur les chemins et dans les bois; que le général forme sur-le-champ ses colonnes, et en donne le commandement aux Généraux Gaveau et Guillot; qu'ils poursuivent sans relâche les brigands, en mettant toujours leurs quartiers généraux dans les villages."

Some years later, in 1803, brigandage having made its appearance anew in La Vendée, Napoleon, writing again to Marshal Berthier, gave him the same instructions. " Mon opinion est, qu'il ne faut laisser nulle part de garnison, mais faire de toutes les forces quatre corps sous les ordres, chaque corps, d'un Général de brigade, indépendemment des corps des généraux Girardon et Dufresse ; que chacun des ces corps doit être partagé en trois autres, chacun de 150 à 200 hommes, infanterie, cavalerie et gendarmerie comprises. Soutenus par l'espionnage, et continuellement en mouvement, ces corps doivent parvenir à étouffer la révolte dans sa naissance."

The wisdom of these suggestions is fully confirmed by actual experience, and frequent and uninterrupted illustrations have proved that continued movements of troops in the country have always produced some such result. Nor is it necessary to add that in all encounters, where encounters have been possible, the brigands have always fared the worst. The few times that they have succeeded in obtaining a victory over our soldiers they have done it by surprise and in disproportionate numbers. How many brave officers in command of small detachments of troops have met death, after unheard-of tortures, in the ambuscades cowardly prepared by those large bands of brigands on horseback, which, for a moment, had spread over the country!

The war against brigandage cost our army the

following losses, between the 1st of May, 1861, and the end of March, 1863 :—In the first eight months of 1861, 8 officers and 89 soldiers killed ; in the whole of 1862, 8 officers and 156 soldiers; in the first three months of 1863, 5 officers and 41 soldiers ; in all, 21 officers and 286 soldiers killed—together, 307. In the first months of 1861, 3 officers wounded, and 45 soldiers ; in 1862, 2 officers and 29 soldiers ; in the first three months of 1863, 7 soldiers ; total, 86 wounded. During all this time only 6 soldiers remained the prisoners of the assassins ; while of 19 others there is no account. Our losses have indeed been excessive and lamentable, when the quality of the victims is compared with that of the murderers, and when it is remembered what cruel ill-usage and savage tortures they had to suffer at the hands of those cannibals. They fell gloriously in an inglorious field, slain by cruel hands—martyrs of civilization and liberty.

The losses endured by the brigands in the same period of time are as follows :—In the first eight months of 1861, 365 shot, 1343 killed in fight, 1571 prisoners; in 1862, 594 shot, 950 killed, 1106 arrested. In the first quarter of 1863, 79 shot, 120 killed, 91 prisoners ; in all, 1038 shot, 2413 fallen in battle—that is, 3451 killed, and 2768 made prisoners. What a sad and painful record of the melancholy inheritance of crime and barbarity come down to us from so many ages of corruption and slavery. Besides, in the first eight months of 1862, 267 brigands gave themselves up; 634 in 1862; 31 in one quarter of 1863; together, 932. The total number, therefore, of brigands put *hors de combat* by death, capture, or voluntary surrender, amounts to about 7151. The number of those who surrendered increased in proportion to the energy of the repressive measures. In the last four months of 1861, there were shot, in Capitanata, 7 brigands, and 30 fell in battle; in the same four months of the following year, 136 were shot, and 322 died in battle. In the first period not one gave himself up; in the second, 281 surrendered.

But to assist the military, it was found necessary that the National Guard should also be called out. For the extirpation of brigandage, the active aid of the whole strength of the country was imperatively required, both for the recognition of places and men, and for the excellent moral effect which it would produce. The National Guards in the southern provinces were certainly not in such a condition as could have been desired. Composed in haste, and without a precise organization, they included elements which by no means conduced to discipline and activity; but all the battalions at the same time contained young volunteers who desired nothing more eagerly than to prove their devotion to the interests of the country, and gallantly to aid in the defence of social order. Of these there have been scores of examples. On many occasions, in all the provinces, the civic militia, when well-directed, has aided the troops, to whom they have acted as guides, and lent assistance. In Capitanata, the National Guards of Pietra, Roseto, Casalnuovo, Alberona, Greci, deserved particular mention; in Basilicata, those of Pietrogalla (which repulsed with much vigour an attack of Borjès), Pescopagano, Bella, and Bernalda; in Terra di Bari, those of Minervino, of Canosa, of Corato, and, most of all, of Gioja; in Terra di Otranto, those of Ostuni, Manduria, Laterza, Nardo, Latiano, and Mesagna. It is gratifying to have to record such facts regarding populations hardly risen from the abjection of the past. Moreover, in many other places troops of cavalry volunteers were organized among the young proprietors of the country, as at Altamura, at Gravina, at Sansevero, at Canosa, and particularly at Troia, whose mounted corps deserved the greatest praise. At Cerignola a rich proprietor named Morya, captain of the National Guard, was also at the head of a troop of young men, full of patriotic spirit, who volunteered for this noble purpose. The Picanti, the Paduli, and the Pomarisi are popular names in Basilicata, as chiefs of patriotic companies, specially called to service against brigandage, which have shown great courage, and on all occasions have shared the fatigues and dangers of the troops. But in reviewing these special non-military corps, particular mention is due to the cavalry organized and commanded by David Mennuni, proprietor of the commune of Genzano, in Basilicata, who has already been mentioned. This company, one hundred strong, was formed in April, 1861, when Crocco and his companions sacked and plundered the province of Melfi, and promoted everywhere sanguinary reactions. On hearing of these things, Mennuni got together, without delay, twenty-two courageous men, who all mounted voluntarily, and undertook to fight the horde of marauders. They gallantly kept their word, and from that day Mennuni and his men have not ceased to perform useful service against brigandage. Well acquainted with the localities, courageous and indefatigable, they scour mountains and forests, and give no peace to the bands, which dread them greatly. David Mennuni is a man of simple habits, modest, prepared for any sacrifice—the true type of the honest patriot.

All this shows the great activity that was displayed in the suppression of brigandage, and the perfect union that subsisted between the government and the sound part of the population. Why then were so many efforts not thoroughly effectual? · Several reasons may be assigned for the persistence of brigandage. First of all, taking into consideration the means of repression used from the very outburst of the Bourbonist reaction, it must be said that, though generally extremely severe, they could not always be successful, as prompt and exemplary punishment seldom followed the discovery of guilt. The most effectual punishment is that which follows the crime at but a short interval; the swiftness of the expiation is a wholesome check on the contagious power of bad example. If brigands taken with arms in their hands were instantly shot without trial, those consigned to the judicial power often remained in prison, waiting for their judgment, for many a month, while some of their accomplices freely passed through the towns, and others followed their career of crime and infamy. This state of things the commissioners very much deplored. In their opinion it was of the highest importance that an end should be put to it, not only because the most sacred interests of justice and humanity were at stake, but also because it was necessary that the people should not lose the respect due to the laws. They proposed, therefore, a bill, intended exclusively to confer on the executive the requisite power to meet more energetically the emergencies of that abnormal condition in which the south of Italy was placed. This fact should not be overlooked. The Government, which is represented by the supporters of the fallen dynasty as one ruling its former dominions with tyrannical despotism, asked, through the representatives of the nation, that even against brigands stricter legality should be observed in the proceedings than was previously thought necessary.

The first thing the Parliamentary Commission insisted upon, in urging the house to adopt some extraordinary dispositions for the repression of brigandage, was that an entirely provisional character should be given to them, in order not to violate the rights guaranteed by the constitution; and secondly, that they were to be withdrawn as soon as the causes which necessitated their adoption no longer existed. This was but justice, for it would indeed be deeply to be regretted if, in a constitutional country, measures of such an exceptional character as those which were suggested were arbitrarily brought forward; and it was only in respect of particular circumstances that the Government was asked to submit, within the shortest delay, such a bill to the house.

'In a free state any act having, even apparently, an arbitrary bearing, would not be justified, even under the most pressing necessity of social defence, unless it were determined, not by the will of any private or public man, but by legal and constitutional considerations. More particularly in this case, as the greatest evil weighing upon the Neapolitan provinces was precisely the lack of confidence in the administration of justice. It was therefore important that to those very exceptional means of repression, demanded by the absolute necessity of putting an end to a great national calamity, should be imparted the strictest legality. But in what would the action of such a bill consist? When in a state of war a country is allowed to adopt such measures as are necessary to maintain the national honour and independence. Now it would be useless to argue that the brigandage of the Neapolitan provinces did not place the Italian kingdom exactly in the same condition as if it were engaged in a real war; for brigandage is the worst of wars— a struggle between barbarism and civilization, the rebellion of crime against society; and therefore the Italian Parliament unanimously declared that the provinces infested by brigands should be placed under the action of special laws, sanctioned by the royal will, and, as soon as it could be safely done, abrogated again by the same supreme authority. The draught for this bill, submitted by the Parliamentary Commission, in accordance with the observations they had gathered during their investigations, had two distinct objects—the prevention of crime and its punishment. I shall briefly trace here the measures by which they proposed to carry out their design.

The suggestion of availing themselves of special preventive measures was the result of a careful investigation of the circumstances which, up to the present moment, had baffled every effort. It is above everything necessary to the success of any operation intended to destroy brigandage, to form accurate lists, in which should be contained, district by district, the names of all the brigands and outcasts who are known to infest the country. These lists were once collected in every district, and designated "Outlaws' Lists." They were then of little value, and were perhaps only used by the Bourbonist kings to ascertain the number of bandits by whom their happy dominions were inhabited. Now, with a totally different view, their revival was advocated, with such alterations as were necessary. The utility of these lists of reference is greater than may at first appear; for through them it is easy to have an idea of the exact number of the contingent furnished to the brigand bands by every village or district. The publication of their names, too, is of great service in aiding the hands of justice, and is also a warning to the brigands themselves. It is true that this may have but little influence over those hardened bandits whose existence has been but a succession of crimes; but it has a totally different effect upon those who may have been unconsciously driven into that guilty life, and who are willing to listen to a warning which may ultimately prevent them from falling into the most abject degradation. To increase the good results that were to be expected from the inauguration of that system, it was also considered advisable that rewards should be granted by the Government to those who delivered into the hands of justice one or more brigands, or who put the police on their track; and that the enumeration of such recompenses should be added to the aforesaid lists.

Another measure, pointed out as one of vital importance, was the mobilization of the National Guard, and the formation of partial flying columns of volunteers, like those we have had already occasion to speak of. It was also observed that it might be deemed necessary, in some of the provinces infested, to order the suspension of certain trades, shut up the farm-houses, concentrate the cattle in some particular place, close all the rural baking-houses scattered about the country, prevent the exportation of gunpowder, cloths, saddles and bridles, and any sort of food whatever, from any town or village, and, if need be, proceed to a general disarmament. Hard measures these, indeed; but if the reader could only know all the good which arose from their application! In the province of Capitanata, for instance, where there are so many shepherds' huts, and so many farm-houses, the advantages of such dispositions are evident, particularly in certain seasons of the year; for the brigands, entirely deprived of the means of getting their provisions through the shepherds or from the farm-houses, were unable to keep the field much longer. But far more dangerous than the bandit who, in the pursuit of his adventurous career, robs and murders on the highway, are the brigands who, abiding in the towns, and many of them in public offices, suggest to their comrades the crimes they are to commit, indicate to them those who are to be the victims of their rapacity, give directions for those ambuscades in which so many brave soldiers have lost their lives, and, constantly providing the bands with food and ammunition, enable them to continue, without intermission, their career of crime and murder. These men, under the threat of dismissal for neglect of duty, were to be kept specially under the supervision of the mayors of the southern towns and the officers of the National Guard.

And such severe measures were certainly necessary when we remember the conduct of the municipality of Grottaglie, who received the band of the famous Pizzichicchio with every mark of honour; or that of the municipality of Carovigno, who sheltered the host of assassins led by the brigand chief La Veneziana; or that of the municipality of San Marco in Lamis, who allowed the murderers of the unhappy Captain Valentini, of the Royal Engineers, to find a safe refuge within the town. In such extreme cases the mere suspension of political officers, or the discharge of the National Militia, not being considered sufficient punishment, the Parliamentary Commission proposed that the Government should follow a system something like that pursued in England towards boroughs which have been convicted of corruption in the exercise of their electoral rights, and deprive the whole district which has been proved guilty of connivance with brigandage of the right of appointing their new magistrates and officials for a certain time—a humiliation which would be severely felt, and could not but produce the most salutary effects. At Foggia, Troia, and many other localities, where, as a measure of precaution, the National Guard had been dissolved, the impressionable population regarded the step, which deprived them of the power of exercising an important civil privilege, as one of the severest punishments that could have been inflicted on them.

A last exceptional power which the commission considered it necessary to confide to the prefects was that relating to local exile, or the confinement, within certain limits, of such individuals as were deemed likely to disturb the public peace—a measure of great importance to those districts where an agitation favourable to brigandage was kept up by one or two troublesome and discontented persons.

The commissioners, after having thus expressed their

opinion as to the means by which brigandage might be repressed, next took into consideration the manner in which it might be most effectively punished. The system followed until that period had been far from successful as a preventive of crime. Brigands caught with arms in their hands had been shot on the spot. Others, given up to the judicial authorities, were almost immediately discharged for want of proof, although it often happened that those thus arrested and set free were in reality the most guilty—the instigators of those who had died for the crimes which subtler villains had prompted them to commit. Immediate execution by martial law can only be justified by an overwhelming necessity; and the soldiers themselves shrank from carrying these summary executions into effect. General Lamarmora, and the most distinguished officers under his command, were opposed to such extreme rigour, except, it might be, in cases of extraordinary atrocity. But as, in the peculiar circumstances of the country, justice often failed to convict the most guilty, what alternative was to be adopted? Even the summary justice of martial law had been ineffectual, for though a large number of brigands had been shot, brigandage was still as flourishing as ever. Was it advisable, then, to leave to the ordinary courts the judgment of the brigands taken in the field with arms in their hands?—or was it desirable that offences arising from brigandage should be entrusted to a special tribunal, armed with all the terrors of the law, but never arbitrary in its decisions? The latter resolution was finally adopted. The disheartened and frightened population thus saw that the sword of an inexorable justice was drawn for their defence. In extreme cases, when bandits were taken with arms in their hands, instead of being summarily shot, they were to be brought to trial before a court-martial, with powers strictly defined by law; and if proved guilty, the sentence of death should be carried out without delay, the punishment being rendered so much the more effective by the certainty and rapidity of its execution. The advantage of such a system was shown in France in the year 1800. Brigandage raging in many departments, the First Consul ordered the formation of flying columns, composed of infantry, cavalry, and gendarmes; an extraordinary military commission, named by the general in command of the division, being attached to each corps, before which the brigands were brought to trial within twenty-four hours after their arrest. The result was, as M. Thiers assures us, that in a short time brigandage was entirely destroyed, and public security on the high roads completely re-established.

Though some of the members of the Parliamentary

Commission were of opinion that capital punishment should be abolished for mere acts of brigandage, the majority, considering the necessity of social security, could not reconcile themselves to a measure which theoretically has so much to recommend it. In a country where such a system as that of brigandage prevails, the abolition of the punishment of death for crimes so atrocious would be tantamount to the abolition of every right of social vindication. The brigands themselves, prompt, merciless, and sanguinary in their deeds, would have seen in such a measure a confession of weakness, which would only have incited them to the commission of greater atrocities. The population of Southern Italy, too, which has felt the full weight of the scourge, would have been thrown into a state of dismay. The danger in which life and property were constantly kept, the interruption of trade, and the stagnation of public prosperity, which have been the consequences of brigandage, would have been greatly increased. The sufferings of the population of the Neapolitan provinces from brigandage—leading them in many cases to tear arrested brigands from the hands of justice and kill them on the spot—have been so great, that any untimely proclamation of mercy would have a most unfavourable effect. If Borjès and Trazigny had not been shot, the irruptions of bandits from the Papal States, the landing of adventurers of every nation, would have greatly increased. Such considerations seemed, to the Parliamentary Commission, sufficiently powerful to induce them to recommend that military tribunals should be authorized to punish with immediate death all bandits taken with arms in their hands, or in flagrant rebellion against the public functionaries, leaving it to the discretion of the authorities to inflict, in less heinous cases, a milder punishment. In the latter, expatriation would be a sufficiently severe punishment to the southern inhabitants, so much attached to their native land, so sensible to the attractions of their beautiful climate, as to abhor the very idea of removal from it. The benefit of a graduation of minor penalties ought certainly not to be extended to those public officials, or members of the clergy, accused of complicity with the brigands, their guilt being such as to exclude every consideration arising from extenuating circumstances. The Italian Parliament wisely supported the view that all who favoured brigandage by any means, but particularly by inducing the soldiers of the Italian army to desert their colours, should be deemed worthy of the severest punishment. The Commission particularly urged that the strictest measures of the law should be carried out against those brigands who hid themselves in the towns and villages, more dangerous in their concealment than those who risked their lives in the open field. And lastly, it was recommended that the goods and property of all who had acquired riches by their complicity with brigandage should be confiscated; for it is a melancholly fact that many families are now in the enjoyment of wealth, the origin of which can be traced to the desire of speedily making a fortune by illegitimate means, the possession of which, therefore, a memorial of wrong and violence, can be justified by no sufficient reason.

It was also advised that some indulgence should be extended to those who surrendered of their own accord; a system which sometimes produces the happiest effects. General Franzini, commander of the military division of Avellino, relates an encounter of his troops with the brigands, in which the latter were so frightened by the valour of the soldiers, that they all swore to the Madonna that they would pay for the celebration of a mass at the nearest church, and then surrender themselves into the hands of justice, provided they succeeded in saving their lives. Fourteen of them put down their weapons and gave themselves up to a captain of Bersaglieri. As it was near Christmas time, they asked permission to go and spend the holidays at home, promising faithfully to come back. General Franzini, curious to know whether a brigand's word could be trusted, granted their demand; and, to the astonishment of all, they punctually returned, not fourteen, but twenty-five, although they were aware that they were all condemned to a more or less severe punishment—in all probability the galleys. The General, touched by their submission, allowed them once more to go home till the first of January, with strict injunctions, however, that they should be back on the second, on which day they reappeared, no longer twenty-five, but forty-six. This incident, though apparently of no great importance, shows that in certain cases a system of conciliation may be very usefully adopted.

The exceptional bill for the repression of brigandage, framed by Parliament on the 15th of August, 1863, after one of the longest and most remarkable discussions on record, during which the interest with which it was generally regarded was manifested in the most unmistakable manner, is generally known as Pica's bill. This bill declared that every one belonging to an armed band of at least three individuals was subject to the action of the military tribunals; that all taken in resistance to the public authorities, with arms in their hands, should be shot, or, in cases where extenuating circumstances were admitted, condemned to the galleys for life. All who should in any way assist the brigands were to be liable to penal servitude for life, and, in case of extenuating circumstances, to twenty years. Government was further authorized to organize as many companies of foot and mounted volunteers as might be thought necessary for the assistance of the troops. The moderation of the measures thus recommended by Parliament must be acknowledged by every considerate reader, and yet it has been asserted by the enemies of Italian progress that they could have proceeded only from the most hateful despotism. Whether or not this was the case, the reader will be enabled to judge for himself, as in Appendix II. I have inserted the principle articles of this important bill.* My own conviction is that it was only by the rigorous application of such measures that the country could be saved from the state of agitation by which its population had been so long disturbed, and that a sure foundation of its commercial, social, and political prosperity could be established for the future.

* See Appendix II.

CHAPTER VIII.

THE LAST STAGE OF BRIGANDAGE—SUCCESSFUL RESULTS OF THE NEW SYSTEM OF REPRESSION—ATROCITIES COMMITTED BY CARUSO—REPORT OF GENERAL PALLAVICINI—SKETCH OF THE LIFE AND CHARACTER OF CARUSO—THE SLAUGHTER OF MELLANICO—RICCIARDELLI—STATE OF THE PROVINCE OF BENEVENTUM—DISASTER NEAR TORRE PALAZZO—GIULIO VIDEMARI—ANECDOTES OF CARUSO—HIS CAPTURE AND DESTRUCTION OF HIS BAND—OPERATIONS AGAINST CROCCO AND NINCO NANCO—ENDURANCE AND PERSEVERANCE OF ITALIAN SOLDIERS.

CHAPTER VIII

HAVING thus, on the best authorities, explained the origin, and narrated the most important and striking episodes in the history of brigandage, I purpose to complete my work by briefly tracing the events of the past few months, during which brigandage has been almost entirely destroyed. While in the history of this period I shall have to narrate anew atrocities instigated by a party shrinking from no act of cruelty or horror, it will be at the same time gratifying to observe the gradual restoration of tranquillity, and the indications of a new life manifesting themselves everywhere throughout the country. The past may have been gloomy, but in the signs of the better times coming, we have indications of a future in which Italy, a country so highly favoured by nature, will be enabled to develope those germs of social and political grandeur which have been crushed during centuries of internal misgovernment and foreign domination.

The appointment of the commission to inquire into the causes and nature of Italian brigandage, and the measures proposed for its repression, showed to Europe that Italian statesmen did not fear to face the danger, and that, in order to conquer it, they were prepared for any sacrifice. The provinces in which the provisions of the bill of August, 1863, were to be enforced, were the two Abruzzi, Basilicata, Beneventum, the two Calabrias, Capitanata, Molise, the two Principati, and Terra di Lavoro. Squadrons of foot and mounted volunteers were subsequently formed in every chief district, and military tribunals, with full power of execution, were established at Potenza, Foggia, Avellino, Caserta, Campabasso, Gaëta, Aquila, and Cosenza. All these provinces were then ravished by brigandage. Among the different bands, that of Caruso, of Torremaggiore, was conspicuous for its daring and ferocity. Four provinces on the coast of the Adriatic, Molise, Beneventum, Avellino, and Capitanata, were exposed to the incursions of Caruso and his lieutenants, Varanelli and Schiavone, themselves the ferocious leaders of bands which had submitted to the orders of that formidable chief. The band under his command, amounting to about a hundred, had its basis of operation on the river Fortore, and in the Forest della Grotte, Caruso's citadel and stronghold. There were still, in August, 1863, considerable bands of brigands in the old principality of Beneventum, and in every part of the Abruzzi, great facilities being afforded by the vicinity of the Papal States. The large and patriotic province of Basilicata was yet infested by numerous bandits, who, in the impenetrable woods of a territory bounded on two sides by the sea, found, notwithstanding the constant presence of the troops, secure refuge. The principal band in that province was that of Crocco, who, with the assistance of such lieutenants as Ninco Nanco, Tortora, and Canosa, commanded a horde of brigands still amounting to no fewer than 150 perfectly armed men, most of them mounted on excellent horses. With the other smaller bands scattered over the country, there were in that province a total of about 250 bandits—a very large number, if one considers that a band of eight or ten men, and even less, was enough to spread disorder and desolation throughout a whole district. Calabria, also, was at that time infested by a considerable number of brigands, who, divided into small "comitive," had succeeded in eluding the vigilance of their pursuers. In the neighbourhood of Naples was the remnant of the two bands Apuzzo and Vitichese, who were hidden in the mountains surrounding Castellamare. All the other provinces, Salerno, Avellino, Bari, Terra di Lavoro, and Lecce, were equally exposed to the ferocity of the "comitive." Such a condition of the Neapolitan provinces in August was appalling, and troops, civic authorities, national guards, and peasants felt the necessity of taking the most decisive measures. The brigands themselves seemed conscious that the time of their destruction was at hand, a conviction which gave them new energy.

The new system of repression was carried out with vigour, and, after three months' trial, the following were the results:—In almost every district the bands were nearly destroyed, many of the chiefs were killed, and others, thanks to the wise system of clemency which was introduced, gave themselves up. All the "comitive" were so far reduced as to be deprived, with a few exceptions, of any great power of inflicting injury. In both the Abruzzi tranquillity had been restored, the bands having been either dispersed or compelled to seek refuge in the Pontifical dominions. Of their chiefs some had fallen into the hands of the soldiers, while others had voluntarily surrendered. The miseries of Basilicata had been greatly alleviated; the terrible band of Crocco and Ninco Nanco, if not yet defeated, had been dislodged, forced to abandon the theatre of their infamous exploits, and to seek refuge in the barren wilderness of the Murgie of Minervino. The "comitive" of Malacarne, Menutti, Occhino, and Rubini, were destroyed, and the two chief brigands, Tina, successor of the ferocious Coppa, and Caruso, of Attella, not to be confounded with the other of the same name, made their submission with all their followers.

Capitanata was in a still more favourable condition. The only gang of bandits which remained there, under the leadership of a brigand named " Coppola Rossa " (the red cap), was dispersed ; so that a province, so terribly wasted in the previous winter, was then perfectly free of the dreadful scourge. In like manner the few brigands who were infesting the neighbourhood of Naples had been reduced to nothing; and the provinces of Salerno, Avellino, and Bari were at last enabled to enjoy a long period of security. The results obtained in Terra di Lavoro were also very brilliant. The terrible bands of de Cosimis, Il Caporale, Giordano, the chiefs of which were killed, or had surrendered, had disappeared or were destroyed. There remained only the " comitive " Fuoco and Giuliano, the latter reported to have fled to Rome, after having been seriously wounded, and the 219 brigands existing in that province in the month of August were reduced in December to 88. The consideration of these facts will show that, with the exception of

Crocco's band, and that of Caruso, who, though a wanderer with only a few men, was nevertheless formidable, main brigandage was put down in Italy. The few " comitive " yet roving about, or concealing themselves in inaccessible passes, were formed of remnants of old bands, to which no new recruits were added.

The three months of energetic repression had thus terminated in results which justified the most encouraging anticipations for the future. We are chiefly indebted for the accomplishment of so great a task to the labours of the troops under the gallant General Pallavicini, and to the Neapolitan National Guard, assisted by the various corps of volunteers. The introduction of the new military jurisdiction had in particular worked admirably. Sentence of death, during that short period, had been passed on only ten brigands—a favourable contrast with the time when every officer in command of a detachment, every commandant of volunteers, and even every captain of National Guards, possessed the power of life and death, and often exercised it with little discrimination.

During these three months 201 brigands surrendered spontaneously to the troops, 179 were made prisoners, and 78 were killed in action. Though much had been done in this short interval, the scourge could not be regarded as entirely eradicated. Two or three of the principal bands still found refuge in the most inaccessible parts of the country. As the exceptional bill had only been enforced for three months, and it was justly feared that if its authority were not continued the new year might be signalized by fresh disorders and devastations, the prolongation of its powers was therefore granted by Parliament.

Among the bands that still defied the authorities was that of the celebrated chief Crocco, who, after having been dislodged from the district of Melfi, where he had been for three years, had taken refuge in the territory of Barletta, in the Murgie of Minervino. As the peasants were no longer disposed to assist either them or any of the other bands, the difficulties with which they had to contend were much increased. The consequence was that they acted with great ferocity towards those who had formerly aided them. Caruso, in particular, knowing he could no longer rely on their blind submission, was inveterate against them. As they would no longer supply him with stores, or give him shelter and protection, he tried to impose upon them by terror, with which view he commited some cold-blooded murders. His last invasion of Capitanata was made at a period when that unfortunate province seemed to be secure from a fresh irruption. When the terrific announcement that Caruso and his dreaded bandits had appeared again in the district of Volturara spread all over the country, the population felt that their brief period of repose was terminated. Caruso's first exploit in Capitanata was characterised by that ferocity for which he was dreaded. His band having received straw, bread,. and five sheep at the farm of a peasant named Antonio Picciuti, he then informed this poor man that, as he would require a further supply on his return, he would, in the meantime, give him such a remembrance of his visit as would prove that his notice was not to be slighted. With these words the bandit seized the hand of the unfortunate man, laid it on a table, and, with a single blow, severed it from the arm.

General Pallavicini, who had the command of the troops employed in pursuit of the brigands, was kind enough to send me a report on the operations which ended in the total destruction of that formidable band —the largest of all, and the only one in which military discipline was maintained. In this document, inedited, and written with the frankness of a soldier, the adventurous life of the brigand is so vividly described, that the reader could sometimes imagine himself in the midst of the very scenes depicted; and not the least interesting part is that in which the writer gives his personal impressions of the chiefs, Caruso, Crocco, and Ninco Nanco.

"*Report of General Pallavicini.*

"Head-quarters of Spinazzola,
April, 1864.

"My dear Maffei,—You ask me to contribute to the publication you intend to make in England on the subject of our brigandage, by giving you a sketch of the life and origin of the most remarkable bandits I had to contend with in this ungrateful struggle, and a description of the last events which brought main brigandage to a close in the South of Italy. I willingly comply with your wish for two reasons—first, because, whatever may have been said or written on this question, the state of demoralization in which this fair country was left by the Bourbons can never be sufficiently known abroad; and secondly, because I am glad thus to be able to pay anew homage to the brave soldiers whom I had the satisfaction to command, and whose valour was certainly worthy of better enemies.

"You must know that, in accordance with the last arrangements made by Parliament, reinforcements were sent to all the troops engaged against the brigands, and that the National Guards were actively organized in all the municipalities. Public spirit was gradually restored; every citizen being determined to fight not only for himself, but also for his country. Villages, and large provincial towns, surrounded themselves with breastworks and loopholes, while isolated houses were fortified with regular parapets—an incredible state of things in Europe in the nineteenth century! In this way everything contributed to a speedy repression of the reactionary inroads, and to the prompt reduction of the brigand bands.

"From 1862 to 1863 the brigands constantly lost in number, and at the end of the former year the only strong 'comitiva' was that of Caruso, which mustered 200 men on horseback. But though their numbers were greatly reduced, those who remained were accustomed to meet dangers with indifference after the experience of three years of hardships. Some of them, gifted with real military qualities, such as the above-mentioned chief, Crocco of Rionero, and Ninco Nanco, who may be numbered first among the leaders whose names attained a more sad renown, had become very skilful in partisan warfare.

"Caruso had at one time been a poor shepherd. From a very early age he had given proof of intelligence, of an indomitable spirit, and of a craving after a life of adventure. When the disturbances broke out in 1860, Caruso joined the revolt, and, from its commencement, distinguished himself not only by his valour, but by his great cruelty. Being arrested, he was incarcerated in the prison of Sansevero, but soon contrived to make his escape, and rejoined his comrades in the field, where, before long, he found himself at the head of a numerous band. Tempted by the wealth of his master, the Prince of Sansevero, he resolved first to attack the benefactor on whose bounty he had lived from his infancy. He dispersed his herds of cattle and droves of sheep, scattered to the winds huge stores of corn, laid waste fertile fields, and burnt to the ground innumerable farmhouses; and after thus wreaking his vengeance on a generous patron, he proceeded to devastate the country in which he was born. In Torremaggiore, his native place, he committed such atrocities that his name was heard with terror by the population. In a short space of time he desolated all Capitanata, and a great part of Molise and of Principato Ulteriore, where, however, his incursions were infrequent, because in the latter province he was under the necessity of obeying the orders of Crocco, who held command both in it and in the extreme part of Basilicata. During the early part of his brigand life, Caruso succeeded in making himself known only as a man of unheard-of barbarity; and it was not until the end of 1862 that he began to be spoken of as a courageous and skilful leader of brigands. At this time the detachment of troops stationed at Santa

Croce di Magliano, a rich district of Molise, was commanded by Captain Rota, of the 36th regiment of the line. When Caruso, with his two hundred brigands, approached the neighbourhood, he obtained minute information as to the strength of this detachment, and the courage and skill of its commandant, who was said to be a man of great impetuosity of character, desiring nothing more ardently than to measure himself with the brigands. Caruso, thinking he might profit by the commandant's want of prudence, posted thirty of his men in the farmhouse of Mellanico, situated on the outskirts of the immense wood of Fortore, and with the rest of his troop concealed himself in the surrounding forest, having previously, however, disguised one of his followers as a shepherd, and sent him to Santa Croce, to inform the commandant of the presence of thirty brigands in the farmhouse. As soon as Rota, who suspected nothing, received the treacherous message, he hastily collected forty-nine men of his detachment, and, full of ardour, advanced at their head to the farmhouse, which had been pointed out to him, where he was welcomed by a volley of musketry from those within. Having surrounded the edifice, he made the necessary arrangements for the assault; but before he could carry them out, Caruso, with all his men, rushed from the wood and surrounded the assailants, who, in no way intimidated by the number of the enemy, made a desperate defence. After an obstinate struggle, the brigands gained the victory. Every one of the little band was struck down by the bullets of the bandits, who, with their swords, dispatched the wounded. When Captain Rota, who, although he had been in the thickest of the fight, had by some chance remained uninjured, saw the last of his comrades fall by his side, he drew his revolver, pointed it at his temple, and shot himself dead.

"Caruso is said by some to have been wanting in personal courage, a charge which is disproved by numerous facts. If he occasionally endeavoured to avoid a fight, it must be recollected that even a succession of victories would, in diminishing the numbers of his band, be equivalent to a defeat. If sometimes during the fray he kept aloof from danger, he was always ready, when an example was necessary to animate his companions, to throw himself into the thickest of the fight. Many of his wounds, some of which at the time of his arrest were scarcely healed, had been inflicted in hand-to-hand encounters, in which he displayed the greatest daring.

"After the slaughter at Mellanico, the troops, still continuing their operations against the brigands, compelled Caruso's band to divide into several small sections, it being impossible for them any longer to keep together more than two hundred horses, on account of the difficulty of procuring forage. Caruso retained with himself about seventy men. A band of the same number was placed under Schiavone, one of their most astute and intelligent leaders. Cascione, at the head of thirty men, established himself in the district of Larino, and the remainder grouped themselves together in little bands of from eight to ten men. One of these, composed of seven individuals, all from S. Marco, Baselice, and other districts of the province of Beneventum, proceeded to the native place of the men, expecting they should there be able to maintain themselves by means of assistance from friends and neighbours. The small knot of brigands, led by one Deodoro Ricciardelli, of S. Marco dei Cavoti, commenced its ravages in the province of Beneventum, destroying the crops in the fields, burning the farmhouses, butchering cattle, levying ransoms, and slaughtering all who were not sufficiently prompt in satisfying their demands. The very smallness of such a band was its greatest safeguard, enabling it to move about freely and expeditiously, without the necessity of making arrangements beforehand for provisions and forage; while the few horses belonging to it could be easily concealed in a wood, in a ravine, or behind any bank.

"While Ricciardelli was scouring Beneventum

with such success, Caruso found himself hard pressed in Capitanata, where, the troops being skilfully distributed, and squadrons of mounted volunteers organized, it was not very easy for a band of seventy horsemen to keep the field. But this vigorous chief had never ceased correspondence with any of the bands which had separated from his own; and, when pressed in Capitanata and in the district of Larino, he felt the necessity of betaking himself to some other quarter. He proposed, therefore, to penetrate into the province of Beneventum, there to avail himself of the local knowledge of Ricciardelli, rather than to resort to the Avellinese, where, as has lately been remarked, Crocco directed the operations of all the hordes of brigands.

"The entry of Caruso into Beneventum was accompanied by a sad catastrophe. Five miles from that place, on the road to Fragne, there stands a farm-house called Torre Palazzo, at which, for the safety of travellers, some regular troops were stationed. In February, 1863, this post was commanded by a lieutenant of the 39th regiment of the line, Camillo Lauri, of Macerata, a young man scarcely twenty-one, who had volunteered as a private soldier in 1859, but for his merits was in a very short time promoted to the rank of an officer.

"After taking possession of Torre Palazzo, Lauri had frequent opportunities of pursuing Ricciardelli's little band of seven, but always without success, the brigands being easily able to evade the pursuit by the swiftness of their horses. On the morning of the 24th of February, while Lauri, after the fatigues of a long and chilly night passed on the watch, was resting on some straw, musket shots and loud shouts suddenly awoke him from his sleep. These proceeded from the seven brigands of Ricciardelli, who, with unwonted audacity, had approached Torre Palazzo, challenging the little detachment. Leaving a few men to guard the farmhouse, Lauri, at the head of seventeen others, rushed out to attack the brigands; who, keeping just out of gunshot, gained the heights of Francavilla (a castle on the hill opposite Torre Palazzo), closely followed by the troops. Just as Ricciardelli and his men had reached the top of the hill and were on the outskirts of the wood of Francavilla, Caruso, with his whole band, and that of Schiavone, who had just joined him, dashed out from its shelter and joined the other brigands, forming altogether a band of one hundred and thirty-five men.

"If, by a deplorable chance, Lauri had not been ignorant of the entry of Caruso into the provinces, it is certain that he would not have allowed himself to be decoyed so far from the post intrusted to his care. But the young officer, convinced that he had only to deal with the little band of Ricciardelli, thought all precautions unnecessary, and, with the object of covering as much ground as he could, had scattered his few men as skirmishers, all of them now so far apart from one another that it was impossible to bring them together at a moment when it was so necessary that the little force should be concentrated. The bandits, being in such numbers, soon despatched the few soldiers, whom they attacked singly; none of the latter, however, perishing without a desperate resistance. The combat over, Caruso had the dead bodies of his own men collected and thrown into a barn, to which he then set fire, being anxious to conceal the price at which he had purchased victory over so small a number of troops. When, warned of the calamity which had befallen his men, the captain of the company to which Lauri belonged hastened to the scene of disaster, he found there only the dead bodies of the combatants, the only living creature being the dog of the dead officer, which, stretched upon the body of his master, was howling dolefully and licking his bloody wounds. The poor animal was carried off by force to Beneventum, but escaped the same night and returned to Francavilla, where, for three days and three nights, he remained upon the spot where Lauri lay buried.

"The terror spread by this affair over the whole of Beneventum is perfectly indescribable, for this province had previously been free from the savage deeds of Caruso. The whole district being totally unprotected by cavalry, with only a few troops scattered here and there, whom it was difficult to concentrate, detachments of brigands began to scour the country, ravaging, murdering, and devastating wherever they appeared, and sometimes advancing even to the gates of the most populous towns. As some peasants, urged by the severity of the scourge to aid the public force, had sometimes, by acting as guides to the troops, enabled them to surprise the band, Caruso, exasperated by his losses, began to act with cruelty against the countrypeople, whom, until then, if he had not befriended, he had at least treated with less inhumanity. Every check on his savage instincts being removed, many a victim was immolated to his lust for blood, the ferocity displayed by him in the latter months of his life being so violent as almost to resemble madness. The pen, indeed, refuses to record the bloody deeds which horrified the whole of Beneventum about the middle of 1863. At Pago, a husbandman, suspected by Caruso of being on good terms with the authorities and the troops, was thrown into a caldron of boiling water, after both his arms and legs had been cut off. At Pontelandolfo, where, by the aid of a mason, Caruso's band had been surprised by the military and three of his men had lost their lives, when the chief learned who the man was that had informed and guided the soldiers, he, three days afterwards, fell suddenly on a place on the main road, about a mile from Pontelandolfo, where more than a hundred men were at work on the roads, and, after the labourers had been drawn up before him, desired that all the regular masons should step forward. Among twelve of these unhappy wretches, almost all under twenty, who advanced, the one who had acted as guide to the troops was not visible. Caruso, in his anger, killed with his own hand every one of them, to punish them for the crime committed by their companion.

"Notwithstanding the valour of our soldiery, Caruso from time to time gave battle to the regular troops, only, however, when numbers and position made him confident of success. Thus, at Sferracavallo, in the house of one Marcone, he assaulted a picket of ten men and a corporal, and cut them to pieces. In a house in Campolettere he surrounded a little band of eighteen men of the 20th regiment of the line, commanded by an officer, and would certainly have despatched them all had not another detachment, which, by a happy chance, was in the neighbourhood, hearing the firing, come to the assistance of this handful of their comrades, of whom nine were already weltering in their blood.

"One fine day in September there was journeying along the road which leads from Torrecuso to Beneventum a party composed of two rich proprietors of Paupisi, six of the National Guard of the same district, and a sergeant of the 39th with eight soldiers. The sergeant was Giulio Videmari, who, although born in Milan, belonged to a wealthy Venetian family. In his infancy he had been deprived of his father, in 1848, during those glorious five days of the revolution of Milan which inaugurated the Italian movement of that year. The orphan Giulio, as he grew up, vowed, like his father, to devote himself to his country; and when the war of 1859 broke out, he left, at seventeen years of age, his aged mother, and hastened to Piedmont to enrol himself under the banner which was so soon to wave from the Alps to the Lilibeo. For some days nothing had been heard of Caruso, and the little band, bound for Beneventum, endeavoured to beguile the tedium of a long journey by amusing tales and merry songs, suspecting nothing of the danger to which they were soon to be exposed. At the same moment the whole band of Caruso was lying in wait near Ponte Finocchio, concealed in a thicket, ready to surprise the passing troops, who soon found themselves surrounded by brigands, in such numbers as to leave them no hope of a successful defence. The two proprietors of Paupisi and the six National Guards thought it best to surrender at once, trusting they might be permitted to purchase their liberty. The two former were not disappointed, and some days afterwards, at the cost of 20,000 ducats, had the happiness of again embracing their families. It was not so, however, with the National Guard, who were all killed by the infamous chief, because, as he said, they had surrendered without an attempt at resistance, and had abandoned the soldiers who were their companions in arms. Videmari, as soon as he saw into what a trap they had fallen, rallied round him his few companions, exhorting them to perish sooner than give themselves up to this horde of assassins. At the first onset four of his men fell mortally wounded, and the four others were rendered incapable of defending themselves. Videmari, with his sword in his right hand and a pistol in his left, was in the centre of a small circle of brigands, who, with all their roughness, struck by the rare beauty and proud air of the youth, did not attempt to injure him. One of them, however, pointing to Caruso, said, 'There is our chief; take off your cap to him and your life shall be saved.' Videmari, however, unwilling to purchase his life on such a condition, turned, in a frenzy of indignation, upon the man who had suggested the humiliating step, exclaiming, 'To me!—to me such an insult;' and, pointing his pistol at the brigand's breast, shot him dead. Then, throwing himself into the midst of his enemies, he smote right and left with his sword, until, exhausted by more than thirty wounds, he fell dead in their presence.

"After the catastrophe of St. Bartolomeo in Galdo, where the band of Caruso, in a fight with the National Guard, despatched more than forty victims—after the affair of Orsara, where twenty-two National Guards fell by the hands of Caruso and his men—the district militia of Beneventum was thoroughly demoralized; and the detachments of regular troops, entirely deprived of the assistance they counted on from the local knowledge of this militia, found the difficulties of the task on which they were employed increase every day. Amid this universal discouragement, Caruso pursued his sanguinary career. At Castelvetere, where there were twenty-seven persons at work in a field, his band overpowered the poor labourers, and binding the men to the trees, violated with great atrocity the women and girls, five of whom were between twelve and fourteen years old! In the midst of laughter and horrible jests the unhappy creatures were afterwards barbarously mutilated, and ultimately put to death. Last, and most miserable, the men were massacred after having been compelled to witness the horrid spectacle of the dishonour and murder of their wives. It is to be remarked that in these and similar other murders in cold blood, Caruso trusted to no other hands than his own the office of executioner. It is calculated that in the month of September, 1863, alone, he put to death two hundred persons *with his own hands!* It has been said, too, that he ate the flesh and drank the blood of his victims, but this is not the fact. Not that such acts would have disgusted him, but he would not have done them, he said, because they seemed to him nothing but vain ostentation. And when one of his men, thinking to gain credit with his chief, wished by similar cannibalism to parade his ferocity, Caruso simply smiled scornfully, as if to signify that such boastings had little weight with him.

"The misery which thus cruelly oppressed the poor province of Beneventum attracted at length the attention of the Government, and, in order to bring to an end the incessant toil to which the military force in the Beneventano was exposed, it considered it expedient to concentrate its efforts in one direction by putting the whole under the command of a single military leader. I was honoured by being selected for this not very easy duty, and at the close of the month of September, I assumed the command-in-chief of the provinces of Beneventum and Molise.

"As the matter now so nearly concerns myself, it would not be correct for me to dilate at length upon the military operations conducted under my command in the Beneventano. I therefore limit myself to an account of those which throw light upon the end of this formidable band of brigands. Without explaining, with too many particulars, how I disposed of the few troops under my orders, I will only say that I distributed in small detachments the infantry of the line, and having left them to guard the more important passes, I then ordered a battalion of Bersaglieri, and the few light horse at my disposal, to beat the country in small flying columns. A few days had scarcely elapsed after I had taken the command of the troops of the district of Beneventum, when a first encounter took place near Francavilla, which produced such confusion in the ranks of the bandits, that from that day the utter destruction of the ferocious band could be anticipated. From that moment I saw the necessity of not leaving the brigands a moment's rest to re-organise their scattered forces, and to collect new recruits. Admirably seconded by the troops, I had the satisfaction to see my efforts crowned with success. The horde of assassins, continually pursued, lost every day men and horses; nor, during this time, was the brigand chief lax in his exertions to escape the fate that constantly drew nearer him, employing the most extraordinary craft in baffling the troops.

" One day that, accompanied by a small detachment of light cavalry, I had been in pursuit of him no less than ten or twelve hours, in the direction of the immense forest of Riccia, it so happened that the pursued band met a poor coalman, who, at the approach of dusk, was making his way home, carrying on his shoulders the result of his day's work. Caruso, going up to the poor fellow, requested him in a familiar tone to allow him to light his cigar at the pipe he was smoking. The brigand, after he had lit his cigar, while, with the one hand, he held out the pipe to return it to its owner, with the other seized his revolver, and fired it in the unhappy man's face. All this was done in an instant, and with the utmost coolness. The followers of Caruso, though long accustomed to his wanton ferocity, could not but express their horror at a deed so atrocious. The bandit merely smiled, and, turning to his companions, said—' Don't wonder; we are followed by those d—— light horse, the deuce if we can escape! It is clear, however, that, on arriving here, the soldiers will stop a few moments to witness the last gasps of this dying man; and we shall thus have time enough to gain the forest, where, in the darkness of night, we may be able to conceal ourselves.' With these words, he thrust his spurs into the flanks of his swift Calabrian steed, and, followed by his companions, was in a moment out of sight. . .

Meanwhile, the pursuit was continued. Exhausted by the fatigues they had to endure, and by the pertinacious pursuit of the soldiers, decimated daily by frequently renewed encounters, the band, once so terrible, was reduced ere long to a few wanderers, who never ventured to show themselves in the daytime.

"One dark night in December, Caruso, with eight companions—all that remained of his once numerous band—repaired to a little farmhouse in the neighbourhood of Montefalcone, a district in which I had previously stationed a small detachment of Bersaglieri, under the orders of Lieutenant Alliaud. As soon as that officer heard of the arrival of the brigands at the farmhouse, he sallied out with twenty-two of his men, and so impetuously attacked the bandits, that they were all killed in a short time, notwithstanding the most desperate defence. The vigilant Caruso, however, again escaped what seemed certain death. While his men, overcome with fatigue, were sound asleep in the farmhouse, he, of iron mould, was watching over their common security; and though he did not observe the approach of the troops in time to withdraw his companions, he himself managed in the darkness to escape unobserved from the dangerous neighbourhood.

"About three months before these events, in going across the district of Cerce Maggiore, Caruso one day, obeying that instinct of slaughter which in him seemed to be a second nature, after plundering and burning a cottage situated in an isolated part of the country, barbarously slew the whole family by which it was occupied. A young girl, hardly sixteen, alone was spared. Gifted with rare beauty, she had awakened a savage passion in the breast of the assassin of her parents and her little sisters! The unconcealed aversion felt by the unhappy girl only increased the ardour of the passion which consumed the terrible lover, who, anxious to save the object of his love from the hardships to which his band was now subjected, committed her to the care of a young brigand, a relation of his own, who, though only twenty years old, was second in ferocity only to the chief, to whom he was entirely devoted. This youth, in fulfilment of the duty imposed on him, placed the poor girl in a miserable straw hut, in the neighbourhood of the village of Molinara.

"After the last irreparable disaster of Montefalcone, Caruso, routed and a fugitive, without a single companion left in the whole world, felt an ardent wish to see once more this object of his affection. Heedless of the dangers by which he was surrounded, despising the terrible risk to which he was exposing his life, he made up his mind to join his Filomena, and either put himself in safety with her, or die by her side. Eluding the vigilance of the troops and National

Guards, he succeeded, after two days of incredible sufferings and danger, in reaching the miserable hut where his beloved was kept prisoner.

"Many days before, however, the syndic of Molinara had been informed of the presence of the young girl in that neighbourhood, and feeling assured that sooner or later the brigand would come to see her, he pretended a perfect ignorance of the fact, in order not to awaken the suspicions of the Cerberus left to guard the unhappy Filomena. Caruso had, in fact, scarcely set his foot into the miserable abode where he sought the gratification of his violent love, when a peasant had already informed the syndic of his arrival. The National Guards of the village during the night surrounded the hut, where, unsuspicious of danger, the brigand was easily arrested, with his last companion. The news of so important a capture spread at once all over the surrounding country with incredible rapidity, and when, the next morning, the two captives were taken to Beneventum, immense crowds of people from the town, and from all the neighbouring villages, assembled to witness the passage of a man whose cruelty had struck the whole province with terror, and who was now a powerless captive in the hands of the National Guards. The day after I ordered a court-martial to assemble for the judgment of this celebrated assassin, and sentence of death was unanimously pronounced against the author of so many atrocities. Caruso listened to the announcement of his terrible fate unmoved, and, without betraying the slightest emotion, maintained the same haughty attitude until the very moment when he was shot outside the walls of Beneventum.

"By the destruction of this dreaded band the province of Beneventum was restored to a state of tranquillity, of which it had been long deprived. The mountainous district on the confines of Terra di Lavoro, a territory affording every facility to the brigands, alone continued to be the receptacle of a band formed of the remnants of those which had just been dispersed. I instantly quitted Beneventum and transported my head-quarters to San Lupo, on the mountain of Cerretto. A few days after my arrival the troops had, in several encounters, defeated and captured half the bandits who scoured the country. The other half suddenly and mysteriously disappeared, and notwithstanding all the efforts of the soldiers they were unsuccessful in their attempts to discover their retreat.

"About eight miles northwards of Cerretto, in the rocks that rise perpendicularly above a small stream flowing at the foot of the mountain of Palombara, is a cavern, spacious enough to protect within its recesses upwards of sixty persons, but of which the entrance is so narrow that only one can enter at a time. During the French domination, at the beginning of the century, this cavern had already served as a refuge for brigands, but had since been so entirely forgotten that its existence was known only to a few shepherds, who used to shelter themselves under its rocky roof in the summer, during those terrible storms which in these regions occasionally burst forth with tropical violence. It was in that cavern that the remaining brigands, fifteen in number, had taken refuge, after they had furnished it abundantly with stores and ammunition. As I had suspected that the bandits might have found some safe place of concealment amid these inaccessible rocks, I urged the municipal authorities of all the surrounding villages to endeavour to obtain, by means of the peasants or the shepherds, some clue by which the retreat of the band might be discovered. I ultimately succeeded in obtaining from a young goat-herd such information as led to the desired discovery. With two companions I hastened towards the spot, and when we were near the mouth of the cavern, the death of a carabineer, struck down by shots from the interior of the cave, convinced me that the brigands were in their lair. Anxious not to sacrifice any of my men by an immediate assault, I took measures to blockade the assassins in their retreat, and thus starve them out. They must have been well supplied with provisions, for even after some days they showed no disposition to yield, but lived gaily, dancing and singing, as if exposed to no danger. After twelve days, however, they expressed their willingness to surrender, provided I was in person on the spot, in evidence of which they prayed me to send them my general's cap. The fifteen brigands were thus finally taken, and the province of Beneventum was happily delivered from the terrible plague of brigandage with which it had been so severely visited.

"I was next entrusted by Government with a moveable column, to operate in the Barese and Basilicata, against the bands of Crocco and Ninco Nanco. In discharge of this duty I betook myself to the little town of Spinazzola, which, as it was the most central point between the Murgie and the Materano, I made my head-quarters.

"Carmine Donatelli, surnamed Crocco, held the supreme command over the brigands of Basilicata; under him were Ninco Nanco, and, lower still, Tortora, Serravalle, Masini, and others. Crocco had the greatest influence not only over all the brigand hordes, but over a great part of the country people, who recognised his extraordinary ability. He was known as the 'General' not only by all the brigands, but also by the peasants. This shrewd man, wise enough to profit by the dangerous occupation to which he had addicted himself, amassed such sums by booty and ransoms, that he is said to have been in possession of half a million francs (£20,000).

"Many conjectures have been made to account for his frequent reappearances, at the head of new bands, after he had suddenly disappeared. Some said that he had taken refuge in Rome, others in some town or suburb of Basilicata, or even in Naples itself; but the secret of the astute chief has never been discovered. All his best lieutenants, Ninco Nanco, Tortora, Tinno, Serravalle, and Coppa, were after a short time either dead or prisoners. Masini alone, at the head of a band of about fifty on foot, still maintained his position in the territory of Marsico, an Alpine and almost inaccessible district.

"Having distributed, as I thought most conveniently, the troops of my column, many days did not pass over before Crocco was beaten by my men in the wood of Montemilone. Not long afterwards the same band was again attacked near Palazzo by another detachment I had sent against it, and in the action that followed, Crocco himself was nearly taken prisoner, after having been compelled to abandon his horse. He succeeded in effecting his escape, however, and, with the aid of the many adherents whom he unquestionably had in the country, he managed to keep himself concealed, for we were unable to obtain any further account of him.

"The band of Ninco Nanco, consisting of about fifty mounted brigands, which now alone remained, frequented the Materano, and the district of Lagopesole, ordinarily preferring, however, to maintain itself in the Murgie, a vast and extremely barren country, lying between Gravina, Altamura, Corato, Andria, Minervino, and Spinazzola. The excessive and unheard of rigours of the winter gave Ninco Nanco reason to hope that the troops would not be able to operate in that difficult country, every inch of which was known to him and his men. The bandit, however, confided in a false hope, for nothing in the world could prevent my following him, whatever inconvenience and fatigue I and my soldiers might have to endure. In the course of less than two months, after having been frequently discomfited, the band was finally overcome, through a skilful manœuvre executed by my cavalry, in consequence of which the bandits fell into a network of posts of the National Guard, by whom they were entirely disorganised. In the desperate fight which ensued, Ninco Nanco, with only three companions, bent his steps towards Avigliano, his native place, in the neighbourhood of which he hoped he might be able to conceal himself with the aid of his relatives and friends. But his refuge was very soon discovered by the Aviglianese authorities; and on the night of the 12th of February the National Guard, with a few carabineers, surrounded and assaulted the farmhouse where he was harboured, and after a short conflict he fell mortally wounded.*

"Among the many acts of cruelty which will consign the name of Ninco Nanco to eternal execration in these provinces, one alone will suffice to reveal all the perfidy of that black heart. Captain Capoduro, commanding a detachment in Basilicata, every attempt to force a fight upon the band proving vain, set on foot negotiations to try to induce the chief to give himself up voluntarily, and throw himself upon the clemency of the sovereign. Capoduro hoped by this means to deliver the country from the

---

* I have seen lately in our papers that Ninco Nanco was not killed as reported, and that he had appeared again at the head of a small band. True or false, this intelligence shows that among the Neapolitan brigands often happens what takes place among the rebel Indian chieftains, whose fate it is impossible to discover, whether they have really fallen, or whether some impostors have assumed their names. Without being able to vouch for the correctness of the fact communicated, the following passage of a letter from Rome was brought under my eyes a few days ago:—"Ninco Nanco lives. At the time it was announced that he had met death on the field of action, he was concealed in the convent of Sant' Angelo (Papal States). The unfortunate assassinated (sic) by Piedmontese fury on that occasion was not Ninco Nanco, but a poor fellow called Gennaro Serritiello."

scourge which had desolated it. Ninco Nanco, after some days of protracted negotiation, declared that he and his whole band were ready to accede to the proposition, but that he wished first to obtain from the captain personally certain secondary conditions. The too trustful Capoduro agreed to the proposal, and, with the Delegate of Public Safety, the sergeant of his own company, and one soldier, went unarmed to the farmhouse which Ninco Nanco had chosen for the meeting. The bandit chief respectfully met the captain at the gate, and begged the party to enter the house, where an abundant repast had been provided for them. At the invitation of Ninco Nanco, the captain and his companions seated themselves at table. During the meal the kind-hearted Capoduro ceased not to exhort the chief, by all kinds of persuasion, to surrender, and ultimately obtained his promise that on that very day the whole band should accompany him to the town, and place themselves at the disposal of the authorities. As if to seal the compact, the treacherous brigand begged of the captain permission to embrace him; and at the very moment when he was giving him this Judas kiss he drew out a revolver which he had kept concealed, and fired at the unfortunate captain, who fell dead at his feet. At this signal the few brigands who were present seized their arms, and at once despatched the three men who had accompanied the unfortunate officer.

"But although a master in the art of treachery, Ninco Nanco was sometimes, on the other hand, a coward in action. Whenever he found himself in sole command of his own band, and at a distance from Crocco, he ceased to attempt resistance to the troops, much less did he dream of attacking them; the only occasions on which his band took an active part in any such conflict being when it was joined to that of Crocco, and under the command of that chief. It was then that the brigand horde attacked and massacred a detachment of cavalry of the regiment of the Saluzzo light horse, about twenty-five men, led by Lieutenant Bianchi, a brave officer, who had always followed close upon the heels of Crocco's band. Crocco, though burning to avenge the losses he had sustained, nevertheless, with his habitual astuteness and prudence, patiently waited until an opportunity offered to strike the blow he meditated. One day when Bianchi was on the march with his twenty-five horsemen, the intrepid officer fell into an ambuscade of brigands, and found himself suddenly assailed by a force so superior in numbers that escape was almost impossible. In a short time many of his men lay stretched on the ground, and Bianchi himself was so seriously wounded that he was unable to defend himself. Many of the brigands were upon him at once, and one of them summoned him to surrender; but Bianchi gave a fitting reply to the bandit, by shooting him dead with his revolver—an act which so infuriated the assassins that they at once despatched him with their knives and daggers.

"When we consider the ferocity and inhumanity of the brigands, the faith and devotion preserved among themselves are incomprehensible. There has never been an instance of a brigand who had been captured choosing to save himself from death either by denouncing any of his companions, or those who had concealed him in times of danger. They rarely abandoned their wounded, but at great personal risk carried them away from the field; and rather than forsake an injured comrade, they would suffer themselves to fall into the hands of the troops. And yet, strange contradiction, when they perceived that they were incurable, they despatched them with the greatest indifference. In the brigand ranks, discipline is maintained by the chiefs by a continuous system of terror. Caruso instantly killed with his own hand any one who hesitated a single moment to execute his orders. Ninco Nanco, on the other hand, dissimulated, but never neglected to find a propitious opportunity to punish anyone who disobeyed him. In the latter months of his life, learning that eight of his followers had concocted a plan to desert him and give themselves up to the authorities, the astute chief, feigning entire ignorance of the matter, appeared more kind and gentle towards those men than he had ever been before; but a few days afterwards, profiting by a moment in which they all lay buried in profound sleep, he, with the aid of the more trusty of his men, put the whole of them to death. The brigand chief Giovanni Coppa even had his own brother shot for having plundered a farmhouse without his orders.

"In every band there was to be found at least one or two women. At one time there were in Schiavone's troop as many as five of these wretched creatures, who, strange to say, preferred the perils of a brigand life to domestic happiness and feminine pursuits. All these novel Amazons displayed the most extraordinary courage in action. I myself have seen one female member of Caruso's band fighting valorously, a revolver in each hand, against my cavalry, at the fight of Francavilla.

"The hardships, fatigue, and privations to which our soldiery were subject in this terrible war, may more easily be imagined than described. In the depths of winter, when the Apennines were covered with ice and snow, the plumes of the Bersaglieri were to be seen waving in the air; in July, in the plains of Puglia, they were indefatigable and energetic, even

when exposed to the fiercest rays of a midday sun.
To the same praises the brave regiments of the line, and
the daring squadrons of light cavalry who acted under
my orders, are also entitled. In this war, in which
the privates were frequently compelled to act for
themselves, the Italian soldier displayed not only
the courage habitual to him, but also a fertility in
expedients, an ingenuity in baffling the stratagems of
the brigands, that prove how well he is adapted for
all the emergencies of war. The possession of so
many of the highest military virtues, as has been
sufficiently proved throughout these trying campaigns, is the proudest boast of our army.

(Signed) "PALLAVICINI."

Such are the startling facts revealed by General
Pallavicini's report. With the fall of Caruso and, at
all events, the disappearance of Ninco Nanco, and
since, though the chief himself escaped the fate that
awaited him, the destruction of the band of Crocco, real
brigandage may be considered as entirely extirpated.
We must not, however, proclaim our victory too soon,
for the danger is still threatening. Political brigandage
has been crushed wherever it dared to show itself, and
of the numerous disciplined bands that used to scour
the country, not one is now to be found in the whole
of the old Neapolitan kingdom. But the vicinity of

the Papal States, the constant retreat of murderers and assassins, must still be a source of danger to Italy; and with the presence within the gates of Rome of the dethroned Bourbon, the greatest stigma on the temporal power of the Pope.

CHAPTER IX.

TRIAL OF THE BROTHERS LA GALA—AN ATROCIOUS DEED—CHARACTER OF THE ROMAN GOVERNMENT—THE ARMY THE EMBLEM OF NATIONAL UNITY—FORMATION OF ROADS AND RAILWAYS—IMPROVED ASPECT OF SOUTHERN ITALY—EDUCATION—SOCIAL AND MUNICIPAL CHANGES—REVIVAL OF COMMERCE—ITALIAN PORTS—GOOD QUALITIES OF THE NEAPOLITANS—STATE OF ROME—THE CONVENTION OF THE 15TH OF SEPTEMBER—TRANSFERENCE OF THE CAPITAL TO FLORENCE—GENERAL CIALDINI'S SPEECH—THE TEMPORAL SUPREMACY OF THE POPE—THE PROGRESS OF ITALY—CONCLUSION OF THE WORK.

CHAPTER IX.

ONE would fain not re-awake a morbid sense of horror, but history has its exigencies, and for the completeness of this work the most remarkable trial of the brothers Cipriano and Giona La Gala, and their associates, which terminated at Naples in last March, is more than any other worthy of being recorded. The brothers La Gala, satiated, it is supposed, with blood and plunder, sought the congenial air of that city which has been converted by the infatuated ministers of a misunderstood religion into the nest of the enemies of Italy, there to rest from their labours under the holy shadow of the temporal government of the Sovereign Pontiff. From his authorities they received a passport duly countersigned in Rome, representing them, with a slight dissimulation of the truth, as travelling gentlemen. They passed safely into the Papal dominions, but were taken out of the French steamer *Aunis*, at Genoa, by the agents of the Italian Government, a proceeding which produced a diplomatic skirmish between Italy and France. The Italian Government had to apologize for violating the protection of a French vessel; and the French Government, not to be outdone in magnanimity, surrendered these travelling gentlemen to take their trial before the Neapolitan courts. The trial lasted a fortnight; one hundred and seventeen questions were submitted to the jury, and the result was the conviction of the prisoners, on the clearest evidence, of atrocities such as probably were never before detailed to the astonished ears of a horrified court of justice and a trembling audience. The chief witnesses were Pasquale Viscusi and Alessandro Ruotolo, two priests. They, together with Giacomo Viscusi, another priest, and uncle of the first-named, had been captured, and saw what they related. After having plundered the house of uncle and nephew, the band commanded by Cipriano carried them off to the mountain called Taburno, and having demanded 12,000 ducats as ransom, finally sent an order to the family for 6,000 ducats. Only a few hundreds were collected, with bread, cheese, and wine. The bread being pronounced too coarse, and the money insufficient, Giona, the brother of Cipriano, threw himself on the old priest Giacomo, compelled him to kneel, and cut off an ear with a knife stolen from the victim's house. Ruotolo, overcome by the sight, invoked the Madonna, whereupon the brigand, in a menacing tone, exclaimed, "Silence! here only the devil is to be invoked!" The ear was despatched to the family, and at length 3,500 ducats were sent, in the delusive hope of recovering their relative. The brigands, disappointed of the sum they had demanded, murdered the poor priest—Giona first, and afterwards all the band, stabbing him with their knives or daggers. The secretary of the "Bourbon General," it must be stated, gave a receipt to the messenger who brought up a portion of the ransom-money, in the following terms: "We, Giona and Cipriano La Gala, declare that we have received the sum of 1,700 ducats from the captives Pasquale and Giacomo Viscusi, and the object for which we have demanded this money is to support the troops in defence of Francis II., and when he shall return to Naples the said Viscusi shall be repaid."

Another witness of this atrocious deed, the uncle of another man murdered on this occasion, himself an old man of seventy years of age, stated that, as soon as Giona had cut off the ear of the priest, Pasquale Papa, brother of one of the prisoners, snatched it from his hand, and began eating a portion of it, when Giona took it from him, saying, "This is not to be eaten, but to be sent to the family." "Did you really see him eat it?" said the President. "Certainly I did," replied the witness; "and, in proof of it, after he had cleaned his teeth, and taken away the threads of flesh, he went about, saying, 'My faith, how savoury are the ears of priests!' while his companion joked him, remarking, 'You like priest's ears?—they are good, eh?'" The same witness, an aged priest, then related the circumstances of the death of his nephew, Francesco de Cesare. Contrary to his counsel, the young man had accepted an invitation to visit the brigands, from the captains of the band, who professed great friendship for him. On his arrival, immediately after they had embraced him, Giona said, "Francesco, you must die." The victim, taking these words as a joke, laughed. Giona, however, calling for a rope, bound his legs; and while Francesco was still laughing, the bandit, drawing a dagger, pierced him with many blows; after which Cipriano shot him with a double-barrelled gun, and the rest of the brigands followed his example. His head was then cut off, and with a pipe in the mouth, was placed in the sill of a window. His limbs were severed from his body, and hung on the neighbouring trees, with a placard on each, bearing the words, "So are spies treated! This is the fate which awaits traitors!" The remainder of the body, cut into morsels, was afterwards roasted over a large fire, and eaten by the cannibal supporters of the Bourbons. "Pasquale Papa," continued the witness, "wanted me to eat some too. 'For the love of God,' I replied, 'I cannot—I revolt at it.' 'You won't, won't you?' was the answer; 'well, to-morrow we will eat your flesh!'"

"Gentlemen," exclaimed the Prisident, addressing the Court, "it is well that all Europe should know who are the defenders of Francis II. and of the temporal power;" and it is in the same spirit that I record here details which a respect for human nature might otherwise induce me to conceal. The trial ended by the condemnation of the brothers Cipriano and Giona La Gala to death, and of their accomplices to the galleys. It might have been supposed that the constant sight of murder, of torture, and of mutilation would have armed these men with that indifference to death which a near acquaintance with its terrors is said so often to produce. But it was not so. They received the sentence with visible marks of fear, shrinking from a fate so infinitely milder than that which they had so often inflicted on their victims.*

* It is known that the King has lately commuted into penal servitude for life the sentence of death pronounced on the brothers La Gala. In exercising his royal prerogative, the King has simply exhibited a mark of deference towards a friendly power, which represented to him what usage and custom sanctioned, when extradition was granted under such peculiar circumstances as those attending the surrender of the prisoners of the *Aunis*. The most important object for the Italian Government was not to bring to the scaffold two mere assassins, but through that great trial to bring to light the enormity of which the supporters of that party, which has its centre in Rome, were capable. This result was obtained, and Italy could well

What a revelation have we of the character of the Roman Government in the facts revealed at the trial of the brothers La Gala. The Bourbonists will doubtless repudiate the acts of Cipriano and his troops;* for unquestionably there are among them humane men, who shudder with horror at such proceedings as those I have narrated. "I have lived honourably," said Cipriano on his trial; "I confess that I have received money from *gentlemen of the Central Committee.*" In doing the work he was hired to do, it cannot be supposed, however, that he received orders

afford to spare the lives of two villains, when, by so doing, she showed her respect for the international rights of a powerful ally. Civilized Europe has judged the cause of those who supplied with money and passports *the travelling gentlemen* of the *Aunis!*

* A foreign legitimist paper, I forget which, in reporting the proceedings of this trial, not only did not shrink from accusing the Italian Government of its severity to these champions of the Bourbons, but, in making some remarks on the episode of cutting off the priest's ears, said: "If the King of Naples had beheaded the Piedmontese diplomatists accredited to his Court, who, availing themselves of the rights afforded by their position, conspired against him and were the instigators of revolution, he would still have been on the throne." Now, as it happens that I was one of the above-mentioned diplomatists, having formed part of the former Sardinian Legation at Naples until the eve almost of the Revolution, I thank my stars that my head is yet upon my shoulders. The rabid paper, in its pious anger, has perhaps forgotten that the real conspirators in the south of Italy were Civilization and Liberty, names before which, sooner or later, reaction and tyranny must inevitably give way.

to eat de Cesari's flesh, but if men employ savages, they must expect the consequences. Let Christian gentlemen in England and elsewhere reflect, then, that when they pay Peter's pence they contribute to the support of a government whose sympathies are with those who employed General Cipriano La Gala, and which, after permitting him to enter Rome, sent him off under the safeguard of a regular passport. By what strange ministers the cause of order and religion has come to be served! How great must be the confidence Francis II. has in the strength of his cause, if he supposes it can survive the support of such men and the damning influence of such revelations!

But enough on this subject. Let us now rather examine the progress and improvement which on every side are clearly discernible. The army is already the emblem of the unity of the country, mustering upwards of three hundred and fifty thousand men from the different provinces of the kingdom, bound together by military brotherhood and by zeal for the national flag. General Lamarmora said, in one of his recent speeches in Parliament, that the fusion of the different elements of the Italian army was so great, that in its ranks one could hardly detect those various shades noticeable even in the old Piedmontese army, arising from the differences of the Subalpine, Ligurian, and Savoyard dialects. If the Neapolitan now desires to speak to the Lombard, and the

Piedmontese to the Sicilian, they must lay aside their vernacular idioms, and use the mother tongue as best they can. The country is thus generally adopting the use of that melodious language which is embodied in Dante's beautiful verses; and the harsh and barbarous dialects, which were only the results of foreign invasions or of fatal internecine divisions, are now gradually disappearing. The army, in fact, is a school of civilization. Few persons can have an idea of the state in which a recruit from the distant districts of Naples or from the interior of Sicily joins the Italian ranks. Superstitious, ignorant, degraded by a worthless priesthood, and demoralized by bad example, his intellectual and social education has been entirely neglected. The same young soldier, after a few months spent under the wholesome discipline of the old chivalrous Piedmontese army, is quite another man when he returns to his home. No longer the degraded peasant whose popular hero was the chief brigand of the district, he brings back habits of order and work. His ideas have been enlarged. The improved system of agriculture he has observed in the rich Lombard fields he tries to introduce among the farmers and peasantry of his native village. Under the honourable uniform of a soldier, the representative of order, obedience, and fidelity speaks to his fellow-countrymen of that chivalrous attachment to the king which is incarnated in every Italian regiment.* The National Guard, too, not seldom, at the beginning of its hasty formation, the accomplices of the brigands, provided they could share the spoil, now reorganized and disciplined, fight admirably. How great must be the moral influence of a force amounting to 1,997,540 men, animated by the same principles of honour and obedience as the army. This fact is an eloquent answer to those who assert that the Italian population are dissatisfied with the present government. If the necessity should ever arise, two hundred battalions could be mobilized in a week, with officers commissioned by the crown, and in everything assimilated to the discipline of the standing army.† The services already rendered by

* Some statistics have been lately published, founded on documents proceeding from the Ministry of War, and tending to show the increase of a military spirit in the army and in the country generally. The decrease in the number of refractory conscripts and of desertions has been remarkable during the last three years; and if those classes of military criminals be yet more numerous in Italy than in some other countries where the army is raised in the same manner, it must be borne in mind that in some provinces—as, for instance, in those taken from the Pope and in Sicily—military service may be looked upon as a new institution, while, in many others, it has been so much altered and transformed, as regards the duties imposed upon the soldier, and the strictness of the discipline enforced, that it may almost be said to be equally a novelty.

† From an official document which I have under my eyes, the National Guards of the kingdom of Italy amount, as I have

this mobilized force in the campaign of 1859, and in the present brigand war, prove that the National Militia, while constituting a real defence of the country, is also a guarantee of its constitutional liberties.

One of the best signs of the improved state of the country is the prevailing tranquillity, and the obedience universally shown to the law. The public administration has been reformed, and works regularly. The tribunals, submitted to a careful investigation, are now found equal to the duties they were founded to discharge.

The complicity of public functionaries with brigands is a scandal happily unknown at present; and if a regular police has not yet been established in every part of the country, a very effective substitute is found in the energy of the gendarmes and the zeal of the population. The country, too, the configuration of which was so favourable to the development of brigandage, is now undergoing a change. Thanks to the military roads that the Italian engineers have cut through its immense mountainous solitudes, the Garganic region is no longer infested by hordes

said, to 1,997,540, of whom 1,230,988 are on active service, and the remaining 766,552 form the reserve. Of these, 726,219 are liable to be mobilized, a proceeding in which the rule observed is, that out of every hundred National Guards, thirty-six men are selected among the youngest and the most apt for military service, to be incorporated in the mobilized battalions.

of bandits. The "Selva delle Grotte" a regular primeval forest, which might have sheltered a whole army in its recesses, is now pierced by many roads and guarded by a block-house, the breast-work of which is sufficient to stop the brigands. The old Papal feud of Beneventum will soon be furrowed by spacious roads, which already stretch out in every direction, defending it against any future incursion, for brigands carefully avoid the vicinity of frequented paths; and the railway uniting Turin and Foggia has at last not only pacified but given life to the most distant regions on the shores of the Adriatic. When Victor Emmanuel inaugurated it, he crossed all the provinces which had once been the theatre of the most cruel deeds of violence without meeting a single bandit. From the Tronto, where he left the railway to Naples, the road followed by the royal cortége resembled a street, crowded with groups of armed peasants, who were to be seen at every step. The foreign ministers, who had accompanied the king, looked with astonishment, perhaps not without fear, on those thousands of muskets which, *by mistake*, or, *as a sign of joy*, might have been fired into the royal carriage. Happily, however, nothing occurred to spoil the significance of that splendid demonstration, and from one end of the country to the other, the armed multitude made the air resound with one cry of joy—" Viva Vittor' Emmanuele!—Viva Italia!"

Southern Italy has now quite a new aspect. The traveller who should leave the railway and venture into the passes of the Apennines, would now find that everywhere the roads are scoured by mounted gendarmes escorting the passengers. Wherever a forest stretches down into the valley, a block-house is erected, and all the approaches are carefully patrolled. On the mountain, once haunted by brigands, is an encampment of Bersaglieri, who, pointing to the loftiest peaks overhead, tell the anxious traveller that the last brigands have found a shelter there, where it is impossible to follow them; but that the coming winter will, in all probability, force them from their last refuge.

The Government understood the mission entrusted to it in those meridional provinces; and in order to counteract the many evils arising from the ignorance and superstition of the peasantry, it hastened to open schools all over the country. The progress of education in Naples will be seen from the following extract from a report made to Parliament by the Chevalier Peruzzi, late Minister of the Interior. In the Neapolitan provinces, in the year 1861, the state of public instruction was as follows:—Boys between six and seven years of age going to school were in the proportion of seven per cent.; at the end of 1863, they had risen to fifteen per cent. In Sicily the proportion was, in 1861, five per cent.

and in 1863, nine per cent. The increase will be still greater in the present year.

From this comparison we find that the provinces in which brigandage has been most prevalent, were precisely those in which public instruction was most neglected; while in those districts where popular education was more advanced, brigandage found little encouragement. Schools have now been established even in the most distant parts. Naples alone possesses upwards of fifty, paid by the municipality. There are also sixteen evening institutions, where thousands of workmen, with the characteristic eagerness of the South, quickly profit by the instruction given them—so that two months after their entrance, they have not only learned to read and write, but have become so far acquainted with the metric and decimal systems, as to be able to sustain very satisfactory examinations. The children of the lower classes have nine infant schools provided for them, in which they may be saved from the dangers of a vagabond life and the bad examples of the streets. Each province has a college, and some two. Technical schools are organized in different places, and the university of Naples, where four years ago reigned silence and solitude, is now the first of Italy. In two of the branches taught in it, mathematics and natural science, it bears comparison with the most celebrated universities in Europe. It numbers the most eminent men among its professors. Law is taught by two able men, formerly ministers of state—M. Manna and M. Pisanelli.* In this great temple of knowledge, more than twelve thousand students are instructed. These facts afford some proof that the Italian Government is prepared to wage a desperate war against ignorance. Nor is it less active in its desire to alleviate the misery of the people. Public mendicity is strenuously opposed by charitable people, whose indefatigable efforts are crowned at every step by happy results. When Francis II. left his capital, the streets were infested by 14,000 beggars; now there are hardly a few hundreds. All the benevolent institutions, once but an agglomeration of administrators, who absorbed all the money intended for the poor, are now faithfully engaged in their relief. The foundling hospital, where formerly seventy-five per cent. died of neglect, is now, under an intelligent direction, the best of Italy, and perhaps of the world.

Vagabonds are relentlessly pursued. A watchful police is constantly making the most strenuous endeavours to prevent the development of every form of social vice. And that the poor may not trust to charity alone, every effort is made to provide them with work, so that they may earn their daily bread. Notwithstanding financial embarrassments and political

* Both members of the late Cabinet.

agitation, the activity of the new Government, in promoting the growth of railways, has been marvellous. The railway which ended at Vietri, goes now from Salerno to Eboli, at the foot of the mountains. Foggia, which was not even in communication with the Abruzzi by a common road, is connected with Turin by a main railway line extending now to Brindisi. The rails which for upwards of twelve years had never extended beyond Capua, are now uninterrupted as far as Rome. The concession of the Calabrian lines has been made to a great company, and the engines are already preparing for their construction. At least two other lines are proposed, for establishing the communication between the Mediterranean and the Adriatic, in two different points of the old kingdom of Naples. Innumerable roads are being constructed in every district. Five from Beneventum alone are intended to put it in communication with the rest of the country. New harbours are inaugurated, light-houses are erected on every part of the coast, and dockyards and arsenals are bustling with activity. The " dolce far niente " of the times of yore exists no longer; the peace of the cloisters themselves has been disturbed, and many a convent now shelters a regiment of young soldiers, instead of idle monks, while others have been turned into vast Government manufactories. Prisons have been rendered wholesome, and, under a stern but moral rule, have ceased to be the loathsome dens so eloquently described by Mr. Gladstone. That iniquitous institution, the Camorra, which the Bourbons only could tolerate and protect, is fast disappearing with them; culprits are now treated like Christians. The economical condition of the country is improving with really marvellous rapidity. The value of everything, but chiefly of land, is almost doubled. The populations of the towns have increased; the Italians of the north have gone in great numbers towards the south, bearing with them those habits of industry by which their prosperity is assured, and which exercise a very beneficial influence on their new neighbours. Civilization has created new wants, which a laborious population is called to provide for. Thus Naples, desiring to have its streets illuminated with gas, required no less than a canalization of one hundred and forty kilometers for the laying of the pipes—an immense work, which was to be accomplished in less than twelve months, and consequently employed a vast number of workmen. The railways have entirely changed the condition of the Puglie and Abruzzi. The traveller who goes back to those provinces finds nothing of the past left. Everything is transformed; labourers have returned to agriculture, the real resource of the country; the long-deserted fields are again covered with luxuriant crops, and shepherds drive their flocks in security along the vast solitary plains. The old weights and measures are abandoned, and the decimal system prevails already where a few years ago in every transaction the old complicated routine was alone understood. Capital is flowing from abroad to second that material revolution which will ere long render impossible the return of brigandage. Agricultural life is awakened by speculation; large companies have been formed for draining the marshes —for canalizing the rivers. Uncultivated moors are attracting the attention of proprietors, who turn them into profitable land; swamps are being drained on an extensive scale; and cotton is now enriching thousands of families. The produce of this cultivation, which in 1863 was five times greater than that of the preceding year, is ten times greater this year, and will be still more the next.

In contemplating the new roads, the most beautiful in the world, which are creeping along the cliffs round the enchanting bay of Naples, joining that almost equally splendid road which is advancing to meet them round the Gulf of Salerno—in observing the immense manufactures which have already been established—and in visiting the many establishments of public utility which have been personally inaugurated by the king, one cannot but look forward with admiration to the wonderful results which liberty must in a few years produce in those beautiful provinces. From one end of Italy to the other "the dry bones are rattling;" a new life is bursting out everywhere, and progress has already utterly changed the aspect of the country. Not only the great commercial centres, but even the old scholastic towns, rich in nothing but the traditions of the past lingering about their abandoned palaces, and peopling their silent streets, overgrown with grass, with phantoms of ancient discord, are now endeavouring to obtain some share of the benefits secured by the progress of commerce. The enterprising spirit of the re-awakened population is carrying them beyond their crumbling walls, and they are availing themselves of resources which they knew not before how to employ. Italian engineers are driving the locomotive through the innermost recesses of both Apennines and Alps for the completion of that great line of railway which will carry to Western Europe all the trade of the East. It was but the other day that, by the opening of the railroad from Pracchia, completing the line from Bologna to Florence and Pistoja, through the mountains of Central Italy, one could exclaim— "The Apennines exist no longer!" And, though a long time may still be required for the completion of a work of such magnitude, we are confident that before many years have elapsed, the miners, advancing simultaneously from both sides of

Mount Cenis, will bring to an end an enterprise which will incalculably benefit the trade of the country, and which was boldly begun under the administration of Count Cavour.

With equal activity the splendid harbours that Providence has scattered all along the Italian shore, are deepened, enlarged, and fortified. A naval establishment of the first rank is now being inaugurated in the Gulf of Spezia. Almost unique in the world, this important work was first contemplated by the great Napoleon, and finally decreed by the illustrious Cavour; and ere long a similar establishment is to be created at the other extremity of Italy, in the Gulf of Taranto, whose salt lake will be transformed into an immense dockyard. Genoa and Naples are enlarging their busy ports, henceforth to be devoted alone to their immensely increased commerce; whilst Leghorn, Messina, Palermo, and a score of their sister seaports, undergo the same transformation. The mouldering cities of the eastern coast, restored to connection with the world by the new railway, which has arrested their decay, are again assuming the appearance of commercial ports. Ancona and Bari have doubled in importance, and the old Brindisi of Roman recollection will in a short time be one of the first stations of the Adriatic for the trade of the East. The fleets of young Italy, already the first after those of Great Britain and France, will soon require new dockyards, for their ironclads will be equal in number, before a few months have elapsed, to those of mighty England. The greatest discipline and perfection of drill reign on board every ship, and when the moment for action arrives, the Italian sailors will prove that they still possess the same daring and skill which won for their forefathers so great a repute. As in the army, the most complete union exists between the seamen of the northern and southern shores. Forgetful of their ancient rivalries, they only remember the glories of those powerful maritime republics that were once the masters of the trade of the world, the descendants of whose populations, whilst burying even the traces of their old fratricidal struggles, are intent only on the peaceful pursuit of trade and commerce.*

* Every one who has been in Italy must remember the huge iron chains which hung on the walls of several streets of Genoa. These were the chains which defended the entrance of the harbour of Pisa, but which did not stop the fury of her mighty rivals the Genoese, who carried them away to adorn the walls of their marble palaces, as a perpetual trophy of the defeat of the Pisans. When the events of 1859 destroyed the boundaries existing between Northern and Central Italy, a deputation of the Genoese municipality proceeded to Pisa, and, as a token of brotherhood, restored them to that city, where they are now suspended in the romantic Campo Santo, the scene of so many glorious traditions of the past. This circumstance has always been present to my memory, as it made a somewhat sentimental impression upon me when I was at Pisa, in the spring of 1860, during the first visit paid to Tuscany by the king after the annexation had taken place, and is connected besides with another recollection, which I will relate. I was then one of the

The national unity is thus cemented by national progress. The pacific invasion of the northern Italians into the south, and of the southerners into the north (Turin numbered in its last census more than 20,000 Neapolitans), the unity of interests in their great industrial enterprises, and the community of views for the advancement of their country, are all so many guarantees for the maintenance of a union so happily inaugurated. The party of intelligence and energy is for united Italy. The internal discords of the Italians, so much talked about by the Ultramontanes, are in reality comparatively unimportant. In presence of the great hopes by which they are united, their shades of difference vanish into nothing. Even the Neapolitan populations, who everywhere take up arms for the defence of the common country, have been unfairly judged. Virtues which they could not

private secretaries of Count Cavour, and I remember that on coming back to the palace with the king and all the royal cortége, after having visited the Campo Santo and the other monuments of that beautiful city, Count Cavour was looking intently from one of the windows of his room at the imposing mass of enthusiastic people who had assembled to cheer the king. All of a sudden, turning to me at a moment when by chance I happened to be near him, he said, with a solemn voice, pausing almost with emotion upon each word: "Yes, there are in this mass of men all the elements of a great nation, and, with the help of God, we will be again a powerful people." The great man appeared as if inspired by a prophetic spirit; and I was so impressed that I shall never forget these words.

possibly have acquired in so short a time were expected of them, whilst their natural merits were purposely left unnoticed. Without recalling that glorious contingent of martyrs given by Naples to the national cause, the Neapolitan people generally deserve the highest praise for the manner in which, in the midst of political and social convulsions, they have remained faithful to the cause of Italy. In their enthusiasm, they have shown themselves capable of any sacrifice. They have been accused of indolence and want of energy, charges for which there is no foundation. Their bravery, too, has been called in question, although more revolutions have taken place in Naples than in any other city. The recollection of their heroic resistance at Venice, in 1849, is still vivid in the mind of every Italian; and the Neapolitan soldiers are now models of valour and discipline in the young army of Italy. Remembering the declarations of General Pallavicini, we may imagine what soldiers men like Caruso and the ruffians who followed him would have made, if they had been educated to the sense of honour and morality! This is the great work which Italy is bound to accomplish by the regeneration of the country. By destroying brigandage, she is fulfilling that task; and a few bandits will not have power to oppose the cherished dream of every generous Italian, from

Dante to Cavour, the realization of which was to form the glory of our present generation.

Since these pages were written, the most important political transaction, since the peace of Villafranca, has taken place between Italy and France. By a convention executed at Paris in last September, the Emperor of the French, wishing to put an end to his anomalous position in Rome, has agreed to evacuate the eternal city in two years; but, at the same time, anxious to satisfy the susceptibility of his own subjects, he has imposed an ostensibly onerous condition on the Italians, who are to profit by the measure, the King of Italy being required to pledge himself both to abstain from encroachments on the Papal territory, and to protect it from external violence. This convention opens a new political era to Italy, and secures real advantages for the future. It is not the place here to discuss the articles of this important treaty. Its prominent point is that, within the short period of two years, one of the two foreign occupations of Italy is to cease, and this most irritating Roman question will thereby find an immediate solution. Italy, at the same time, in return for these unmistakable advantages, engages not to attack the Pontifical territory, nor to allow it to be attacked. However, it is evident that if, through its own inherent weakness the Pontifical Government should fall, each of the two contracting powers may reserve for itself complete freedom of action. In other words, if, notwithstanding the most scrupulous observation of the convention, the temporal power of the Pope should prove unable to maintain itself in face of the dangers to which it is exposed, Italy may then have full liberty to follow the course most conducive to her own interests, and most accordant with her own dignity as an independent state. It is true that France, as it has been said, has the same power, but, whatever may happen, she will no doubt remember that she has solemnly proclaimed the principle of non-intervention. The Government of Victor Emmanuel, looking forward with confidence to the destinies of the country, will faithfully abide by its engagement. As sincere Catholics, its members will not hesitate to pay homage to the spiritual supremacy of the Pope, being desirous that there should be a reconciliation between the Venerable Head of the Church and the regenerated Italian kingdom. If the Holy See, however, persists in its fatal obstinacy, it then remains to be seen whether in this nineteenth century a cause associated with the bigotry and superstition of the past is to triumph over the civilization and intelligence of a new era.

Meantime, the capital is to be transferred from Turin to Florence. Whatever may have been said against this measure, every liberal Italian has seen in it a solemn sanction to the renovated state of things in the country. With the single exception of Turin, all the Italian cities have considered the removal to Florence as the last step towards the fulfilment of the highest aspirations of the nation; and poor Turin itself, since the sad events of September, has, by its exemplary conduct, redeemed the errors of one moment of forgetfulness.* As regards the strategical reasons by which this change was urged, it would be bold in me, after the magnificent speech delivered on that subject by General Cialdini, in the Italian senate, to express an opinion. In exposing the danger to which the capital would be exposed if

* This was written before the scandals of the night of the 30th of January last. I thought at first of altering words apparently contradicting the facts I am alluding to, but, after consideration, I have determined to leave them as they are. The cowardly demonstration which took place before the palace of King Victor Emmanuel on the night he had opened the state rooms for the reception of a host of distinguished guests, would not be to the honour of the old loyal capital, if it could be taken as the expression of the feelings of its faithful inhabitants. But let the shame of so base a plot fall on its authors, and not on the Piedmontese people, who had no share in it. Although not of Piedmontese extraction, I was born and educated in that little country, whose glorious destiny it has been to initiate the independence of Italy, and, justly proud of my birthplace, I am anxious to redeem its fame. I know but too well who, on that night, instigated the disgraceful manifestation, which had been prepared beforehand by hostile parties. The feelings vented in a manner so little honourable to all concerned, proceeded from a *very few* members of an aristocratic coterie; for-

situated in a district that would certainly be the scene of war whenever Italy had to encounter an enemy, the eminent soldier suddenly revealed himself as a politician of a superior order. Taking a loftier view of the question than had been entertained before, he said that, since the cession of Savoy and Nice, the security of Turin as a capital, open on two sides to foreign invasion, had become greatly endangered. The question of the National defence, he added, had been his constant preoccupation since the beginning of 1862; and after stating that, in case of any

getful of their traditions of allegiance to the august house of Savoy, and from some narrow-minded individuals belonging to the bourgeoisie, who gave way to a selfish spirit of municipalism. The event has been most painful to every Piedmontese devoted to his king and country, and especially at such a moment, when the monarch, for the sake of Italy, was about to accomplish a great sacrifice, that of leaving the city of his affections. The outburst of indignation which followed the event, both from the Turinese themselves, and from the inhabitants of every town of old Piedmont, must have convinced the king, and our brethren of other parts of Italy, that the Piedmontese race is not to be confounded with the rioters of the 30th of January, an unworthy minority, whose violent attacks within and without Parliament have excited the indignation of Italy. The people of Turin have proved to Victor Emmanuel, on his reappearance among them, that they are still true representatives of the genuine old stock; and both the municipal instigators of disorder, and the agents of disunion from abroad, must have been convinced that, in conspiring against Italian unity in this sad moment of transition, they had forgotten the sound patriotism and the political sense of the Piedmontese nation.

misunderstanding with France, Austria might pour forth her legions from Verona, the General, entering fully into the military discussion, continued:—

"I, however, want to show how a well-intended system of general defence implies the transfer of the capital behind the Apennines. As the system I wish to develop is very simple, no special knowledge or technical terms being required to explain it, but only general notions of the topographic configuration of Italy, I shall briefly address the Senate upon it. Italy is for two-thirds of her surface skirted by her two seas; the other third attaches itself to the Continent by the circle of the Alps, at the foot of which lie the plains of Lombardy and Piedmont. The Apennines turn their chain towards the Adriatic, forming a great curtain, which extends from Genoa to Calabria. Opposite the magnificent curtain of the Apennines, and facing it, lies the beautiful valley of the Po, in which stands Austria, shut up within the formidable positions of her Quadrilateral. The defiles of this valley are not in our power, nor can we provide for their defence by building fortresses. 'The valley of the Po' means the enemy dwelling in your houses, with the door wide open for him to enter at his pleasure. And in such a position you still persist in having your capital in this city. Senator Farini, I am sorry to say, expressed the desire of retaining the capital at Turin, because it would thus be under the perpetual protection of France. He is desirous of having the capital under the protection of France. I, on the contrary, desire it to be where it will have for its only protection the arm and the valour of the Italians. The honourable senator has cited the opinion expressed by Napoleon at St. Helena in support of his opposition to the bill, and said that the great captain wrote that 'Florence is not central enough to become the capital of Italy.' I know it, and for this reason I desire to have Rome; but is Turin more central than Florence? Behind the Apennines you will have a country quite surrounded by the sea, and shut up by the Apennines themselves, and that will be the safest spot for your capital, at least, if you are not afraid of the army of mercenaries which the Pope may organize in your rear. All hesitation on this subject would be fatal. Let us remove our military stores, our arsenals, our reserves—in a word, all our resources—behind the Apennines; let us at the same time fortify its defiles from Genoa to La Cattolica. Once let those seven or eight defiles be fortified, and you may depend upon it they will become for Italy so many Thermopylæ, which it will be impossible for our enemies to force. Let us also prepare easy means to effect the crossing of the Po; and, when this system of general defence shall have been adopted, the future lot of Italy will no longer be decided by the result of one great battle. All armies may lose a battle, but were we to lose one in the valley of the Po, after the system which I suggest was adopted, we should retire slowly behind the Po and the Apennines, where we should be able to reorganise our armies, and we should again come out to the valley of the Po to deliver another battle. With the capital behind the Apennines, the action of the Government will be more felt, because the Government will be able to initiate a more useful policy when it has the consciousness of safety. Those orators who spoke so much of the valley of the Po as the natural theatre of Italian battles, forgot that the battle fought by Hannibal on the Trebia did not decide the fate of Rome; but though he had conquered on the Thrasymene and at Cannæ, the greatest captain of the world was obliged at last to give up the enterprise. I have insisted on these facts in order to prove how wrong is the opinion that there is not safety for Italy out of the valley of the Po. And if such was the military condition of Italy at the time of Hannibal, what will be her strength now that we have railways and telegraphs at our disposal, and when the nation, united as it is, has the consciousness of her strength and of her future greatness? Let foreign writers say that Italy is the land of the dead.

Yes, but the dead have at last risen from their tombs in the shape of 350,000 armed men, and of 200 battalions of mobilised National Guards. The dead have strong and well-manned fortresses to defend their fatherland; they have a fine fleet to assert their rights over the waters of their national seas. Those very Italians of whom it was said, 'Les Italians ne se battent pas,' have already won many battles, and, whether under the grey coat of the regular soldier, or under the red shirt of the volunteer, have taught the illustrious general* who, in a moment of bad humour, uttered those words, that they know how to fight and conquer. (General and repeated enthusiastic cheers.) Some orators have said that the transfer of the capital will weaken our defence on the Po; but they have forgotten that the consequence of the transfer will be a freer action, because we shall not have the capital to defend. The natural affection which those orators have for Turin, and their grief at seeing it dispossessed of a crown, make them develop the most strange and singular opinions. I have heard also most respectable and learned men assert that both the Po and the Apennines are no obstacles, and that the minor rivers are of more importance. These arguments, however, are so strange, that it would be

---

* General Lamoricière, whose army was completely routed at Castelfidardo.

totally useless to refute them. Let us speak clearly. I also have a heart which is keen to feel great sorrows as well as great affections; and God forbid I should say even a word which could offend this noble city, those sorrows, and those affections. But when the future of the country is at stake, it is necessary to impose silence upon the heart, and let logic speak loudly. The eye moistened by tears cannot see clearly; the heart broken and the mind pre-occupied by sorrow cannot judge aright. Ought we to stop because the gloomiest forebodings have been uttered? Had we listened to the prophets of misfortune, we certainly should not have done all that we have accomplished. Let us recognise that a mysterious force pushes Italy along a determined way, and that our revolution follows its slow, peaceful, and irresistible course. I sincerely deplore the losses Turin is destined to sustain, as on the field of battle I deplored the losses of soldiers and of friends. But, because dear friends and soldiers fall, ought a general not to fight any more? Turin cannot be the capital of Italy—I say it with sorrow—because it is placed at the foot of the Alps, at the extremity of the kingdom. Let us proclaim it, as it has already been proclaimed, the most magnanimous city of Italy, and let the Turinese remember the noble words once uttered by Baron

Ricasoli, 'The greatest fortune which may happen to a man, to which a citizen may aspire, is that of rendering a great service to his country.' I, therefore, vote in favour of a bill which transfers the capital behind the Apennines, because, above all, I desire my country to be strong enough to defy foreign insolence. I vote for it because my country, once strong, will exercise the influence to which she is entitled. As for the Convention, I can understand that to some people it does not appear clear enough to satisfy them of its necessity. It is more a question of trust; but for my part I vote it, because by it we get rid at least of one foreign occupation. Those foreigners, though our allies, are still foreigners, and noble France will, I am sure, understand and appreciate the meaning of these words. I vote for the bill because it rouses Italy from that apathy in which she has remained during the last two years, and because we assert once more the fact of our glorious revolution by transplanting our capital to one of the annexed provinces. Allow me to conclude with one deeply-felt consideration. The debates, to which I have attentively listened, leave in my mind a painful impression—the fear of seeing civil dissensions arise. But instead of speaking of the interests of such and such town or province, would it not be better to speak of the interest of our fatherland? Instead of talking of sacrifices, would it not be better to comfort those who have the duty of making them? Were you, honourable senators, to say that these sacrifices are claimed by the glory, the welfare of Italy, the people would believe you. Were you to tell your countrymen that liberty and independence are blessings which are never purchased too dearly, your fellow-countrymen would believe you. The school of sacrifice makes the soul of a people stronger. Prometheus had the power of making a man out of clay, sacrifice alone has the power of turning men into heroes. (Prolonged applause.)"

These patriotic sentences will not have been uttered in vain. The Italian crown, though transported to a more central part, will not cease to be the dearest care of the Subalpine people; and, if the day should ever come when the mother country shall call forth all her sons, old Piedmont will answer the summons with her traditional spirit. But let even that name die away—let it be forgotten. From the ruins of seven states has risen a nation, and its name is Italy!

The new kingdom has already taken its place among the civilised states of Europe, and, admirably seconded by the good sense and energetic will of the people, is prepared to achieve the work it has so gloriously begun. The Government, while maintaining an immense army, has recently, in the midst of great financial embarrassment,* undertaken several works of great importance—such as those we have already indicated, the creation of an ironclad navy, the armament of all the fortresses of the kingdom, and the construction of railways. If money has been too freely expended, we must impute it to the desire of our rulers to put the national defence in that state of perfection required by the position of the country. The municipalities, aware of the burdens which, in the reorganization of the kingdom, the Government found it necessary to lay on the people, generously answered the demand of one year's land-

* This pecuniary difficulty is, however, greatly exaggerated. The total National Debt of the Italian Kingdom of every description, including the old debts of the various States of which it is composed, represents an annual charge of about £10,000,000, or a capital of £200,000,000 in five per cent. rentes. It is thus evident that the financial position of the country, so far from being as bad as has been generally supposed, is such that, if Italy perseveres for a few years in a prudent policy, her exchequer will be in as favourable a condition as that of any European Power. The population of Italy is also not merely one of agricultural peasants, as in less advanced countries, but to a great extent one of town-dwellers, practising the arts of commerce and industry. There can be no reason why such a population should not, in the course of a few years, support a rate of taxation per head equal to that of the leading European states. At present, the average taxation per head is only 25 francs in Italy against 58 in Great Britain, 50 in France, 22 in Austria, 20 in Russia, 58 in Holland, and 37 in Spain.

tax in anticipation*—a fact which proves the harmony existing between the governors and the governed.

If now, directing our attention to the Pontifical State, we compare the condition of its population with that of the rest of Italy, how sad is the spectacle! While the world is advancing, that intolerant government which remains in the hands of the priesthood stands still. The Sacra Consulta arrogantly tramples upon the great principles of liberty of conscience and of thought. The empire of ideas is scorned, mediæval despotism is in full vigour, and barbarous customs, prevalent in the times of the Inquisition, still remind us that the *Sant' Uffizio* has not lost the power it has so long wielded. In that part of Italy children under ten years of age have been forced from the arms of their parents, professing creeds condemned by the head of

* Signor Sella, the Minister of Finance, on the last day of 1864, delivered to the king a report explaining the reasons that forced the Government to anticipate the land-tax for 1865, and setting forth the patriotic manner in which the nation had met the sudden and onerous demand. Within the time fixed, nearly five-sixths of the whole amount of the tax was paid into the coffers of the State. " Sire," the Minister concluded, " the country has nobly responded to the confidence that you and the Parliament have placed in it. It has been said, especially out of Italy, that this has been a new *plebiscitum* of the national unity; and truly the nation could not give to the world more distinct testimony of the faith it has in you, and of its firm resolution to maintain its honour, and to advance at any sacrifice the accomplishment of its glorious destinies."

the Roman Church, in order to bring them up forcibly in another religion. Under the pretext of a faith which they insult, men of bad character can still oppress the weak and the defenceless, and priests can commit the greatest abuses, safe from the hands of justice. Who does not remember the scandalous affair in which the priest Arcangeli played so disgraceful a part, in endeavouring to bring about a clandestine marriage between the Frenchman Balmette, a young man of rather weak mind, and a woman of indifferent reputation? Although his father protested before the tribunals against this so-called marriage, in which there had been no publication of bans, yet it was all in vain, for, in presence of ecclesiastical authority, that of the civil power is disarmed. Even the representations of the French Embassy at Rome were totally disregarded, and the father of the unfortunate young man was unable to liberate his son from the meshes of the culpable intrigue into which he had been drawn. Could anything more strikingly illustrate the unhappy results of that union of the temporal and ecclesiastical power, of which the Roman Government affords so unfavourable an example? And yet, however incredible such a fact may appear to those unacquainted with Rome, we learn from two letters of Monsieur Belot de la Digne, a superior French officer now in command of the gendarmerie at Marseilles, but formerly for six years prévôt of the army of occupation—letters which were presented to the magistrates, by Mons. Jules Favre, in the proceedings which took place before a French court—"that nothing is more common, and that many cases of a similar kind have been known. " J'ait fait arrêter à Rome," concludes the writer of these letters, in the original, " des assassins de la pire espèce qui, sous le prétexte de réaction Napolitaine, avaient commis des crimes atroces dans les provinces, séquestrant les gens qu'ils arrêtaient, les rançonnant, puis les faisaient mourir après des mutilations qui duraient plusieurs jours. Ces assassins, j'ai conservé leurs noms et le souvenir exact de leurs cruautés. Ils avaient tous des papiers en règle délivrés par la police Romaine, et quelques uns trouvaient asile dans les couvens. J'ai fait arrêter des voleurs dans les églises, au grand scandale du clergé, quand on les prenait en flagrant délit ; mais la police Romaine, alors qu'elle devait les rendre, les mettait en liberté le lendemain ; il est bon de faire connaître ces faits, que j'affirme sur l'honneur, pour que l'on sache bien à quoi s'en tenir sur la justice d'un pays qui n'a aucune espèce de resemblance avec le nôtre."

Rome, as the French have learned at their own expense, and as it has been previously stated, has been the centre of all the intrigues and plots of European reaction; and while the army of the Emperor protected the sovereignty of the Pope, Rome has turned a deaf ear to every warning from France, whose soldiers have frequently been the victims of those brigands of whom the Pope, by his connivance, has made himself the accomplice. The following case, which occurred recently, is a striking example of the truth of our statement. Between Castro and Lofi, on the Papal territory, a brigadier and a soldier of the French gendarmerie met four brigands, the chief of whom wore the military cap of a French captain. "Ils parvinrent," says the original account, "à s'emparer de ce chef et d'un des autres brigands, et ils les emmenaient enchainés, lorsque arrivés au bas de Castro, toujours sur le territoire pontifical, ils furent tout-à-coup enveloppés par une bande de trente brigands armés jusqu'aux dents, qui les sommèrent de rendre leurs armes et leurs prisonniers. Ils s'y refusèrent, en répondant que le soldat Français mourait à son poste, mais ne se rendait jamais. Une lutte inégale s'engagea alors. Le brigadier tomba frappé de plusieurs balles. Le gendarme Tribillac ne tarda pas à succomber aussi; ses vêtements ont fait connaître qu'il avait reçu trois balles dans les reins, dont une est sortie par la poitrine. Les brigands, s'acharnant sur les deux cadavres, leur brisèrent la tête à coups de crosse de fusil, puis leur volèrent tout ce qu'ils avaient sur eux, jusqu'aux galons du brigadier. Ils prirent également leurs mousquetons. Ceci se passait à midi, à cinquante mètres de la gare du chemin de fer de Castro. Les brigands prirent la fuite vers la montagne des Abruzzes. La brigade des gendarmes, c'est à dire les trois hommes qui restaient, ne furent prévenus de la mort de leurs camarades qu'à sept heures du soir. Un détachement d'infanterie alla relever les corps de ces deux malheureux, qui se trouvaient à six milles environ de Ceprano. Ce fut une explosion d'indignation dans toute la division, car on savait que les brigands trouvent un refuge assuré près des autorités pontificales, qui, le soir même du crime (ceci est authentique), délivrèrent des permis de port-d'armes à tous les bandits qui n'en avaient pas encore. Le brigadier Legrand avait vingt-trois ans de services et était proposé pour la croix de la Légion d'Honneur ; le gendarme Tribillac avait dix-neuf ans de services, et était sur le point d'obtenir la médaille militaire."

The assassins belonged to the crew who have been so long fighting in the cause of Francis II. in Southern Italy. This shows how anomalous is the situation of that country where at any moment facts like this may produce the most serious and unforeseen consequences. In the meanwhile the French have felt the necessity of taking most determined measures. The more energetic action adopted by General Montebello has already produced very satisfactory results; and it is reported that he has come to an understanding with the Italian Generals for a more active co-operation. But brigandage must be attacked in Rome itself. Its most active supporters are not all at Ceprano or at Velletri, but in the streets of the Holy City, in the residences of the cardinals and other dignitaries of the Church. The liberation of many convicts belonging to the pontifical provinces, now annexed to the kingdom of Italy, has lately favoured the increase of brigandage. This measure, opposed at first by the General Director of Police, was subsequently carried into effect by order of Cardinal de Mérode and of Monsignor Sagretti, president of the Sacra Consulta. Excited by such events, the greatest activity now reigns in the French army, which keeps incessant watch over those frontiers confided to its care, until the term fixed by the Convention of the 15th of September shall relieve it from that onerous duty.

What course the Pontifical Government will then follow with reference to the new state of things created by the Convention, it is difficult to foresee. If, for the present, the Pope has taken no material precaution, he has just issued an encyclical letter which has struck the world with painful astonishment, and good Catholics have been deeply grieved to see the head of the Church persevering in that path of mediæval intolerance which has already done so much injury to the cause of true religion. Even in past times the temporal supremacy was not always recognized, and since then so great has been the progress of enlightenment, that nation after nation has shaken off the yoke that bound the civil to the spiritual rule, a system which could have originated only in those days when culture was found amongst the clergy alone. Many centuries have elapsed since that period, each of them sweeping away some figment of Papal temporal authority, until a mere shadow of the Pontiff's former power is left. Still, as if all that had passed signified nothing, he declares, in his Syllabus, a deadly war against every principle of freedom, proclaiming those absurd theories which many centuries ago were only obeyed with reluctance, under the influence of fear and religious superstition. Liberty of conscience, the will of nations, civil jurisdiction, the independence of the human mind, everything that savours of freedom, is denounced by the Pontiff, and all who reject the divine right of kings are condemned as heretics. In thus anathematizing those principles to which the emperor owes his throne, has the Pope committed a mere act of folly, or does he desire to become the soul of a new Holy Alliance? Time will show. We may perhaps hope that, taught by the disapproval with which the encyclical letter was received even by ardent Ultramontanes, the Supreme Pontiff will yet adopt a more generous system, and leave a way open for reconciliation with liberal Catholics. When the Holy See perceives that its most sacred interests are not at variance with the liberties of nations, it will gain many valuable adherents, who at present hesitate to connect themselves with the head of a church so inimical to human progress. Italy will not neglect anything to obtain this most desirable end, persevering, meanwhile, in the work of internal organization; and surmounting the difficulties created by her as yet incomplete nationality, she will not suffer any obstacle to oppose the achievement of a work so useful to every civilized government.

By courageously resisting the encroachments of Pontifical intolerance—by striving to free the Church from its temporal bonds, and thus destroying what has been a stumbling-block to many consciences, and at the same time the cause of the most embittered discords that history has to record—Italy fulfils a noble mission, the results of which will prove highly beneficial to the cause of humanity. And it is perhaps in the unfathomable designs of Providence that this great transformation, so much in harmony with the most sublime ends of religion, should be left to the care of that country which has twice initiated the civilization of the world. In the accomplishment of so grand a work, Italy is not moved by the outcries of the reactionist party, for she knows that in fighting for the realization of the great idea, first put forth by her immortal Cavour, of a free Church in a free State, she is serving the interests of humanity as well as those of religion; and she is heedless of the insinuation of envious enemies that her unity is an idea which can never be maintained, and that she will only be a perpetual source of disorder amidst the community of nations.

History will ere long pronounce its verdict as to the justice of such assertions. In the meantime, let men of impartial principles consider that there is not a country in Europe which, in establishing its position among nations, has not been placed for a time under some conditions resembling those of Italy, which have greatly troubled its internal tranquillity, and momentarily impeded its advancement. France may recollect the state in which her provinces of the South and West once were. England was embarrassed at no distant period by the disorders of Ireland. While we do not forget the dangerous phases which the Islands of Corsica and Sardinia have passed through, let us, at the same time, bear in mind that state of violence and misrule which was the normal condition of Naples and Sicily during the sway of that Government which the legitimists and reactionists of Europe would again impose on their free citizens, who have for ever cast it off.

At the commencement of their glorious revolution the Italians pledged themselves that their united country would be as great a security for the peace of Europe, as when, divided into different states, it had been a standing peril. They have kept their word. Under the rule of that dynasty which is the symbol of the monarchical traditions of eight centuries, and under the influence of constitutional institutions founded on the principle of nationalities, Italy, developing within herself all the best elements of modern civilization, is thus really becoming, as her work of regeneration advances to accomplishment, an effective guarantee of peace, of progress, and of political equilibrium among the great powers of Europe.

APPENDIX.

I.

In the month of December of the year which has just elapsed, the Italian Government submitted to Parliament a bill for the continuance of some of the articles of the special laws against brigandage, which, according to the last concession, were to expire on the 31st of the same month. The ground for this proposal was that, as the scourge that had long afflicted the Neapolitan provinces had, since the adoption of the above temporary measures, been so effectually quelled, it would be unwise, all at once, in so short a period, to deprive the country of laws the operation of which had been so beneficial. Though brigandage has been everywhere subdued, and many of the Neapolitan provinces are now entirely free from those bands that once infested them, as I will show by official statistics, yet prudence suggests that, on account of the remnants of the old *comitive* which still infest some of the other provinces, where, owing to the immense distances, the want of roads, the difficulties of the mountainous regions, and the immensity of the woods, they can still find a refuge, the martial laws previously adopted by Parliament should still be maintained in vigorous operation. If, after the results obtained in the year 1864, the special measures against brigandage were to be withdrawn, "the Government would be imperfectly armed, and its action would be less effectual against the crimes of brigandage, to which the circumstances of these provinces have given a special character, and a more than ordinary gravity and extension. Preserving still, however, for a short time, the military tribunals for this species of crimes, it is to be regarded as certain that, as a consequence of the moral effect produced by this system of repression on the minds of these populations, by the promptitude of its judgments, and, in fine, by all those expedients of which it can avail itself, brigandage in a very short time will be entirely destroyed." The Italian Government, therefore, asked for a further grant of these extraordinary powers for the whole of 1865, in order not to lose, by an untimely withdrawal, the benefits of a work so patiently accomplished. The term of another year may perhaps appear a long one to impatient minds, and, in fact, it was not the intention of Government to fix so protracted a period. However, after serious consideration, they came to the resolution to ask for such a prolongation of these laws, pledging themselves to propose the abolition of the martial tribunals as soon as the public safety would permit it.

I am now able to give two official statistical tables, showing the state of the different provinces, with the exact number of brigands killed in action, made prisoners, or who spontaneously surrendered during the whole year 1864, and the first two months of the year 1865, compared

APPENDIX. 307

with the total number who still remain in the whole of the ex-kingdom of Naples. These documents show, by the irrefragable evidence of figures, both the efficacy of the means of repression used by the Italian Government, and the progressive alleviation in the severity of the measures adopted as the object for the attainment of which they are employed draws nearer accomplishment.

The first table, referring to the whole of the year 1864, includes the following dates:—

PROVINCES.	Killed in Action.	Taken Prisoners.	Surrendered.	Total.
Abruzzo Citra (Chieti)	4	12	1	17
Abruzzo Ultra 1st (Teramo)	1	38	3	42
Abruzzo Ultra 2nd (Aquila)	2	17	3	22
Basilicata (Potenza)	205	90	44	339
Beneventum	11	7	3	21
Calabria Citra (Cosenza)	8	18	4	30
Calabria Ultra 1st (Reggio)	...	...	...	...
Calabria Ultra 2nd (Catanzaro)	9	18	11	38
Capitanata (Foggia)	11	19	2	32
Molise (Campobasso)	4	28	1	33
Napoli	...	31	1	32
Principato Citra (Salerno)	22	13	18	53
Principato Ultra (Avellino)	26	24	8	58
Terra di Bari (Bari)	18	26	4	48
Terra di Lavoro (Caserta)	16	85	18	119
Terra d'Otranto (Lecce)	9	27	11	47
Total	346	453	132	931

Thanks to these results, at the beginning of January,

1865, the provinces of Teramo and of Reggio di Calabria were entirely delivered from brigandage; and moreover those of Molise, Beneventum, Capitanata, Bari, and Lecce, on the borders of which the brigands were ever at work, without succeeding, however, in their attempts to penetrate into them or to maintain their position there. A band of thirteen brigands was then in Abruzzo Citeriore; one of twenty, on horseback, between our frontier and that of the Pontifical Government, in the province of Aquila; 83 divided into thirteen *comitive* in Basilicata; 28 in the province of Cosenza, often reinforced by bands from neighbouring provinces; 32 in the province of Catanzaro; 9, the band of Vuola, in the province of Napoli, and more properly in the district of Castellamare;* 30 in the province of Salerno; 18 in the province of Avellino; and 175 collected in eleven *comitive*, in Terra di Lavoro, generally encamped in Pontifical territory, but constantly molesting the borders, especially of the provinces of Aquila and Molise.

This number of 410, the sum total of brigandage in all the Neapolitan provinces, must, according to the following statistical table for the months of January and February, be diminished by 80:—

* The mountains and woods surrounding Castellamare are very favourable to the concealment of the few bandits that still remain, who, finding safety in their limited number, are thus enabled to avail themselves of many opportunities of escape. By the same or other similar reasons, the prolonged presence of some brigands in the other provinces can be explained.

Provinces.	Killed in Action.	Taken Prisoners.	Surrendered.	Total.
Abruzzo Citra (Chieti)	...	1	...	1
Abruzzo Ultra 1st (Teramo)	...	1	...	1
Abruzzo Ultra 2nd (Aquila)	...	...	...	...
Basilicata (Potenza)	6	6	31	43
Beneventum	1	...	1	2
Calabria Citra (Cosenza)	...	2	...	2
Calabria Ultra 1st (Reggio)	...	...	...	...
Calabria Ultra 2nd (Catanzaro)	...	1	...	1
Capitanata (Foggia)	...	...	...	...
Molise (Campobasso)	...	1	...	1
Napoli	...	...	1	1
Principato Citra (Salerno)	...	3	1	4
Principato Ultra (Avellino)	1	2	4	7
Terra di Bari (Bari)	...	1	...	1
Terra di Lavoro (Caserta)	1	13	1	15
Terra d'Otranto (Lecce)	1	...	...	1
Total	10	31	39	80

And here, although the evidence of figures (showing that one-fifth of the brigands have been destroyed in two months) may be amply sufficient to prove the benefits that have been secured up to this time, we would add a few observations with the view of showing the greater benefits that we may yet anticipate at no distant period. Every one knows that brigandage had two principal centres—one in Terra di Lavoro, the other in Basilicata, permanent camps, where it received, organized, and increased its forces, and from whence it directed their movements or reinforced the contingents, constantly reviving the boldness and inspiring the hopes of the bands in the other provinces. The basis of operations in the Terra di Lavoro, on account of its proximity to the Pontifical frontier, and of the favour accorded to the bandits constantly reappearing there, was very difficult to destroy; but now in consequence of the long experience acquired by our troops, supported by the effective co-operation of the French, these districts are so thoroughly watched and guarded that such brigands as find refuge in the Roman territory have little chance of again re-entering ours. The province of Aquila, for more than a month, has been quite clear of them; and as the communications with the Papal States will be henceforth better guarded, the one hundred and fifty-five, which still infest the Terra di Lavoro, will not be able to escape so readily from the pursuit of justice. The centre of Basilicata was still more formidable, because it included a greater number of adherents, was possessed of greater power, was more firmly established, and the resistance there was consequently more desperate. That basis, however, is now quite destroyed. Of five hundred brigands which held the country in 1864, there are now only forty-nine, and the haste and frequency of the last voluntary presentations are sufficient proof of the condition in which these desperadoes now find themselves.

Another re-assuring fact is that with regard to these spontaneous presentations. In the statement for 1864, there were only one hundred and thirty-two, or one-seventh of the total number of 931. In that for the first two months of the present year, the voluntary presentations assume a proportion of one half—thirty-nine in eighty. Whilst this result, on one hand, proves the efficacy of the means of repression which have been adopted, on the other hand, he on whom the obligation of repressing brigandage was imposed may rejoice that he has been able to reduce it by a half without having recourse to those rigorous measures which the state, in its supreme necessity, put in his power.

In a country not long ago swarming with brigands, an inheritance of evil unparalleled in history, these results are certainly satisfactory; and all the more so, if one considers that they have been attained neither by the sanguinary repressions of a Manhès, nor by such pactions with the assassins as the Bourbonist kings were not ashamed to enter into. The Italian government may indeed justly congratulate itself that, notwithstanding the unjustifiable support given to the cause of reaction by the clerical congregation of Rome, it has never been tempted to have recourse to any means of repression but such as were strictly legal.

Not one of the least gratifying events of the year which has just elapsed is the remarkable number of brigands, who, sometimes in whole bands, have voluntarily surrendered to the authorities—a fact which shows that they contemplate with little confidence the ultimate triumph of their cause, and that that confidence would be still less if they knew that their king and supporter is no longer an inhabitant of Rome. One by one, almost all the more important chiefs, with the exception of Crocco, whose disappearance is still a mystery, and of a few others, have perished, and the province of Basilicata saw, in November last, the end of that terrible Schiavone, the leader of so many sanguinary and destructive expeditions. The close of the year

1864 has been indeed fatal to the heroes of the Court of the Palazzo Farnese—a good omen, let us hope, for the future. The recent events in Basilicata form the subject of the following very interesting letter, written by an eye-witness:

"Melfi, 30th November.

"In my last letter I announced to you the capture of the brigand chiefs Schiavone and Petrella, and of three other bandits. To-day it is my duty to inform you that, according to the sentence of the Council of War immediately convoked in Melfi, these five malefactors were yesterday shot.

"Schiavone and his companions died, as all the brigands die, with indifference. It appears that the life of the bandit must necessarily be attended with this contempt for existence.

"The population appears perfectly satisfied with the severity that has been employed. Since 1860 and 1861 these scoundrels have been burning and slaughtering in every direction.

"In consequence of the important revelations made by Schiavone, General Pallavicini was enabled to arrest the too celebrated Filomena Pennacchio, the mistress of that chief.

"I have seen Filomena; she is a fine woman. No longer clothed in the brigand costume, or in the midst of brigands, her former boldness has disappeared, and from her manner one would rather judge her to be a simple-minded girl than a being rejected by society. Since September last Filomena has been concealed in Melfi, in a house where she was assisted in maintaining correspondence with Schiavone.

"General Pallavicini has succeeded in inducing Filomena to make revelations, which have led to important discoveries. She told him she had been harboured, with Schiavone, for several months in the house of Lieutenant Michele Raho, of the National Guard of Bisaccia, and that Crocco also had received shelter there. The most exact indications regarding a place of concealment in the house of Signor Donato Raho, the uncle of Michele, were supplied to the General.

"Last night the troops from Bisaccia, according to the instructions and indications given by the General, surrounded the houses of the Signors Raho, and, after closely searching them, arrested the chief Agostino Sacchitiello, the brigands Vito Sacchitiello and Pasquale Gentile, the mistress of Crocco, a certain Maria Giovanna, of Ruvo, and the mistress of Sacchitiello, whose name I don't remember. According to these facts the great *manutengolismo* (support given to brigandage) is no longer to be doubted; on the contrary, it must be acknowledged that this has been the greatest obstacle to the successful issue of the military operations.

"The results I have mentioned to you, along with the advantages previously obtained, will secure to these provinces a long period of tranquillity, for this evil thing which has been destroyed will no longer arise, as in the past, because with the bandit chiefs the true supports of brigandage have fallen; and, moreover, the revelations which the military authorities will obtain from Sacchitiello, and from the mistress of Crocco, will lead to the deliverance of these districts from *manutengolismo*, and will henceforth render impossible the reorganization of these malefactors in bands.

"The year just passed has been marked by great successes against brigandage in this province, and will ever be joyfully remembered by the people who were, and partly still are, oppressed by a scourge so dreadful. At the commencement of the year 1864 the province was desolated by fully five hundred brigands, divided into thirty-two bands, some of which were led by chiefs of name, each with some political emblem.

"In the beginning of this year, 1865, not more than seventy-five brigands remain in Basilicata, dispersed in small *comitive*, destitute of any peculiar character, led by men without moral power, and with no political object. Now, as you may imagine, so many successes have far exceeded every expectation, so far transcending anything we could have anticipated a year ago; nor certainly could such a result have been obtained without the assistance and co-operation of all the civil and military powers who have taken part in this work. That which has often been spoken of as something desirable, as a design, namely, that the war against the brigands should be carried on by the action of the police rather than by the movements of soldiers and the charge of the bayonet, has been at last accomplished in Basilicata. It was our good fortune to find a chief of the province singularly versed in these arts, and a chief of police of great experience. These two men came to a good understanding together as soon as they met, and since that time have spread their nets with such dexterty, that in a single year they have succeeded in arresting twenty famous chiefs and four hundred brigands. I know well that those who are ever unwilling to recognize the authors of any great or good deed declare that there is not, after all, so much to boast of, since with the aid of all the forces of which every public functionary could dispose, and especially with that powerful instrument of military and civil tactics —the electric telegraph, they have only had to fight against miserable robbers. The reply to this is that even miserable robbers have their arts and stratagems, against which it is often a work of great difficulty to contend; and among the rest that specially of connivance, and of the *manutengoli*, a sort of secret police which they have, against which the government long contended in vain."

In the beginning of January of this year, the last bandits of that dreaded gang known under the name of the Banda Masini, made their submission.

"Some days ago," says an official account, "Nicola Massini, pressed by the troops and the National Guards, and deprived henceforth of the means of existence, sent word to the syndic of Paterno, stating that it was his wish, with six others who remained of that band, consisting formerly of twenty brigands, to surrender; a wish, however, which he accompanied with such conditions, that Lieut.-Colonel Borghesi, who commanded in the military district of Marsico, did not think he could accede to them. Finally, on the 13th, he came with his six men to Marsico Vetere, and surrendered to Signor Borghesi, who has sent him to Potenza, where he will be tried by the military tribunal which sits there. This fact should not be considered one of little importance, for, although the Comitiva Massini, having lost its head, had sunk almost to nothing, it was yet to be feared that his cousin Nicola could either attract to himself the remains of other small bands, or himself form a junction with those now in the district of Melfi and of Matera. This event, in connection with others of a similar nature which have rapidly succeeded in a short space of time, will aid more than ever in the destruction of the last branch of this pestiferous plant, and will certainly deprive it of every hope of budding again in the future."

The campaign of Basilicata, one of the greatest strongholds of brigandage, and of the surrounding districts, was probably one of the most important conducted by General Pallavicini. The death of Schiavone was soon followed by that of another dreaded chief, Coppolone, a man stained with innumerable crimes.

After the destruction by General Pallavicini of brigandage in the valley of the Ofanto, there remained only the bands of Ingiongiolo, Coppolone, and Bellettieri, which overran the lands of Matera, the forest Imperatore, and the defiles of the Basente and of the Bradano.

These *Comitive* often joined together, but in presence of danger again separated, and dispersed in opposite directions.

Coppolone, for the most part, infested the country from Ginosa to Otranto, where, as the proprietor of property, he had certain fixed interests.

The attention of General Pallavicini was then turned to these three brigands, whose discomfiture will signalize the destruction of brigandage in the Potentino and in Terra di Otranto. The operations commenced in the first days of February, and were then, in consequence of the bad weather, suspended for some days, and then again resumed.

On the 19th, Lieutenant Severi, with a detachment of Bersaglieri, attacked the band of Coppolone in the forest Imperatore. That chief, who, in consequence of the death of his horse, was nearly taken prisoner, succeeded by the desperate defence which he made, in effecting his escape. But he did not come out of the conflict uninjured. Wounded in several places, he died in two days, and was interred by his companions in the vicinity of Ginosa; so that there remained now only Ingiongiolo and Bellettieri, against whom General Pallavicini had to carry on his operations. And there was no doubt as to his complete success. In fact, a few more well-directed operations completed in a short interval what had been so luckily begun, and on the 9th of the last month the gallant General brought his expedition to a fortunate termination, at the same time addressing the following proclamation to his soldiers:

"*Officers and Soldiers,*

"The succession of military movements, in spite of the obstacles presented by the severity of the season, the operations of many small bodies of troops, which maintained themselves permanently in the woods, the continual clearances, the levellings, the life of abnegation you have led for several months, have at last been rewarded with the most complete success.

"The districts of Melfi, of Lacedonia, and of Bovino, long the principal scenes of the devastations committed by the brigands, contain no longer either armed comitive or brigands. Thanks to the incessant prosecution of the war in these last months, the names of Crocco, Tasca, Tortora, Schiavone, Petrella, Di Tore, Sacchitiello, Collarulo, Teodoro, Totoro, and Volunino, which had long sounded as words of terror to entire districts, were for ever cancelled from the registers of crime. With the chiefs fell also the numerous brigands who had composed these bands.

" Often, during the course of our operations, the general commanding the sixth military department communicated to me his great satisfaction on account of the fortunate results which had rewarded the efforts of the troops. These successes, and the more important ones gained during last February, have evoked other brilliant eulogiums, both from the general in command and from the Minister of War and of the Interior. I cannot have a more favourable opportunity to communicate to you the expression of gratification on the part of our superiors, since, at the same time, I can also make myself the interpreter of the gratitude of the inhabitants—a gratitude which is signified to-day by the most grateful manifestations.

"Officers and Soldiers,—whoever was witness of the fatigues and of the difficulties which you endured with exemplary patience, can estimate your labour at its just value. You all exhibited zeal and activity, all gave admirable proof of perseverance, since in every district, and by everybody, the most brilliant and glorious deeds were performed.

" Recognising in you one of the principal causes of the fortunate condition of these districts, the most honourable reward which the soldier can desire falls to you. To your unwearied efforts in the pursuit of the criminals, the country is indebted for their conquest and destruction. To the intelligent directions of the three commandants of the district, Lieutenant-Colonels Barbavara, Peyssard, and Gorini, your labour is indebted for the results obtained. Praise, then, to them, and praise also to the commanders of the different troops. They, knowing how to evoke the generous sentiments and the best spirit of those subject to them, acted so as to merit the entire satisfaction of the Government, and the love and gratitude of these provinces.

"GENERAL PALLAVICINI.
"Melfi, March 9th, 1865."

From day to day new proofs are gathered, as if such were wanting, of the connivance of the enemies of Italian unity with the brigands. Among the most curious documents discovered in the possession of the Bourbonist bandits, are undoubtedly those found upon some of them, taken but a few months ago in the environs of Naples. In last November, the police of that city was informed that some of the outlaws, who once formed the " comitiva " of Pilone, had left Rome, whither they had fled for safety, and had reached the neighbourhood of Mount Vesuvius in small numbers, their object being to avoid suspicion, and wait there for the arrival of their chief. A search was ordered at once, which ended in the capture of four of them, who were taken before the magistrate of Torre Anunziata, to whom they made the followin depositions :—

They had all been enlisted by Pilone in July, 1862, and they had chiefly scoured the country comprised between

Resina, Portici, Torre del Greco, Torre Anunziata, and the opposite side of Vesuvius down to Ottajano. They had repaired to Rome when the band was defeated at Torre Anunziata—an event which all confessed had been preceded by constant interviews between their chief and many gentlemen friends of the fallen dynasty, besides several priests from Naples and various other localities, from whom Pilone received food, money, and provisions for the use of the band. After the reported breaking up of the gang, those who were able to escape embarked on board some small fishing-boats and gained Terracina, where the Pontifical authorities, on hearing they were the remnants of the band of Pilone, furnished them with duly legalized passports, and enabled these respectable excursionists to reach Rome without molestation. At Rome the police renewed their papers, and, full of paternal solicitude, sent them on to Velletri, recommending them to the directors of the railway at that place. Things thus went on for some time as smoothly and quietly as possible, till the end of last September, when a favourable opportunity of returning to their last occupation of murdering and plundering in the dominions of the King of Italy apparently presenting itself, they again had recourse to the accommodating Roman police, who, knowing no doubt their laudable intentions, gave them a fresh passport, under the protection of which they went to Porto d'Anzo, where they were at once received by the brigand recruiting agent stationed there, and, always under the safeguard of the keys of St. Peter, embarked on board a ship taking coals to Naples. Landing three days afterwards, under the disguise of coalmen, in the neighbourhood of that fairy queen of the Mediterranean, they made at once for their old haunts in the mountains, where, having wandered for some time, they at last fell, as has been stated, into the hands of justice.

Every brigand was found to have in a tin box, besides the Pontifical passport, some holy medals, the image of the Virgin, and of two or three other saints, *the list of the last drawing of the lottery,** and finally a prayer in Latin, which had been given by Pilone to each member of his band, with the assurance that it would save them from every danger. This prayer is so characteristic, that I cannot resist the temptation of quoting it here *in extenso* :—

"*(Sic) Jesus Maria Joseph, sancti Apostoli Petrus et Paulus, et B. Franciscus Salvatoris et SS. Crescentius et Philippus.*

"V. M. I. Qui Verbum Caro factum est, et abitavit in nobis nascens et M. V. per ineffabilem pietatem et misericordiam suam, et intercessionem B. M. V. et Angelorum Ioannis Mattei et Lucae, sanctorumque Vincentii et B. P.

---

* Those who have been in Italy must recollect the immoral institution of the public lotteries, a remnant of the old system. The present Government has proposed a bill for their suppression, to the effect that at the death of each individual to whom such a concession has been granted, it shall neither be renewed nor given to any one else. In a few years, therefore, the system will entirely disappear, and, indeed, in the North of Italy, very little of it now remains, but at Naples, where, under the Bourbons, lotteries flourished, some time must elapse before they altogether disappear.

Francisci sit tibi clemens et propitius. Amen. Ora pro eo S. Maure.

"Salvum fac servum tuum, Deus meus, sperantem in te Esto e Domine turris fortitudinis. Et filius iniquitatis non apponat nocere ei. Mitte ei Domine auxilium de sancto. Et de Sion tuere eum. Exurge Domine adjuva eum. Et libera eum propter nomen tuum et in virtute tua libera eum ab omni malo propter gloriam nominis tui Domine: libera eum, propitius esto peccatis ejus propter nomen tuum. Non enim est aliud nomen sub coelum datum hominibus in quo oportet nos salvos fieri, quam in nomine Domini Nostri Jesu Christi.

"Igitur per perfectum et triumphale nomen Jesu, scilicet J. N. R. J. fugite partes adversae ab hac dicta creatura. Durum est vobis contra stimulorum calcitrare, et durissimum est vobis virtuti sanctissimi nomini Jesu resistere: sit nomen Dei et Domini nostri Jesu Christi benedictum ex hoc nunc et usque in saeculum.

"Deus et Pater D. N. J. C. invoco nomen sanctum tuum et nomen ejusdem D. N. J. C. filii tui insuper et clementiam tuam supplex et posco ut hunc famulum tuum defendere ac liberare digneris ab omni peccato, ab ira tua, a flagello terraemotus, ab omni mala voluntate, a spiritu fornicationis, a fulgure et tempestate, a morte perpetua, a peste, fame, et bello, ab omni infestatione Satanae, omnique periculo animae et corporis in omni tempore et loco. Tandem Domine Jesu da ei tuam sanctam gratiam, charitatem, et pacem. Amen. Fiat, fiat, fiat.

"Benedicat tibi Deus, custodiat te, ostendat . . . . . . et misereatur tui; convertat Dominus vultum . . . . pacem.

Amen. Super aegros manus imponent et bene habebunt. Jesus Mariae filius, mundi solus et Dominus, meritis Beati patris Francisci, Salvatoris, et beati Ubaldi sit tibi clemens et propitius. Amen.

"Dominus Jesus Christus apud te sit, ut te deducat, intra te sit, ut te conservet, ante te sit, ut te reducat, post te sit, ut te custodiat, super te sit ut benedicat qui cum Patre et Sancto Spiritu in virtute et regnat in saecula saeculorum. Amen.

"Benedictio Dei Omnipotentis. Patris et filii et Spiritus Sancti descendat super hunc Dei famulum et omnes diabolicas virtutes omnesque Daemonum fallaces insidiam ab eo repellere dignetur. Amen.

"Domine Jesu Christe sit hic famulus tuus sanctissimi nominis tui intus et foris munitus, intus in corde, foris in fronte et anima et corpore dite tutus. Amen.

"Sub tuum praesidium confugio o clemens, o pia, o dulcis Virgo Maria. Sanctissima Dei Genitrix quibus te laudibus afferam nescio, o Maria Mater Gratiae, mater misericordiae, tu me ab hoste protege et in hora mortis suscipe, dignare me laudare te, filio aeterni Patris Mater Jesu Christi, sponsa Spiritus Sancti, Regina Coelorum et Domina angelorum da mihi virtutem contra hostes tuos. Amen.

" Initium Sancti Evangelii secundum Joannem : *si legge il Vangelo.* In principio erat verbum, &c.

"Deinde benedicit quinque grana incensi ponenda in Cruce.

" *Dicens absolute hanc orationem.*

"Veniat quaesumus omnipotens Deus super hoc incensum larga tua benedictionis infusio et hunc nocturnum splendorem invisibilis regenerator accende ut non solum sacrificium quod hac nocte licitum est arcam luminis tui administratione refulgeat, sed in quemcumque locum ex hujus sanctificationis mysterio aliquid fuit deportatum expulsa diabolicae fraudis nequitia, virtus tuae majestatis assistat per Christum Dominum nostrum. Amen."

What will the defenders of the temporal power say to this sacrilegious profanation?

* * * * * *

It was but the other day (the 22nd of March), when the telegraph informed us that on some brigands acting on the Roman frontier, against whom General Montebello had sent large reinforcements, had been found *documents from which it appeared that an understanding existed between the court of the ex-King of Naples and the chiefs of the brigands* —a fresh piece of intelligence indeed! But I need say no more. These two facts put together resume all that has been patiently collected and stated in this work. The religious as well as the political support given to brigandage has been fully proved. To impartial minds it now belongs to pronounce a verdict.

II.

The Exceptional Bill, mentioned in the present volume, for the repression of brigandage, was framed by Parliament on the 15th of August, 1863, and, from the honourable gentleman by whom it was proposed, is commonly known as Pica's bill. The following are the articles of that important measure:—

Art. 1.—Until the 31st of December, 1863, in those provinces declared by royal decree to be in a state of brigandage, any one belonging to an armed band of at least three persons, which may scour the country for mischievous purposes, shall be, as well as his accomplices, judged by martial tribunals according to the prescriptions of military law.

Art. 2.—Any one guilty of brigandage, opposing an armed resistance to the public authorities, shall be condemned to be shot, or, in cases of extenuating circumstances, sentenced to hard labour for life. Those who shall not display resistance, as well as those who shall in any way assist the brigands, by collecting and distributing arms, ammunition, food, or by giving them intelligence, or any help whatever, shall be likewise condemned to penal servitude for life, or, in cases of extenuating circumstances, to twenty years of the same penalty.

Art. 3.—Any one giving himself up to the authorities out of his own will, within a month from the date of the decree, shall receive a diminution of penalty, from one to three degrees.

Art. 4.—The Government shall also have authority, at the expiration of the above term, to grant a diminution of the penalty to any one surrendering spontaneously, whenever it may be deemed convenient.

Art. 5.—The Government will have power to confine, for a time not exceeding two years, in a determined place, those vagabonds, or suspected people, *camorristi*, or *manutengoli* (supporters of brigandage), who may be designated by a committee composed of the provincial authorities.

Art. 6.—The individuals contemplated in the preceding article, if they break their confinement, will be liable to be punished according to the existing laws.

Art. 7.—The Government will be authorized to appoint armed companies of foot, or of mounted volunteers, to commission their officers, to fix their attributions, and subsequently to disband them.

Art. 8.—The pensions to be granted to the volunteers or National Guards, on account of wounds received in the repression of brigandage, will be regulated by the law on Military Pensions, of the 27th June, 1850. The Minister for War will issue a decree to determine the circumstances that will entitle to the receipt of a pension.

Art. 9.—A credit of one million francs (£40,000) is opened to the Home Office for the extraordinary expenses occasioned by the repression of brigandage.

Victor Emmanuel.
U. Peruzzi.

Turin, 15th August, 1863.

This bill has been in vigour since the 20th August, 1863, Parliament renewing its powers at the end of every grant, and it is now voted for the whole of the current year. The state of the country is such, however, that it is to be hoped no further prolongation will be deemed necessary.

THE END.

13, Great Marlborough Street.

MESSRS. HURST AND BLACKETT'S NEW WORKS IN PREPARATION.

MEMOIRS AND CORRESPONDENCE OF FIELD-MARSHAL VISCOUNT COMBERMERE, G.C.B., &c. From his Family Papers. 2 vols. 8vo, with Portraits and other Illustrations.

THE LIFE OF HIS EMINENCE CARDINAL WISEMAN. Any Persons possessing Manuscripts, Letters, &c., or having the knowledge of any facts of importance connected with the Life of His Eminence, are requested to communicate by letter with the Right Rev. H. E. MANNING, D.D., care of Messrs. HURST & BLACKETT, 13, Great Marlborough Street.

HISTORIC PICTURES. By A. BAILLIE COCHRANE, M.P. 2 vols. 21s. (*Now Ready.*)

RELIGIOUS LIFE ON THE CONTINENT. By Mrs. OLIPHANT, Author of "The Life of the Rev. Edward Irving." 2 vols. 8vo.

YACHTING ROUND THE WEST OF ENGLAND. By the Rev. A. G. L'ESTRANGE. 1 vol. 8vo, Illustrated.

VIOLET OSBORNE. By the LADY EMILY PONSONBY, Author of "The Discipline of Life." 3 vols. (*Now Ready.*)

BRIGAND LIFE IN ITALY. By COUNT MAFFEI. 2 vols. (*Now Ready.*)

ADVENTURES AMONGST THE DYAKS OF BORNEO. By FREDERICK BOYLE, Esq. 1 vol. 8vo, with Illustrations.

IMPRESSIONS OF LIFE AT HOME AND ABROAD. By Lord EUSTACE CECIL, Lieut.-Colonel Coldstream Guards. 8vo.

ALEC FORBES OF HOWGLEN. By GEORGE MAC DONALD, M.A., Author of "David Elginbrod," &c. 3 vols.

MY LIFE AND RECOLLECTIONS. By the Hon. GRANTLEY F. BERKELEY. Vols. 3 and 4, completing the Work.

SOCIAL LIFE IN FLORENCE. By COUNT CHARLES ARRIVABENE, Author of "Italy under Victor Emmanuel." 2 vols.

SPORT AND SPORTSMEN: A BOOK OF RECOLLECTIONS. By CHARLES STRETTON, Esq. 2 vols.

AGNES. By MRS. OLIPHANT. 3 vols.

WILLIAM SHAKESPEARE. By CARDINAL WISEMAN. 1 vol. 8vo, 5s. (*Now Ready.*)

13, GREAT MARLBOROUGH STREET.

MESSRS. HURST AND BLACKETT'S LIST OF NEW WORKS.

A JOURNEY FROM LONDON TO PERSEPOLIS; including WANDERINGS IN DAGHESTAN, GEORGIA, ARMENIA, KURDISTAN, MESOPOTAMIA, AND PERSIA. By J. USSHER, Esq., F.R.G.S. Royal 8vo, with numerous beautiful Coloured Illustrations. 42s. Elegantly bound.

"This work does not yield to any recent book of travels in extent and variety of interest. Its title, 'From London to Persepolis,' is well chosen and highly suggestive. A wonderful chain of association is suspended from these two points, and the traveller goes along its line, gathering link after link into his hand, each gemmed with thought, knowledge, speculation, and adventure. The reader will feel that in closing this memorable book he takes leave of a treasury of knowledge. The whole book is interesting, and its unaffected style and quick spirit of observation lend an unfailing freshness to its pages. The illustrations are beautiful, and have been executed with admirable taste and judgment."—*Post.*

"This work is in every way creditable to the author, who has produced a mass of pleasant reading, both entertaining and instructive. Mr. Ussher's journey may be defined as a complete oriental grand tour of the Asiatic west-central district. He started down the Danube, making for Odessa. Thence, having duly 'done' the Crimea, he coasted the Circassian shore in a steamer to Poti, and from that to Tiflis. This was the height of summer, and, the season being favourable, he crossed the Dariel Pass northwards, turned to the east, and visited the mountain fastnesses of Shamil's country, recently conquered by the Russians. Thence he returned to Tiflis by the old Persian province of Shirvan, along the Caspian, by Derbend and the famous fire-springs of Baku. From Tiflis he went to Gumri, and over the frontier to Kars, and the splendid ruins of Ani, and through the Russian territory to the Turkish frontier fortress of Bayazid, stopping by the way at Erivan and the great monastery of Etchmiadzin. From Bayazid he went to Van, and saw all the chief points of interest on the lake of that name; thence to Bitlis and Diarbekir. From Diarbekir he went to Mosul by the upper road, visited Nineveh, paid his respects to the winged bulls and all our old friends there, and floated on his raft of inflated skins down the Tigris to Baghdad. From Mosul he made an excursion to the devil-worshipping country, and another from Baghdad to Hilleh and the Birs Nimrud, or so-called Tower of Babel. After resting in the city of the Caliphs, he followed the track of his illustrious predecessor, Sindbad, to Bassora, only on board of a different craft, having got a passage in the steamer Comet; and the English monthly sailing packet took him from Bassora across the gulf to Bushire. From thence he went to Tehran over the 'broad dominions of the king of kings,' stopping at all the interesting places, particularly at Persepolis; and from Tehran returned home through Armenia by Trebisonde and the Black Sea."—*Saturday Review.*

"This is a book of travel of which no review can give an adequate idea. The extent of country traversed, the number and beauty of the coloured illustrations, and the good sense, humour, and information with which it abounds, all tend to increase the author's just meed of praise, while they render the critic's task all the harder. We must, after all, trust to our readers to explore for themselves the many points of amusement, interest and beauty which the book contains. We can assure them that they will not meet with a single page of dulness. Mr. Ussher handles such topics as Persepolis, Nineveh, and the cities of the Eastern world, with singular completeness, and leaves the ordinary reader nothing to desire. The coloured illustrations are really perfect of their kind. Merely as a collection of spirited, well-coloured engravings they are worth the cost of the whole volume."—*Herald.*

"Mr. Ussher went by the Danube to Constantinople, crossed thence to Sebastopol, and passed through the Crimea to Kertch, and so on to Poti. From Poti he went to Teflis, and made thence an excursion to Gunib and Baku on the Caspian. The record of this journey is the most interesting part of the book. Having returned to Teflis, Mr. Ussher visited Gumri and Kars, and went thence to Lake Van, and so by Diarbekr and Mosul to Baghdad. From Baghdad he went to Babylon and Kerbela, and returning to Baghdad, descended the river to Basra, and crossed to Bushire. Thence he went by Shiraz and Isfahan to Tehran, and returned to Europe by the Tabreez and Trebisonde route. The reader will find the author of this pleasant volume an agreeable companion. He is a good observer, and describes well what he sees."—*Athenæum.*

"A truly magnificent work, adorned with gorgeously-coloured illustrations. We are lured over its pages with a pleasant fascination, and derive no little information from so agreeable a cicerone as Mr. Ussher."—*Sun.*

13, GREAT MARLBOROUGH STREET.

MESSRS. HURST AND BLACKETT'S
NEW WORKS—*Continued*.

THE LIFE OF JOSIAH WEDGWOOD. From
his Private Correspondence and Family Papers, in the possession of JOSEPH MAYER, Esq., F.S.A., FRANCIS WEDGWOOD, Esq., C. DARWIN, Esq., M.A., F.R.S., Miss WEDGWOOD, and other Original Sources. With an Introductory Sketch of the Art of Pottery in England. By ELIZA METEYARD. Dedicated, by permission, to the Right Hon. W. E. GLADSTONE, Chancellor of the Exchequer. Vol. 1, 8vo, with Portraits and numerous Illustrations, price 21s. elegantly bound, is now ready. The work will be completed in one more volume.

COURT AND SOCIETY FROM ELIZABETH
TO ANNE, Edited from the Papers at Kimbolton, by the DUKE OF MANCHESTER. *Second Edition.* 2 vols. 8vo, with Fine Portraits.

"The Duke of Manchester has done a welcome service to the lover of gossip and secret history by publishing these family papers. Persons who like to see greatness without the plumes and mail in which history presents it, will accept these volumes with hearty thanks to their noble editor. In them will be found something new about many men and women in whom the reader can never cease to feel an interest—much about the divorce of Henry the Eighth and Catherine of Arragon—a great deal about the loves affairs of Queen Elizabeth—something about Bacon, and (indirectly) about Shakspeare—more about Lord Essex and Lady Rich—the very strange story of Walter Montagu, poet, profligate, courtier, pervert, secret agent, abbot—many details of the Civil War and Cromwell's Government, and of the Restoration—much that is new about the Revolution and the Settlement, the exiled Court of St. Germains, the wars of William of Orange, the campaigns of Marlborough, the intrigues of Duchess Sarah, and the town life of fine ladies and gentlemen during the days of Anne. With all this is mingled a good deal of gossip about the loves of great poets, the frailties of great beauties, the rivalries of great wits, the quarrels of great peers."—*Athenæum.*

"These volumes are sure to excite curiosity. A great deal of interesting matter is here collected, from sources which are not within everybody's reach."—*Times.*

"The public are indebted to the noble author for contributing, from the archives of his ancestral seat, many important documents otherwise inaccessible to the historical inquirer, as well as for the lively, picturesque, and piquant sketches of Court and Society, which render his work powerfully attractive to the general reader. The work contains varied information relating to secret Court intrigues, numerous narratives of an exciting nature, and valuable materials for authentic history. Scarcely any personage whose name figured before the world during the long period embraced by the volumes is passed over in silence."—*Morning Post.*

THE LIFE OF THE REV. EDWARD IRVING,
Minister of the National Scotch Church, London. Illustrated by his Journal and Correspondence. By Mrs. OLIPHANT. *Fourth and Cheaper Edition, Revised,* in 1 vol., with Portrait, 5s., bound.

"We who read these memoirs must own to the nobility of Irving's character, the grandeur of his aims, and the extent of his powers. His friend Carlyle bears this testimony to his worth:—'I call him, on the whole, the best man I have ever, after trial enough, found in this world, or hope to find.' A character such as this is deserving of study, and his life ought to be written. Mrs. Oliphant has undertaken the work and has produced a biography of considerable merit. The author fully understands her hero, and sets forth the incidents of his career with the skill of a practised hand. The book is a good book on a most interesting theme."—*Times.*

"Mrs. Oliphant's 'Life of Edward Irving' supplies a long-felt desideratum. It is copious, earnest, and eloquent. On every page there is the impress of a large and masterly comprehension. And of a bold, fluent, and poetic skill of portraiture. Irving as a man and as a pastor is not only fully sketched, but exhibited with many broad, powerful, and life-like touches, which leave a strong impression."—*Edinburgh Review.*

"A truly interesting and most affecting memoir. Irving's life ought to have a niche in every gallery of religious biography. There are few lives that will be fuller of instruction, interest, and consolation."—*Saturday Review.*

13, Great Marlborough Street.

MESSRS. HURST AND BLACKETT'S NEW WORKS—*Continued*.

MY LIFE AND RECOLLECTIONS. By the Hon. Grantley F. Berkeley. 2 vols. 8vo, with Portrait. 30s.

Among the other distinguished persons mentioned in this work are:—Kings George III. and IV., and William IV.; Queens Charlotte, Caroline, and Victoria; the Prince of Wales; the Dukes of Kent, Cumberland, Sussex, Cambridge, d'Aumale, Wellington, Norfolk, Richmond, Beaufort, Bedford, Devonshire, St. Albans, Manchester, Portland; the Marquises of Anglesea, Buckingham, Downshire, Waterford, Tavistock, Londonderry, Clanricarde, Breadalbane, Worcester; Lords Mulgrave, Conyngham, Clanwilliam, Wynford, Palmerston, Bathurst, Cantelupe, Roden, Eldon, Grey, Holland, Coleraine, Rokeby, Munster, Chelmsford, Ducie, Alvanley, Chesterfield, Sefton, Derby, Vane, Mexborough, George Bentinck, Edward Somerset, Fitzclarence, Egremont, Count d'Orsay; the Bishop of Oxford, Cardinal Wiseman; Sirs Lumley Skeffington, William Wynn, Percy Shelley, Godfrey Webster, Samuel Romilly, Matthew Tierney, Francis Burdett; Messrs. Fox, Sheridan, Whitbread, Brummell, Byng, Townsend, Bernal, Maginn, Cobden, Bright, O'Connell, Crockford, &c.; the Duchesses of Devonshire, Gordon, Rutland, Argyle; Ladies Clermont, Berkeley, Shelley, Guest, Fitzhardinge, Bury, Blessington, Craven, Essex, Strangford, Paget; Mesdames Fitzherbert, Coutts, Jordan, Billington, Mardyn, Shelley, Misses Landon, Kemble, Paton, &c.

"A book unrivalled in its position in the range of modern literature."—*Times*.

"There is a large fund of amusement in these volumes. The details of the author's life are replete with much that is interesting. A book so brimful of anecdote cannot but be successful."—*Athenæum*.

"This work contains a great deal of amusing matter; and that it will create a sensation no one can doubt. Mr. Berkeley can write delightfully when he pleases. His volumes will, of course, be extensively read, and, as a literary venture, may be pronounced a success."—*Post*.

"A clever, freespoken man of the world, son of an earl with £70,000 a-year, who has lived from boyhood the life of a club-man, sportsman, and man of fashion, has thrown his best stories about himself and his friends into an anecdotic autobiography. Of course it is eminently readable. Mr. Grantley Berkeley writes easily and well. The book is full of pleasant stories, all told as easily and clearly as if they were related at a club-window, and all with point of greater or less piquancy."—*Spectator*.

HAUNTED LONDON. By Walter Thornbury. 1 vol. 8vo, with numerous Illustrations by F. W. Fairholt, F.S.A. 21s., elegantly bound.

"Haunted London is a pleasant book."—*Athenæum*.

"Pleasant reading is Mr. Thornbury's 'Haunted London '—a gossiping, historical, antiquarian, topographical volume, amusing both to the Londoner and the country cousin."—*Star*.

"Mr. Thornbury points out to us the legendary houses, the great men's birthplaces and tombs, the haunts of poets, the scenes of martyrdom, the battle-fields of old factions. The book overflows with anecdotical gossip. Mr. Fairholt's drawings add alike to its value and interest."—*Notes and Queries*.

"As pleasant a book as well could be, forming a very handsome volume—a volume worthy of being pronounced an acquisition either for the table or the bookshelf. A capital title is ' Haunted London '—meaning by that not merely localities like Cock Lane, but all London. For is it not haunted, this London of ours? Haunted happily, by ghosts of memories that will not be laid. What footsteps have not traversed these causeways, inhabited these dwelling-houses, prayed in these churches, wept in these graveyards, laughed in these theatres? And of all these Mr. Thornbury discourses—shrewdly, like an observant man of the world; gracefully, like a skilled man of letters; lovingly, like a sympathizing fellow-creature; courtier and playwright, student and actress, statesman and mountebank, he has an eye for them all. Saunter with him down any street he may seem fain to conduct you through, and before you get to the end of it we wager you will be wiser than at starting—certainly, beyond any doubt of it, you will have been entertained."—*Sun*.

13, Great Marlborough Street.

MESSRS. HURST AND BLACKETT'S NEW WORKS—*Continued.*

A PERSONAL NARRATIVE OF THIRTEEN YEARS' SERVICE AMONGST THE WILD TRIBES OF KHONDISTAN, FOR THE SUPPRESSION OF HUMAN SACRIFICE. By Major-General JOHN CAMPBELL, C.B. 1 vol. 8vo, with Illustrations.

"Major-General Campbell's book is one of thrilling interest, and must be pronounced the most remarkable narrative of the present season."—*Athenæum.*

THE DESTINY OF NATIONS, AS INDICATED IN PROPHECY. By the Rev. JOHN CUMMING, D.D. 1 vol. 7s. 6d.

"Among the subjects expounded by Dr. Cumming in this interesting volume are The Little Horn, or The Papacy; The Waning Crescent, Turkey; The Lost Ten Tribes; and the Future of the Jews and Judea, Africa, France, Russia, America, Great Britain, &c."—*Observer.* "One of the most able of Dr. Cumming's works."—*Messenger.*

MEMOIRS OF JANE CAMERON, FEMALE CONVICT. By a Prison Matron, Author of "Female Life in Prison." 2 vols. 21s.

"This narrative, as we can well believe, is truthful in every important particular—a faithful chronicle of a woman's fall and rescue. It is a book that ought to be widely read."—*Examiner.* "There can be no doubt as to the interest of the book, which, moreover, is very well written."—*Athenæum.*
"Once or twice a-year one rises from reading a book with a sense of real gratitude to the author, and this book is one of these. There are many ways in which it has a rare value. The artistic touches in this book are worthy of De Foe."—*Reader.*

TRAVELS AND ADVENTURES OF AN OFFICER'S WIFE IN INDIA, CHINA, AND NEW ZEALAND. By Mrs. MUTER, Wife of Lieut.-Colonel D. D. MUTER, 13th (Prince Albert's) Light Infantry. 2 vols. 21s.

"Mrs. Muter's travels deserve to be recommended, as combining instruction and amusement in a more than ordinary degree. The work has the interest of a romance added to that of history."—*Athenæum.*

TRAVELS ON HORSEBACK IN MANTCHU TARTARY: being a Summer's Ride beyond the Great Wall of China. By GEORGE FLEMING, Military Train. 1 vol. royal 8vo, with Map and 50 Illustrations.

"Mr. Fleming's narrative is a most charming one. He has an untrodden region to tell of, and he photographs it and its people and their ways. Life-like descriptions are interspersed with personal anecdotes, local legends, and stories of adventure, some of them revealing no common artistic power."—*Spectator.*

HISTORY OF ENGLAND, FROM THE ACCESSION OF JAMES I. TO THE DISGRACE OF CHIEF JUSTICE COKE. By SAMUEL RAWSON GARDINER. 2 vols. 8vo.

ADVENTURES AND RESEARCHES among the ANDAMAN ISLANDERS. By Dr. MOUAT, F.R.G.S., &c. 1 vol. demy 8vo, with Illustrations.

"Dr. Mouat's book, whilst forming a most important and valuable contribution to ethnology, will be read with interest by the general reader."—*Athenæum.*

MEMOIRS OF QUEEN HORTENSE, MOTHER OF NAPOLEON III. Cheaper Edition, in 1 vol. 6s.

"A biography of the beautiful and unhappy Queen, more satisfactory than any we have yet met with."—*Daily News.*

13, Great Marlborough Street.

MESSRS. HURST AND BLACKETT'S NEW WORKS—Continued.

REMINISCENCES OF THE OPERA. By Benjamin Lumley, Twenty Years Director of Her Majesty's Theatre. 8vo, with Portrait of the Author by Count D'Orsay. 16s.

"Mr. Lumley's book, with all its sparkling episodes, is really a well-digested history of an institution of social importance in its time, interspersed with sound opinions and shrewd and mature reflections."—*Times.*

"As a repertory of anecdote, we have not for a long while met with anything at all comparable to these unusually brilliant and most diversified Reminiscences. They reveal the Twenty Years' Director of Her Majesty's Theatre to us in the thick and throng of all his radiant associations. They take us luringly—as it were, led by the button-hole—behind the scenes, in every sense of that decoying and profoundly attractive phrase. They introduce us to all the stars—now singly, now in very constellations. They bring us rapidly, delightfully, and exhilaratingly to a knowledge so intimate of what has really been doing there in the Realm of Song, not only behind the scenes and in the green-room, but in the reception-apartment of the Director himself, that we are *au courant* with all the whims and oddities of the strange world in which he fills so high and responsible a position. Reading Mr. Lumley, we now know more than we have ever known before of such Queens of the Lyric stage as Pasta, Catalini, Malibran, Grisi, Sontag, and Piccolomini—of such light-footed fairies of the ballet as Taglioni, Fanny Elssler, and Cerito—of such primi tenori as Rubini, Mario, Gardoni, and Giuglini—of such baritones as Ronconi and Tamburini—or of such bassi profondi as the wondrous Staudigl and the mighty Lablache. Nay, Mr. Lumley takes us out of the glare of the footlights, away from the clang of the orchestra, into the dream-haunted presence of the great composers of the age, bringing us face to face, as it were, among others, with Rossini, Mendelssohn, Meyerbeer, Verdi, Balfe, and Donizetti. He lets us into the mysteries of his correspondence—now with Count Cavour, now with Prince Metternich—for, in his doings, in his movements, in his negotiations, Sovereigns, Prime Ministers, Ambassadors, and Governments are, turn by turn, not merely courteously, but directly and profoundly interested! Altogether, Mr. Lumley's book is an enthralling one. It is written with sparkling vivacity, and is delightfully interesting throughout."—*Sun.*

"Everyone ought to read Mr. Lumley's very attractive 'Reminiscences of the Opera.' In the fashionable, dramatic, and literary worlds its cordial welcome is assured. It is a most entertaining volume. Anecdote succeeds to anecdote in this pleasant book with delightful fluency."—*Post.*

WILLIAM SHAKESPEARE. By Victor Hugo. Authorized English Translation. 1 vol. 8vo, 12s.

"M. Victor Hugo has produced a notable and brilliant book about Shakespeare. M. Hugo sketches the life of Shakespeare, and makes of it a very effective picture. Imagination and pleasant fancy are mingled with the facts. There is high colouring, but therewith a charm which has not hitherto been found in any portrait of Shakespeare painted by a foreign hand. The biographical details are manipulated by a master's hand, and consequently there is an agreeable air of novelty even about the best known circumstances."—*Athenæum.*

LIFE IN JAVA; with SKETCHES of the JAVANESE. By William Barrington D'Almeida. 2 vols. post 8vo, with Illustrations. 21s., bound.

"'Life in Java' is both amusing and instructive. The author saw a good deal of the country and people not generally known."—*Athenæum.*

"Mr. D'Almeida's volumes traverse interesting ground. They are filled with good and entertaining matter."—*Examiner.*

"A very entertaining work. The author has given most interesting pictures of the country and the people. There are not many authentic works on Java, and these volumes will rank among the best."—*Post.*

A LADY'S VISIT TO MANILLA AND JAPAN. By Anna D'A. 1 vol., with Illustrations.

"This book is written in a lively, agreeable, natural style, and we cordially recommend it as containing a fund of varied information connected with the Far East, not to be found recorded in so agreeable a manner in any other volume with which we are acquainted."—*Press.*

13, GREAT MARLBOROUGH STREET.

MESSRS. HURST AND BLACKETT'S NEW WORKS—*Continued.*

THE WANDERER IN WESTERN FRANCE. By G. T. LOWTH, Esq., Author of "The Wanderer in Arabia." Illustrated by the Hon. Eliot Yorke, M.P. 8vo.

A WINTER IN UPPER AND LOWER EGYPT. By G. A. HOSKINS, Esq., F.R.G.S. 1 vol., with Illustrations.

POINTS OF CONTACT BETWEEN SCIENCE AND ART. By His Eminence CARDINAL WISEMAN. 8vo. 5s.

GREECE AND THE GREEKS. Being the Narrative of a Winter Residence and Summer Travel in Greece and its Islands. By FREDRIKA BREMER. Translated by MARY HOWITT. 2 vols.

MEMOIRS OF CHRISTINA, QUEEN OF SWEDEN. By HENRY WOODHEAD. 2 vols., with Portrait.

ENGLISH WOMEN OF LETTERS. By JULIA KAVANAGH, Author of "Nathalie," "Adele," "French Women of Letters," "Beatrice," &c. 2 vols.

THE OKAVANGO RIVER: A NARRATIVE OF TRAVEL, EXPLORATION, AND ADVENTURE. By C. J. ANDERSSON, Author of "Lake Ngami." 1 vol., with Portrait and numerous Illustrations.

TRAVELS IN THE REGIONS OF THE AMOOR, AND THE RUSSIAN ACQUISITIONS ON THE CONFINES OF INDIA AND CHINA. By T. W. ATKINSON, F.G.S., F.R.G.S., Author of "Oriental and Western Siberia." Dedicated, by permission, to HER MAJESTY. Second Edition. Royal 8vo, with Map and 83 Illustrations, elegantly bound.

ITALY UNDER VICTOR EMMANUEL. A Personal Narrative. By COUNT CHARLES ARRIVABENE. 2 vols. 8vo.

THE LIFE OF J. M. W. TURNER, R.A., from Original Letters and Papers furnished by his Friends and Fellow Academicians. By WALTER THORNBURY. 2 vols. 8vo, with Portraits and other Illustrations.

THE CHURCH AND THE CHURCHES; or, THE PAPACY AND THE TEMPORAL POWER. By Dr. DÖLLINGER. Translated by W. B. MAC CABE. 8vo.

CHEAP EDITION OF LES MISÉRABLES. By VICTOR HUGO. The Authorized Copyright English Translation, Illustrated by Millais. 5s., bound.

"The merits of 'Les Misérables' do not merely consist in the conception of it as a whole, it abounds page after page with details of unequalled beauty."—*Quarterly Review*

CHRISTIAN'S MISTAKE. By the Author of "John Halifax, Gentleman." 1 vol.

"A more charming story, to our taste, has rarely been written. Even if tried by the standard of the Archbishop of York, we should expect that even he would pronounce 'Christian's Mistake' a novel without a fault."—*Times.*

Under the Especial Patronage of Her Majesty.

Published annually, in One Vol., royal 8vo, with the Arms beautifully engraved, handsomely bound, with gilt edges, price 31s. 6d.

LODGE'S PEERAGE
AND BARONETAGE,
CORRECTED BY THE NOBILITY.

THE THIRTY-FOURTH EDITION FOR 1865 IS NOW READY.

LODGE'S PEERAGE AND BARONETAGE is acknowledged to be the most complete, as well as the most elegant, work of the kind. As an established and authentic authority on all questions respecting the family histories, honours, and connections of the titled aristocracy, no work has ever stood so high. It is published under the especial patronage of Her Majesty, and is annually corrected throughout, from the personal communications of the Nobility. It is the only work of its class in which, *the type being kept constantly standing*, every correction is made in its proper place to the date of publication, an advantage which gives it supremacy over all its competitors. Independently of its full and authentic information respecting the existing Peers and Baronets of the realm, the most sedulous attention is given in its pages to the collateral branches of the various noble families, and the names of many thousand individuals are introduced, which do not appear in other records of the titled classes. For its authority, correctness, and facility of arrangement, and the beauty of its typography and binding, the work is justly entitled to the place it occupies on the tables of Her Majesty and the Nobility.

LIST OF THE PRINCIPAL CONTENTS.

Historical View of the Peerage.
Parliamentary Roll of the House of Lords.
English, Scotch, and Irish Peers, in their orders of Precedence.
Alphabetical List of Peers of Great Britain and the United Kingdom, holding superior rank in the Scotch or Irish Peerage.
Alphabetical list of Scotch and Irish Peers, holding superior titles in the Peerage of Great Britain and the United Kingdom.
A Collective list of Peers, in their order of Precedence.
Table of Precedency among Men.
Table of Precedency among Women.
The Queen and the Royal Family.
Peers of the Blood Royal.
The Peerage, alphabetically arranged.
Families of such Extinct Peers as have left Widows or Issue.
Alphabetical List of the Surnames of all the Peers.

The Archbishops and Bishops of England, Ireland, and the Colonies.
The Baronetage alphabetically arranged.
Alphabetical List of Surnames assumed by members of Noble Families.
Alphabetical List of the Second Titles of Peers, usually borne by their Eldest Sons.
Alphabetical Index to the Daughters of Dukes, Marquises, and Earls, who, having married Commoners, retain the title of Lady before their own Christian and their Husband's Surnames.
Alphabetical Index to the Daughters of Viscounts and Barons, who, having married Commoners, are styled Honourable Mrs.; and, in case of the husband being a Baronet or Knight, Honourable Lady.
Mottoes alphabetically arranged and translated.

"Lodge's Peerage must supersede all other works of the kind, for two reasons: first, it is on a better plan; and secondly, it is better executed. We can safely pronounce it to be the readiest, the most useful, and exactest of modern works on the subject."—*Spectator.*
"A work which corrects all errors of former works. It is a most useful publication."—*Times.*
"A work of great value. It is the most faithful record we possess of the aristocracy of the day."—*Post.*
"The best existing, and, we believe, the best possible peerage. It is the standard authority on the subject."—*Herald.*

NOW IN COURSE OF PUBLICATION,

HURST AND BLACKETT'S STANDARD LIBRARY

OF CHEAP EDITIONS OF

POPULAR MODERN WORKS,

ILLUSTRATED BY MILLAIS, HOLMAN HUNT, LEECH, BIRKET FOSTER, JOHN GILBERT, TENNIEL, &c.

Each in a single volume, elegantly printed, bound, and illustrated, price 5s.

VOL. I.—SAM SLICK'S NATURE AND HUMAN NATURE.

"The first volume of Messrs Hurst and Blackett's Standard Library of Cheap Editions forms a very good beginning to what will doubtless be a very successful undertaking. 'Nature and Human Nature' is one of the best of Sam Slick's witty and humorous productions, and well entitled to the large circulation which it cannot fail to obtain in its present convenient and cheap shape. The volume combines with the great recommendations of a clear, bold type, and good paper, the lesser, but attractive merits, of being well illustrated and elegantly bound."—*Post.*

VOL. II.—JOHN HALIFAX, GENTLEMAN.

"This is a very good and a very interesting work. It is designed to trace the career from boyhood to age of a perfect man—a Christian gentleman, and it abounds in incident both well and highly wrought. Throughout it is conceived in a high spirit, and written with great ability. This cheap and handsome new edition is worthy to pass freely from hand to hand as a gift book in many households."—*Examiner.*

"The new and cheaper edition of this interesting work will doubtless meet with great success. John Halifax, the hero of this most beautiful story, is no ordinary hero, and this his history is no ordinary book. It is a full-length portrait of a true gentleman, one of nature's own nobility. It is also the history of a home, and a thoroughly English one. The work abounds in incident, and many of the scenes are full of graphic power and true pathos. It is a book that few will read without becoming wiser and better."—*Scotsman.*

"The story is very interesting. The attachment between John Halifax and his wife is beautifully painted, as are the pictures of their domestic life, and the growing up of their children; and the conclusion of the book is beautiful and touching."—*Athenæum.*

VOL. III.—THE CRESCENT AND THE CROSS.
BY ELIOT WARBURTON.

"Independent of its value as an original narrative, and its useful and interesting information, this work is remarkable for the colouring power and play of fancy with which its descriptions are enlivened. Among its greatest and most lasting charms is its reverent and serious spirit."—*Quarterly Review.*

"A book calculated to prove more practically useful was never penned than 'The Crescent and the Cross'—a work which surpasses all others in its homage for the sublime and its love for the beautiful in those famous regions consecrated to everlasting immortality in the annals of the prophets, and which no other writer has ever depicted with a pencil at once so reverent and so picturesque."—*Sun.*

VOL. IV.—NATHALIE. BY JULIA KAVANAGH.

"'Nathalie' is Miss Kavanagh's best imaginative effort. Its manner is gracious and attractive. Its matter is good. A sentiment, a tenderness, are commanded by her which are as individual as they are elegant. We should not soon come to an end were we to specify all the delicate touches and attractive pictures which place 'Nathalie' high among books of its class."—*Athenæum.*

[CONTINUED ON THE FOLLOWING PAGES.]

HURST AND BLACKETT'S STANDARD LIBRARY
(CONTINUED).

VOL. V.—A WOMAN'S THOUGHTS ABOUT WOMEN.
BY THE AUTHOR OF "JOHN HALIFAX, GENTLEMAN."

"A book of sound counsel. It is one of the most sensible works of its kind, well-written, true-hearted, and altogether practical. Whoever wishes to give advice to a young lady may thank the author for means of doing so."—*Examiner.*

"These thoughts are worthy of the earnest and enlightened mind, the all-embracing charity, and the well-earned reputation of the author of 'John Halifax.'"—*Herald.*

VOL. VI.—ADAM GRAEME OF MOSSGRAY.
BY THE AUTHOR OF "MRS MARGARET MAITLAND."

"'Adam Graeme' is a story awakening genuine emotions of interest and delight by its admirable pictures of Scottish life and scenery. The eloquent author sets before us the essential attributes of Christian virtue, their deep and silent workings in the heart, and their beautiful manifestations in life, with a delicacy, a power, and a truth which can hardly be surpassed."—*Post.*

VOL. VII.—SAM SLICK'S WISE SAWS AND MODERN INSTANCES.

"We have not the slightest intention to criticise this book. Its reputation is made, and will stand as long as that of Scott's or Bulwer's Novels. The remarkable originality of its purpose, and the happy description it affords of American life and manners, still continue the subject of universal admiration. To say thus much is to say enough, though we must just mention that the new edition forms a part of Messrs Hurst and Blackett's Cheap Standard Library, which has included some of the very best specimens of light literature that ever have been written."—*Messenger.*

VOL. VIII.—CARDINAL WISEMAN'S RECOLLECTIONS OF THE LAST FOUR POPES.

"A picturesque book on Rome and its ecclesiastical sovereigns, by an eloquent Roman Catholic. Cardinal Wiseman has here treated a special subject with so much generality and geniality, that his recollections will excite no ill-feeling in those who are most conscientiously opposed to every idea of human infallibility represented in Papal domination."—*Athenæum.*

VOL. IX.—A LIFE FOR A LIFE.
BY THE AUTHOR OF "JOHN HALIFAX, GENTLEMAN."

"We are always glad to welcome Miss Mulock. She writes from her own convictions, and she has the power not only to conceive clearly what it is that she wishes to say, but to express it in language effective and vigorous. In 'A Life for a Life' she is fortunate in a good subject, and she has produced a work of strong effect."—*Athenæum.*

VOL. X.—THE OLD COURT SUBURB. BY LEIGH HUNT.

"A delightful book, that will be welcome to all readers, and most welcome to those who have a love for the best kinds of reading."—*Examiner.*

"A more agreeable and entertaining book has not been published since Boswell produced his reminiscences of Johnson."—*Observer.*

VOL. XI.—MARGARET AND HER BRIDESMAIDS.

"We recommend all who are in search of a fascinating novel to read this work for themselves. They will find it well worth their while. There are a freshness and originality about it quite charming, and there is a certain nobleness in the treatment both of sentiment and incident which is not often found."—*Athenæum.*

HURST AND BLACKETT'S STANDARD LIBRARY
(CONTINUED).

VOL. XII.—THE OLD JUDGE. BY SAM SLICK.

"The publications included in this Library have all been of good quality; many give information while they entertain, and of that class the book before us is a specimen. The manner in which the Cheap Editions forming the series is produced deserves especial mention. The paper and print are unexceptionable; there is a steel engraving in each volume, and the outsides of them will satisfy the purchaser who likes to see a regiment of books in handsome uniform."—*Examiner.*

VOL. XIII.—DARIEN. BY ELIOT WARBURTON.

"This last production of the author of 'The Crescent and the Cross' has the same elements of a very wide popularity. It will please its thousands."—*Globe.*

VOL. XIV.—FAMILY ROMANCE; OR, DOMESTIC ANNALS OF THE ARISTOCRACY.
BY SIR BERNARD BURKE, ULSTER KING OF ARMS.

"It were impossible to praise too highly this most interesting book. It ought to be found on every drawing-room table. Here you have nearly fifty captivating romances with the pith of all their interest preserved in undiminished poignancy, and any one may be read in half an hour."—*Standard.*

VOL. XV.—THE LAIRD OF NORLAW.
BY THE AUTHOR OF "MRS MARGARET MAITLAND."

"The Laird of Norlaw fully sustains the author's high reputation."—*Sunday Times.*

VOL. XVI.—THE ENGLISHWOMAN IN ITALY.

"We can praise Mrs Gretton's book as interesting, unexaggerated, and full of opportune instruction."—*The Times.*

VOL. XVII.—NOTHING NEW.
BY THE AUTHOR OF "JOHN HALIFAX, GENTLEMAN."

"'Nothing New' displays all those superior merits which have made 'John Halifax' one of the most popular works of the day."—*Post.*

VOL. XVIII.—FREER'S LIFE OF JEANNE D'ALBRET.

"Nothing can be more interesting than Miss Freer's story of the life of Jeanne D'Albret, and the narrative is as trustworthy as it is attractive."—*Post.*

VOL. XIX.—THE VALLEY OF A HUNDRED FIRES.
BY THE AUTHOR OF "MARGARET AND HER BRIDESMAIDS."

"We know no novel of the last three or four years to equal this latest production of the popular authoress of 'Margaret and her Bridesmaids.' If asked to classify it, we should give it a place between 'John Halifax' and 'The Caxtons.'"—*Herald.*

VOL. XX.—THE ROMANCE OF THE FORUM.
BY PETER BURKE, SERJEANT AT LAW.

"A work of singular interest, which can never fail to charm. The present cheap and elegant edition includes the true story of the Colleen Bawn." *Illustrated News.*

VOL. XXI.—ADELE. BY JULIA KAVANAGH.

"'Adèle' is the best work we have read by Miss Kavanagh; it is a charming story, full of delicate character painting."—*Athenæum.*

HURST AND BLACKETT'S STANDARD LIBRARY
(CONTINUED).

VOL. XXII.—STUDIES FROM LIFE.
BY THE AUTHOR OF "JOHN HALIFAX, GENTLEMAN."

"These 'Studies from Life' are remarkable for graphic power and observation. The book will not diminish the reputation of the accomplished author."—*Saturday Review.*

VOL. XXIII.—GRANDMOTHER'S MONEY.

"We commend 'Grandmother's Money' to readers in search of a good novel. The characters are true to human nature, the story is interesting, and there is throughout a healthy tone of morality."—*Athenæum.*

VOL. XXIV.—A BOOK ABOUT DOCTORS.
BY J. C. JEAFFRESON, ESQ.

"A delightful book."—*Athenæum.* "A book to be read and re-read; fit for the study as well as the drawing-room table and the circulating library."—*Lancet.*

VOL. XXV.—NO CHURCH.

"We advise all who have the opportunity to read this book. It is well worth the study."—*Athenæum.*

VOL. XXVI.—MISTRESS AND MAID.
BY THE AUTHOR OF "JOHN HALIFAX, GENTLEMAN."

"A good wholesome book, gracefully written, and as pleasant to read as it is instructive."—*Athenæum.* "A charming tale charmingly told. All the characters are drawn with life-like naturalness."—*Herald.* "The spirit of the whole book is excellent. It is written with the same true-hearted earnestness as 'John Halifax.'"—*Examiner.*

VOL. XXVII.—LOST AND SAVED.
BY THE HON. MRS NORTON.

"'Lost and Saved' will be read with eager interest. It is a vigorous novel."—*Times.* "A novel of rare excellence; fresh in its thought, and with a brave soul speaking through it. It is Mrs Norton's best prose work."—*Examiner.*

VOL. XXVIII.—LES MISERABLES. BY VICTOR HUGO.
AUTHORISED COPYRIGHT ENGLISH TRANSLATION.

"The merits of 'Les Misérables' do not merely consist in the conception of it as a whole; it abounds, page after page, with details of unequalled beauty. In dealing with all the emotions, doubts, fears, which go to make up our common humanity, M. Victor Hugo has stamped upon every page the hall-mark of genius."—*Quarterly Review.*

VOL. XXIX.—BARBARA'S HISTORY.
BY AMELIA B. EDWARDS.

"It is not often that we light upon a novel of so much merit and interest as 'Barbara's History.' It is a work conspicuous for taste and literary culture. It is a very graceful and charming book, with a well-managed story, clearly-cut characters, and sentiments expressed with an exquisite elocution. The dialogues especially sparkle with repartee. It is a book which the world will like. This is high praise of a work of art, and so we intend it."—*Times.*

VOL. XXX.—LIFE OF THE REV. EDWARD IRVING.
BY MRS OLIPHANT.

"A good book on a most interesting theme."—*Times.*
"A truly interesting and most affecting memoir. Irving's life ought to have a niche in every gallery of religious biography. There are few lives that will be fuller of instruction, interest, and consolation."—*Saturday Review.*
"Mrs Oliphant's Life of Irving supplies a long-felt desideratum. It is copious, earnest, and eloquent. Irving, as a man and as a pastor, is not only fully sketched, but exhibited with many broad, powerful, and life-like touches, which leave a strong impression."—*Edinburgh Review.*

www.ingramcontent.com/pod-product-compliance
Lightning Source LLC
Chambersburg PA
CBHW031849220426
43663CB00006B/550